PORTUGAL

Signpost
Guides

Titles in this series include:

For further information about these and other Thomas Cook publications, write to Thomas Cook Publishing, PO Box 227, Thorpe Wood, Peterborough PE3 6PU, United Kingdom

Signpost
Guides

PORTUGAL

The best of Portugal's sophisticated
cities and rural backwaters, from
lively Lisbon and the fishing villages
of the Atlantic coast to the castles
and mountains of the Minho and
Trás-os-Montes

Barbara Radcliffe Rogers and
Stillman D Rogers

The
Globe
Pequot
Press

Guilford, Connecticut

Thomas
Cook
Publishing

Published by Thomas Cook Publishing
The Thomas Cook Group Ltd
PO Box 227
Thorpe Wood
Peterborough PE3 6PU
United Kingdom

E-Mail: books@thomascook.com

The Globe Pequot Press, PO Box 480, Guilford, Connecticut, USA, 06437

Text: © 2000 The Thomas Cook Group Ltd
Maps and diagrams: © Road maps supplied and designed by Lovell Johns Ltd., OX8 8LH.
Road maps generated from Bartholomew digital database © Bartholomew Ltd, 1999.
City maps prepared by RJS Associates, © Thomas Cook Group Ltd.

ISBN 0 7627 0689 9

Library of Congress Cataloging-in-Publication Data is available.

Publisher: Stephen York
Commissioning Editor: Deborah Parker
Map Editor: Bernard Horton

Series Editor: Christopher Catling
Copy Editor: Felicity Laughton
Proofreader: Sara Peacock
Written and researched by: Barbara Radcliffe Rogers and Stillman D Rogers

About the authors

Barbara Radcliffe Rogers and Stillman D Rogers have been visiting in Portugal for more than three decades. They wrote their first Portugal guidebook in 1989. Their own personal interests are in ancient sites – especially Celtic castros – and architecture, from graceful Roman bridges to Lisbon's stunning Art Deco and postmodern buildings. They return to Portugal year after year because there is still so much to discover there.

Authors of *Exploring Europe by Boat*, *New Hampshire Off the Beaten Path*, *The Rhode Island Guide*, *The Adventure Guide to Canada's Atlantic Provinces* and several other books on New England, Atlantic Canada and elsewhere in the world, they have contributed to three previous Thomas Cook guides.

Acknowledgements

Our heartiest thanks go to all the people who helped us in our travels and writing: Evelyn Hayward and Maria João Ramires for their help in making travel arrangements at late notice, Mafalda Burnay for her thorough commentaries on Portuguese history as we travelled, John Rab for his superb scouting and Jamie Samoes for leading us to secret corners of his land which we would never have found without him – such as the atmospheric castle hidden deep in a valley near Lousão.

While our hosts all over Portugal were friendly and helpful, a few stand out: the manager and staff at the Buçaco Palace and the staff of Hotel de São Francisco in Chaves, the Astoria in Coimbra, the Hotel de Lagos, and the Pousada São Gonçalo in Amarante. Our thanks also to Enatur for finding us *pousada* rooms during their busiest Easter weekend.

Thanks to the endlessly patient Chistopher Catling, who endured a manuscript delivered piecemeal, its chapters out of order. And to Lura for helping with the photography (and for being such a good-humoured travelling companion) and to Julie, an old Portugal hand and good companion herself, for pitching in with the manuscript preparation. And to both for taking over other assignments while we wrote. Thanks to Dee for holding down our own fort as we explored those of King Dinis.

Finally, thanks to Portuguese people everywhere who restrained their laughter at our comic-opera renditions of their language, and who pointed us on our way with unfailing politeness and solicitude. And to the many who toiled in their vineyards so that we might relax each evening, after a long day's driving, over some of the world's best wines.

Contents

About Signpost Guides

Thomas Cook's Signpost Guides are designed to provide you with a comprehensive but flexible reference source to guide you as you tour a country or region by car. This guide divides Portugal into touring areas – one per chapter. Major cultural centres or cities form chapters in their own right. Each chapter contains enough attractions to provide at least a day's worth of activities – often more.

Star ratings

To make it easier for you to plan your time and decide what to see, the principal sights and attractions are given a star rating. A three-star rating indicates an outstanding sight or major attraction. Often these can be worth at least half a day of your time. A two-star attraction is worth an hour or so of your time, and a one-star attraction indicates a site that is good but often of specialist interest.

Chapter contents

Every chapter has an introduction summing up the main attractions of the area, and a ratings box, which will highlight the area's strengths and weaknesses – some areas may be more attractive to families travelling with children, others to wine-lovers visiting vineyards, and others to people interested in finding castles, churches, nature reserves or good beaches.

Each chapter is then divided into an alphabetical gazetteer, and a suggested tour. You can select whether you just want to visit a particular sight or attraction, choosing from those described in the gazetteer, or whether you want to tour the area comprehensively. If the latter, you can construct your own itinerary, or follow the authors' suggested tour, which comes at the end of every area chapter.

The gazetteer

The gazetteer section describes all the major attractions in the area – the villages, towns, historic sites, nature reserves, parks or museums that you are most likely to want to see. Maps of the area highlight all the places mentioned in the text. Using this comprehensive overview of the area, you may choose just to visit one or two sights.

One way to use the guide is simply to find individual sights that interest you, using the index, overview map or star ratings, and read what our authors have to say about them. This will help you decide whether to visit the sight. If you do, you will find plenty of practical information, such as the street address, the telephone number for enquiries and opening times.

Alternatively, you can choose a hotel, perhaps with the help of the accommodation recommendations contained in this guide. You can

Symbol Key

- ℹ Tourist Information Centre
- ⇄ Advice on arriving or departing
- Ⓟ Parking locations
- Ⓡ Advice on getting around
- ➲ Directions
- ⓣ Sights and attractions
- Ⓒ Accommodation
- Ⓜ Eating
- ⬤ Shopping
- Ⓢ Sport
- Ⓐ Entertainment

Practical information

The practical information in the page margins, or sidebar, will help you locate the services you need as an independent traveller – including the tourist information centre, car parks and public transport facilities. You will also find the opening times of sights, museums, churches and other attractions, as well as useful tips on shopping, market days, cultural events, entertainment, festivals and sports facilities.

then turn to the overall map on page 10 to help you work out which chapters in the book describe those cities and regions that lie closest to your chosen touring base.

Driving tours

The suggested tour is just that – a suggestion, with plenty of optional detours and one or two ideas for making your own discoveries, under the heading *Also worth exploring*. The routes are designed to link the attractions described in the gazetteer section, and to cover outstandingly scenic coastal, mountain and rural landscapes. The total distance is given for each tour, as is the time it will take you to drive the complete route, but bear in mind that this indication is just for the driving time: you will need to add on extra time for visiting attractions along the way.

Many of the routes are circular, so that you can join them at any point. Where the nature of the terrain dictates that the route has to be linear, the route can either be followed out and back, or you can use it as a link route, to get from one area in the book to another.

As you follow the route descriptions, you will find names picked out in bold capital letters – this means that the place is described fully in the gazetteer. Other names picked out in bold indicate additional villages or attractions worth a brief stop along the route.

Accommodation and food

In every chapter you will find lodging and eating recommend-ations for individual towns, or for the area as a whole. These are designed to cover a range of price brackets and concentrate on more characterful small or individualistic hotels and restaurants. In addition, you will find information in the *Travel facts* chapter on chain hotels, with an address to which you can write for a guide, map or directory. The price indications used in the guide have the following meanings:

€	budget level
€€	typical/average prices
€€€	de luxe

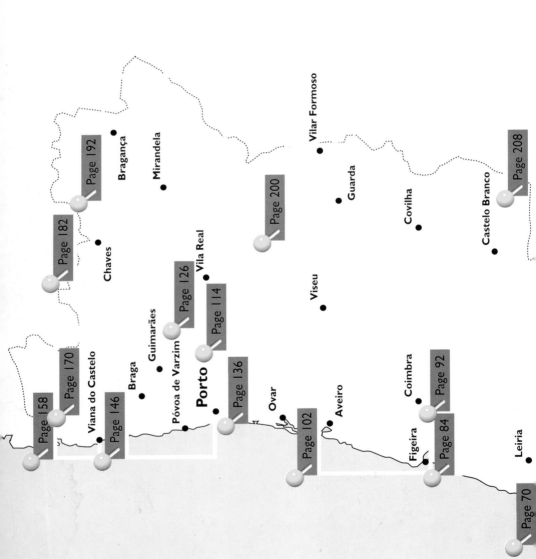

Vilar Formoso

Page 192

Bragança

Mirandela

Page 208

Page 182

Guarda

Chaves

Page 200

Covilha

Castelo Branco

Page 126

Vila Real

Page 114

Guimarães

Viseu

Coimbra

Page 170

Page 92

Póvoa de Varzim

Viana do Castelo

Braga

Porto

Page 136

Page 158

Page 146

Ovar

Aveiro

Figeira

Page 84

Page 102

Leiria

Page 70

Portalegre

Elvas

Redondo

Estremoz

Evora

Page 228

Page 220

Page 238

Serpa

Beja

Castro Verde

Page 246

Almodovar

Ayamonte

Faro

Abrantes

Entroncamento

Coruche

Grândola

Odemira

Page 256

Albufeira

Torres Novas

Santarém

Page 274

Lagos

Torres Vedras

Lisbon

Page 42

Setúbal

Page 264

Cascais

Page 58

Introduction

Above
Romanesque carvings in Bravães

UNESCO has singled out eight places in Portugal as World Heritage sites, but we could easily name a dozen more contenders. Castles are almost commonplace, each different from the last. Some have entire villages – living or in ruin – inside them, others are hardly more than remote fortified watchtowers. Whole villages – even city centres – are filled with buildings whose ages are reckoned in centuries.

Portugal's location and the geological forces that shaped it make it a beautiful land, with mountains of incredible vertical drop, barren and stony at their tops, lush and green with vineyards carved into their lower slopes. Among them are wild places alive with birds and flowers – one mountain so blossom-covered each spring that its name translates to 'yellow mountain'. The mountains seem bigger than they are; as you snake along precipitous roads into the deep river-carved valleys it is easy to forget that Portugal's highest elevation doesn't quite reach 2 000 metres.

But Portugal offers a great deal more than castles and dramatic scenery. Hidden in its valleys, scattered along its rolling plains and dotting the craggy coast are brilliant gardens, long wave-swept beaches, unparalleled prehistoric sites, stone villages from the Middle Ages, colourful local festivals that have not become tourist events, Romanesque and later churches decorated with exquisite craftsmanship.

Much of Portugal's art is in its churches, even in the remotest village parish, where you may find painted altar panels and ceilings, brilliant *trompe-l'oeil*, entire walls of eye-boggling woodcarving covered in gold, intricately carved wooden choir stalls with mischievous little faces on their misericords. It is the Portuguese love of delightful and incongruous surprises, as much as their love for elaborate decoration, that charms in these churches, which are each village's art gallery.

The Algarve is known best for its white sand beaches, often backed by wildly eroded cliffs, but a day's wandering can take you to mountain villages, high hiking trails with views to the sea or a castle that Richard the Lion-Heart wrested from the Moors. The cliffs at Sagres or Lagos, or on Cabo Espiche, near Lisbon, give the beaches a dramatic backdrop, and you will always find a boat ready to take you for a sailor's view.

Some of Europe's most and charming small cities are within a few hours' drive of Lisbon: Guimarães, Tomar, Castelo de Vide, Amarante, Viana do Castelo and Evora, its entire centre still encircled by walls.

But most endearing and inviting of all is the almost unfailing kindness and courtesy of Portuguese. Among the most civilised countries on the continent, Portugal's manners are those of the heart, not just those learned by rules. They love their land and love to share it; they are very good at being genuine.

Compared with the hordes of tourists who flood into Venice or the Riviera each year, Portugal is relatively undiscovered. Its location far from traditional Grand Tour routes has kept it isolated, less pricey and – best of all – uncatalogued. While hardly a sight in Italy goes with its raptures unsung, you can still discover wonderful places in Portugal which no guidebook mentions.

It is this sense of discovery that makes Portugal so appealing to the inquisitive independent traveller. After a few days you will begin to notice things – two parallel stone walls with a few tell-tale flat stones still visible between, two millennia since the Romans so carefully laid them. After exploring a few hillforts, you will begin to scan hilltops for likely sites, like Celtic advance-men looking for a defensible place to settle. Driving through the wildflower-painted Alentejo, you will eye a hummocky outcrop in a meadow and say 'There's a dolmen under there'. Portugal is full of places waiting to be discovered.

Below
Rio Torto dolmen

Travel facts

Accommodation

Lodgings, except Turihab and similar properties (see below) are rated by government-issued stars, which bear little relation to criteria the traveller cares about. The system is of little use, and the various classifications – *albergaria, estalagem, residencial,* etc – make it even less helpful. But wherever you choose to stay, you can usually expect a clean room, possibly dowdy or dated in decor, but comfortable.

Hotels are just that, although they may be as grand as the Buçaco Palace or quite modest. **Apartment hotels** have tiny kitchens in each room or suite. *Pousadas* are government-run hotels, some in historic castles or monasteries, others new. They are deluxe, although rooms vary greatly in size. Their good restaurants always offer local specialties.

Albergarias and *estalagems* are inns, whose prices increase with their location and number of stars. *Pensões* are more modest, although often quite nice, whose prices generally reflect their quality. **Turismo de Habitação (also called Turihab, Turismo No Espaco Rural and Solars de Portugal)** is a programme of private homes, which may be palaces, *solares,* renovated medieval village houses, in-town manor houses, or simple farms offering one to ten rooms. Prices range according to the elegance and pedegree of the home, but are generally quite reasonable.

Newer in Portugal, but offering interesting chances to meet local rural families is ECEAT, the **European Centre for Eco-Agro Tourism**. These environmentally conscious **farms** have rooms and campsites, often meals, and are most common in the Serra da Estrela and western Algarve. For a directory, contact *ECEAT, PO Box 10899, 1001 EW, Amsterdam; tel: (3120) 668 1030, fax: (3120) 463 0594, e-mail: eceat@antenna.nl*

At the lowest price range are **Pousadas de Juventude**, of which Portugal has 20 under the International Hostelling programme, and campsites, the most elaborate of which are managed by Orbitur; *tel: (01) 815 48 71, fax: (01) 814 80 45.*

Rates are generally lower in Portugal than for similar hotels elsewhere in Europe, and drop significantly, especially at top-end establishments, November–March, except at Easter and New Year.

Thomas Cook or any other good travel agent can handle room bookings when purchasing air tickets and car or other local transportation. Although international chains are not as well represented in Portugal as elsewhere in Europe, a few have hotels throughout the country, and can be reached on toll-free numbers.

Best Western

Aus (1 800) 222 422
Ire (800) 709 101
NZ (09) 520 5418
SA (011) 339 4865
UK (0800) 393 130
US (1 800) 528 1234

Comfort Inn

Aus (008) 090 600
Can (800) 888 4747
Ire (800) 500 600
NZ (800) 8686 888
UK (0800) 444 444
US (1 800) 228 5150

Ibis

Aus (001) 300 656565
NZ (0800) 444 422
UK (0181) 283 4500
US (1 800) 221 4542

A few quirks of Portuguese hotels: Even some posh places have light switches in hallways, so if the elevator door opens into a dim corridor, look for a switch next to the elevator door and for subsequent timed switches along corridors. Also, expect to forfeit one passport per room when you register, but do not expect the desk to remember it when you check out – leave a note in your car to remind you each morning.

Airports

Portugal's three international airports are in Lisbon, Porto and Faro. If you are headed directly to the western Algarve, it is faster to take a through EVA bus to Lagos or Portimão than to fly to Faro from Lisbon. Lisbon's airport is so well located that with quick directions from the well-staffed information desk, motorists can be on their way to the Algarve or to the north on a newly built motorway in five minutes, without ever encountering the city.

Below
Working donkeys can still be seen

Children

Portuguese people of all ages love chidren and make much of their own and yours. Children are your passport to invitations and to experiences you would not have without them. All but the poshest Lisbon restaurants will gladly bring children's seats and half portions; cranky children are the object of sympathy, not disapproval. Most lodgings can supply a baby cot, especially if you ask when reserving a room.

Climate

The Atlantic moderates what would otherwise be a hot, dry Mediterranean climate. Anywhere near the coast, the temperature will drop at night on even the hottest day. Rain is rare in the summer, but July and August can be very hot, especially in the Alentejo. Inland temperature variations are greatest in the mountains, where summer evenings encourage travellers to

CASINO DA PÓVOA

Enjoy...
a Great Evening!

pull out a jumper. While winters do not bring bitter cold, they bring snow enough for skiing to the Sera da Estrela, and freezing temperatures even in lower-altitude northern cities.

Currency

The unit of currency is the escudo, divided into 100 centavos and written with a '$' where the decimal point would go. A price tag of 10.50 escudos would read 10$50. Coins commonly seen are 5$00, 10$00, 20$00, 50$00, 100$00 and 200$00. Bills are 500$00, 1 000$00, 2 000$00, 5 000$00 and 10 000$00.

Some, but by no means all, menus and rate cards are printed with both escudos and Euros as Portugal moves toward conversion.

Currency exchange facilities in the Lisbon airport (to the right from arrivals) are open 24 hours. Avoid the currency changing machines adjacent to baggage claim.

Also avoid carrying large amounts of cash. Safer are traveller's cheques and credit or debit cards, either of which are easily converted everywhere. Traveller's cheques from Thomas Cook and other major issuers are accepted at banks and large hotels, also by stores in cities and major tourist areas. If possible, bring at least one, preferably two, major credit cards. Visa is the most commonly accepted in Portugal. Most *pensões*, Turihab properties and many small restaurants do not accept cards.

Automated teller machines offer the best currency exchange rates and never close. Check with your card issuer before leaving home to find out what international network you can use in Portugal. Multibanco machines are commonly found, on nearly every street corner in cities. Although you pay transaction fees to both banks involved, you will get the best rate for that day, at the commercial exchange rate.

Expect trouble trying to cash Eurocheques except in large Lisbon banks. Banks are usually open Mon–Fri 0830–1445.

Eating and drinking

Food is cheap and plentiful in Portugal. Local people eat out a lot, so except in heavily visited areas, such as Lisbon and the Algarve, restaurants will offer a very good value at low prices. Fish and shellfish, except for grilled sardines, are more expensive than meat. A standard plate will have meat or fish with potatoes (chips with meat, boiled with fish) and sometimes rice as well. Servings are large, often double what you would be served at home, and vegetables are scarce in restaurants, even when markets are filled with them.

The variety of dishes changes very little from one restaurant to the next. You will see the same 10–15 choices on every menu, the only difference being the variety of fish and an occasional local

Information

For general information on Portugal, contact the tourism department, **ICEP**:

Canada: 60 Bloor St West, Suite 1005, Toronto, Ontario M4W 3B8; tel: (416) 921-7376.

South Africa: PO Box 2473–Houghton, 2193 Johannesburg; tel: (11) 484-3487.

UK: 22 Sackville St, London W1X 2LY; tel: (0171) 494 1441.

USA: 590 Fifth Ave, New York, NY10036; tel: (212) 354-4403.

Insurance

Experienced travellers carry insurance that covers their belongings and holiday investment as well as their bodies. Travel insurance should include provision for cancelled or delayed flights and weather problems, as well as immediate evacuation home in the case of medical emergency. Thomas Cook and other travel agencies offer comprehensive policies.

Right
Caniçada shepherdess

speciality, such as trout in the north. At midday there will nearly always be a daily special menu, which is a three-course meal with a glass of wine or beer at a low price. This is often good value, although the portions will be smaller. Half portions are available at about ⅔ the full-portion price.

Meal hours vary, but are generally lunch 1230–1400, dinner 1900–2100 in the north, 1300–1500, 2000–2200 in the centre and south, except resort areas and cities, which will be later. Most *pousadas* serve dinner until at least 2100.

If breakfast is not included in lodging price, cafés are better value than hotel breakfasts. For plain breadrolls, ask for *pão e manteiga*. These tasty crisp breadrolls won't be displayed in the counter with the cheese- and sausage-filled pastries, which also make good breakfasts.

There is a blurred line between bars and restaurants, which are usually together. The town's best restaurant may be upstairs, behind or beside the noisiest local pub, with a totally different atmosphere.

Health

Portugal is generally a healthy place to travel; drinking water is normally safe (although savvy travellers usually drink bottled varieties to avoid discomforts caused by changes in water). No immunisations are required to enter Portugal. For minor medical problems, ask at a chemist's; for more serious illness or injury, the TIC or your hotel can suggest English-speaking doctors. Be sure to bring enough of any prescription to last the entire trip, and also a copy of the prescription in generic form. Portugal and Britain have reciprocal agreements for health care in emergencies, but you must fill out forms before leaving home.

Information

Towns of any size have TICs, which are open varying hours. Except in the largest towns, these usually close for lunch. Some can make lodging reservations, all can suggest options. They are usually very helpful, although only regional offices are well stocked with brochures, and you usually have to request these rather than gather them from display racks.

Before driving too far in search of an attraction mentioned in a local brochure, ask at the TIC; occasionally these brochures rave about places no one has ever heard of, giving directions that make no sense even to locals.

Language

Even for those with a facility for foreign languages, Portuguese is difficult. Those with knowledge of other Romance languages,

especially Italian or Spanish, will be able to read it, but probably not understand it. The pronunciation is quite unusual, with nasal sounds and slurred sibilants. As a rule of thumb, ~ over a vowel gives it a nasal upturn, much like the 'on' ending in French. To make matters worse, Portuguese is filled with false cognates: *Puxe* (pronounced 'pushe') means 'pull' and *coppa* is a glass, not a cup; *caraffa* is a corked bottle of wine, not a carafe.

If someone does not speak English, try French, which is widely spoken, not Spanish, which is still not looked on favourably, except in border towns. Always ask, for good manners' sake, if they speak English, or another language, before launching into it. In heavily travelled areas, most people will speak some English, in other areas those who deal most with travellers will. Unfailingly, Portuguese people are good natured about their language and your blunders with it, and are very pleased when you try even a smiling *Bom dia*.

Apart from Lisbon, for which the international spelling instead of the Portuguese 'Lisboa' is used, all place names in the book are in Portuguese, not to confuse you, but to make it easier to recognise signs. This also makes it possible to ask directions from local residents, who would be less likely to recognise an English translation when shown the words. When a meaning is not obvious (as it is in *museu* and *castelo*), the work is translated or described in text immediately following.

OAPs

Older people – and this includes total strangers as well as neighbours – are usually treated with respect by young people, even more so in smaller towns. They will extend courtesies and kindnesses – even protectiveness – that they extend their own grandparents, who are usually very much a part of their lives and homes. This makes Portugal an especially comfortable destination for older travellers. That said, you will rarely find discounts for senior citizens, and may find that Avis is the only car hire agency that will provide cars for drivers over the age of 70 .

Opening times

Expect all but the largest museums, shops and offices to close for lunch. Closing times vary from 1200 to 1300, reopening is most often at 1400, but may be later in the south.

Packing

The old rule of 'less is better' applies here. Pack comfortable clothing that you can layer for warmth in the mountains or in the evening, when temperatures can drop quickly even on a hot day. The

Public Holidays

Jan 1, Carnival (Shrove Tuesday, six weeks before Easter), Good Friday (before Easter Sunday), Apr 25, May 1, Corpus Christi (May or Jun), Jun 10, Aug 15, Oct 5, Nov 1, Dec 1, Dec 8, Dec 24, Dec 25.

Above
Linhares

Portuguese are a bit more formal than many other Europeans about going out in the evening, even in beach resort areas, but are not overly dressy otherwise. Jeans are acceptable daywear anywhere, but shorts are frowned upon in churches and at evening meals.

A small daypack can be handy for carrying picnic lunches, guidebooks and daily-use items, and can double as a spare carry-on for souvenirs on the trip home. On the way to Portugal it can be folded flat in your suitcase.

Public transport

Surprisingly, coaches are often better than trains, with more frequent and convenient connections, shorter travel times, lower fares and more comfortable seats. Their stations (except in Lisbon) are often more convenient to town centres. Even some time after privatisation, companies and routes are still shifting and confusing; direct coaches from Lisbon to the Algarve are operated by EVA.

Safety

Portugal's crime rate is the lowest in Europe, and crimes against tourists are usually from pickpockets, purse-snatchers and car thieves. Especially in Lisbon and the Algarve, be careful of handbags and cameras; carry money and documents in body-wallets, with only enough for immediate needs in an exposed wallet. Lock cars and remove or cover any sign of being a tourist, such as maps or guidebooks. Tourists' cars are a greater target than local cars, since they are assumed to have luggage in the boot.

Perhaps the greatest danger is of being struck by a car on narrow streets and lanes where there is barely room for cars, let alone cars and pedestrians. Before you step out into a street, be sure you're not sharing it with a car.

When swimming on Atlantic beaches, be especially careful of undercurrents, which can easily sweep swimmers out to sea. Swim only on beaches signposted as safe or obviously intended for swimming. Never swim where others are not in the water.

Shopping

Most shops are open from 0900 or 0930 to 1230 or 1300 and again from 1400 or 1500 to 1900. Midday break is longer in the south than in the centre and north. Shops in resort areas often stay open later.

Local crafts to look for include ceramics and pottery, *azulejos* (painted tiles), embroidery, lace (be careful, since most is now imported), leather goods, baskets and knitted items. Cork mats, although harder to find, are good value. The best selection of crafts will be from *artesanatos*. Port wine, olives and honey are also good souvenirs to take home. *Azulejo* house numbers and signs in English are occasionally seen in *artesanatos*, but a greater selection will be found in studios or specialty shops. Arraiolos rugs are found in Lisbon, but prices are somewhat lower in Arraiolos or nearby Evora.

Telephones

Inconsistent, often out of order and badly in need of updating, coin-operated telephones in Portugal will challenge both your patience and your linguistic skills. Carry a telephone card (from a post office or news stand), or go to a café and ask to use their telephone. These are metered and you can pay when you finish – and if you have problems, someone can help you.

Telephone numbers are changing – often randomly and without notice – to 6 or 7 digits. If you can't get through, check to see if a number has been added to the beginning. Printed materials lag far behind reality, since these number changes are made without advance notice. Again, ask a tourist office or hotel desk to help or go to a café.

To call or fax Portugal from outside the country, dial international access, then the country code (351) then the area code without the initial 0, then the number.

Time

Portugal is in the same time zone as the UK in winter and on GMT plus one hour between the last Sunday in March and the last Sunday in September. It is one hour later than Spain all year.

To the Portuguese, time is not especially important, so be prepared for delays and for doors closed even when the sign on them says they should be open.

Travellers with disabilities

Except in the Algarve, where a few more places have wheelchair access, facilities for mobility-impaired travellers are minimal at best. All three airports are wheelchair accessible, and major hotels usually have a few rooms adapted, but travel is very difficult otherwise. For current information, contact RADAR, 12 City Forum, 250 City Rd, London EC1V 8AF; tel: (0171) 250 3222.

Right
Obidos

Driver's guide

Touring in Portugal is a crash course (if you'll pardon the unfortunate adjective) in defensive driving. Roads are often either too narrow or too good, encouraging outrageous speeds. They have among the highest road fatality rates in Europe, possibly because so many drivers are first-generation, and did not grow up around cars, still a comparatively new toy to many drivers.

The most immediate problem will be for those from left-hand drive countries, such as the UK and South Africa. When you are in normal traffic, it will begin to seem natural as you follow other drivers. But at roundabouts (*rotundas*) or on dual-carriageways, it becomes more difficult, because your natural instincts give you the wrong signals. Be especially alert and continue to remind yourself of this danger.

The most difficult time for some is in starting out in the morning on a road without other traffic. You can drive for some distance without realising that you are on the wrong side. To solve this, attach a card to your keys, with the words "Drive Right!" printed in large

Below
Wine boats on the River Douro in Porto

Driving

What look like verges are often drainage ditches covered by grass or weeds, so be careful when pulling off to the roadside – if in doubt ask a passenger to get out and check first.

You may be puzzled by signs warning of *Bandas Sonoras* – these are rumble strips of rough pavement on the motorways.

letters. Whenever you leave the car, and need to pocket your keys, this will be in your way. Remove it and tape it to your steering wheel. That reminds you as soon as you enter your car, at which time you return the card to your keys. A roll of tape is a small price to pay for avoiding a head-on collision.

The most important rule of the road is to give way to the right. In the absence of a traffic light, traffic officer or other indication, the vehicle on the right has the right-of-way, except at roundabouts where the vehicle in the circle has right-of-way over entering traffic.

Accidents

In case of accident, remain at the scene until police arrive, stay calm and request an English-speaking interpreter to assist you in making a statement. One of the advantages of the Portuguese fascination for mobile telephones is that accidents are reported and help summoned almost immediately.

Breakdowns

Membership to an affiliated national auto club entitles you to road assistance from ACP, the Automovel Club de Portugal; confirm this with your own club before leaving home.

Car hire

Although it is often possible to rent a car spontaneously, especially in the Algarve, you will usually have the best rate – not to mention the assurance of your choice of car awaiting you – by reserving before you leave home. The best rates will be in a package with air fare, booked through Thomas Cook or other reliable travel agency.

Most car hire (rental) companies require a credit card deposit, even if the hire has been prepaid. Before leaving the car park, be sure you have all necessary registration and insurance documents and that you know how to operate the vehicle. Try to spend the first night in a hotel near the airport rather than jumping from an international flight into a strange car on the wrong side of the road.

Documents

Drivers from EU nations and the United States need only their own current driving licence; others should have an International Driving Permit in addition to their original permit. You must get these in your own country, usually through an automobile club. If driving your own car, you must have its registration and insurance documents in the car at all times. It is also important to get a card from your insurer to prove that you have third-party coverage.

Driving conditions

Roads range from state-of-the-art motorways to cobbled lanes a few centimetres wider than your car. Most roads are paved, unless you (like your authors) wish to chase down remote prehistoric sites, in which case you may drive many unpaved roads and farm lanes. The most nerve-wracking problem, apart from Portuguese drivers, is the number of mountain roads with precipitous drop-offs and no guard-rails. Avoid these roads in the rain or in winter, and at night. In fact, it is wise to avoid night driving entirely, allowing enough time for daylight arrivals.

Fuel

Petrol (unleaded is *sem chumbo*) and diesel are sold by the litre, at fairly high prices. Very few stations are self-service, and a tip of 50 escudos is welcome. Major brand stations generally accept credit cards, but most others take only cash.

Information

The best and most up-to-date road map is issued by ACP, the Automovel Club de Portugal; second is Michelin's. The ICEP road map is convenient to have in planning overall routes, since it is smaller and gives a better view of the country as a whole. Roadmaps disagree wildly, so it is best to carry several if you plan to use any but major roads. One of the maps you carry should show topography; often that shortcut may be straight (or not so straight) over a mountain range.

Don't expect to see route numbers on roadsigns, although they will often be there. Instead, know the towns and cities on your route. Labelling is quite good, especially from major roads, and each town or village has a sign announcing its beginning and end. This makes it quite easy to follow a map. The more exploring you plan to do, the more detailed your map should be and the more maps you should have.

Routes out of cities are often difficult to find, with signage not becoming adequate until you reach a roundabout at the outskirts. Always ask someone for directions before leaving a city. And when asking directions, remember to watch as well as listen: right, left, straight and roundabouts are all described with a wave of the hand.

Parking

Many parking areas have meter boxes which provide tickets when fed coins. These are quite simple to figure out, even without being able to read the instructions. Put the ticket inside the car, on the dashboard. Elsewhere you may meet parking 'attendants' who expect tips. It is hard to tell if they really are, but they seem happy with 50 escudos,

Right
Alentejo cork tree

Above
Corn store on granite
pillars in Lapella

and if you've tipped them, they'll at least feel responsible for making sure another car doesn't block you in.

If you are blocked in, go to the closest business and enquire for the driver, then to the nearest café. By then you will have a group of several people all calling up to balconies overhead and rushing about to find the driver, who will appear, touch his forelock and move, while all those people give you and him directions at once and wave you on your way.

Seat belts

Seat belts are mandatory for driver and all passengers; those under 12 must be in the back seat.

Speed limits

Maximum speeds are 120 kph on motorways, 90 kph on dual carriageways and other roads, 60 kph in thickly settled areas. Other limits are posted. Do not expect Portuguese drivers to pay any heed to these.

Contact your local Thomas Cook shop to arrange your

CONTINENTAL MOTORING ASSISTANCE

- Assistance due to breakdown / accident

- Hire car

- Legal protection

- Comprehensive Personal Travel Insurance

- And much more . . . . .

Full details available at Thomas Cook Shops in the UK.

Getting to Portugal

British Airways; *tel: (0181) 897 40 00.*

Air Portugal (TAP); *tel: (0171) 839 10 31.*

Eurolines *52 Grosvenor Gardens, Victoria, London SW1 0A4; tel: (0171) 730 82 35.*

British Rail International *tel: (0171) 834 2345.*

Brittany Ferries *Millbay Docks, Plymouth; tel: (01752) 221 321.*

Right
The Discoverers' Monument, Lisbon

Below
Lisbon's Praça Martim Moniz

By air

British Airways (BA) and Air Portugal (TAP) fly daily from London to Lisbon (2½ hours), Porto (2 hours) and Faro (3¼ hours). TAP flies to the same cities from Manchester. TAP connects Lisbon with Dublin.

TAP also offers connections between Lisbon and New York, Boston, Montreal and Toronto, all about 6½ hours.

By train and bus

Connections from London to Lisbon by rail require train and station change in Paris, arriving in Lisbon or Porto about 24 hours after leaving Austerlitz station in Paris. Consult the latest edition of Thomas Cook European Rail Timetable for exact schedule or contact British Rail.

Train connections from Spain are best from Madrid (about 8 hours) to Lisbon, and from Galicia (La Coruña) to Porto and Lisbon. Trains from Sevilla cross into Portugal at Vila Real de Santo António, about an hour from Faro, several times daily.

Coaches operated by Eurolines connect London to Lisbon, Porto, Faro, Lagos and several other cities in Portugal. Their coaches also connect Portugal to Madrid, about 11 hours.

By car

The shortest driving route from the UK takes advantage of the 28-hour ferry ride from Plymouth to Santander, in Spain, to cut off days of driving through France and Spain. From Santander, Lisbon is still 950km away, and the ferry is pricey. Going across the channel to France by ferry or Channel Tunnel leaves about 1900km of driving through France and Spain to reach Lisbon. Rail Europe/SNCF offers a 'piggy-back' ride for your car while you ride the train to Madrid, cutting off many long hours of driving.

Above
Roman column, Evora

Setting the scene

The place

Only 560km long and 220km wide, Portugal shares borders only with Spain and the Atlantic Ocean, two neighbours that have profoundly influenced Portugal's history and culture. The Tejo (Tagus) river forms a watery belt, separating the more mountainous north from the rolling plains of the south (although, even in the south, sudden outcroppings create steep perches for castellated towns).

The granite and shale of the northern mountains were thrust up as the earth's crust folded and crumpled. As the land was later worn down, the harder rock resisted, forming the *serra*, or mountain ranges. More folding in the Terciary era again thrust up mountains, this time the largest of them, the Serra da Estrela, just under 2000 metres at its highest. Faults and fissures left hot springs, and a tendency to earthquakes, such as the one which destroyed Lisbon in 1755.

Rivers working over countless millennia have carved deep, often precipitous river valleys, some with gorges, into the mountains. The Zêzere is the only major river that rises in Portugal; the others flow in from Spain. The Douro forms part of the eastern border in the north and the Guadiana in the south. The Minho forms part of the northern border.

Portugal's 840km of coastline alternates between eroded cliffs and sandy beaches and dunes. Near Aveiro and in the central and eastern Algarve, rivers form lagoons and large marshy areas rich in birdlife. The most dramatic sea cliffs are between Lagos and Sagres in the western Algarve and at Cabo Espiche on the Setúbal Peninsula south of Lisbon

The past

The first people known have lived on the Iberian Peninsula were Lusitanian Celts, who tended small farms and kept sheep north of the Douro River. They also raided each other's walled hilltop towns of round stone houses, remains of which can be seen all over northern Portugal, especially at Citânia Sanfins and Citânia Briteiros, between Porto and Braga. Other prehistoric remains are dolmen, found all over the country, and menhirs and cromlechs found near Evora.

In about the 9th century BC, Greeks and Phoenicians, then Carthaginians, began trading along the Atlantic coasts, seeking tin for bronze. From their trading posts, and by mixing with locals, Carthage controlled the countryside by the 3rd century BC. During the Second Punic War, the Romans took control of the peninsula and spent two centuries razing and Romanising the Celt's hillforts. They built administrative and social centres at Lisbon, Santarém, Evora, Beja, Mértola and Braga. Significant remains of their civilisation are today found in Evora and Santiago do Cacém and near Coimbra. Four centuries of Roman rule left a coherent legal system, cities, roads and efficient agriculture.

The 3rd and 4th centuries AD brought successive invasions from the north: Vandals, then bands of Suevi and Visigoths, who settled, assuming control by the 5th century. This turmoil is dramatically visible at Roman Conimbriga, where a hastily erected defensive wall incorporates columns and statuary ripped from homes and public buildings. The Visigoths established government, but an 8th-century dynastic squabble led one contender to request help from the Moor, Tariq ibn Ziyad, giving rise to problems that would plague Portugal and Spain for many centuries.

Arriving in 711, the Moors quickly overran their hosts and the Visigothic settlements, controlling the peninsula south of the Mondego by 716 AD. By mid-century the Moors had colonised, introducing new irrigation techniques, rice and fruit cultivation. The initial Moorish leaders were liberal overlords for their age, allowing Christians (called mozarabs) and Jews some self-government, and to rent farmland and practise their religions. But more zealous Islamics followed in 1099 and 1146, and hardships increased.

The seed of the Moors' undoing had been planted, however, in 718 AD when Pelayo, son of a slain Visigoth, defeated a Moorish troop sent to destroy him. He was declared King of Asturias, and his tiny northern kingdom made constant war on the Moors, taking Galicia, then as far south as Porto by 868. By the 11th century, Portucale was recognised as a separate county. War against the Moors raged across Iberia, until a coalition of Castile, Galicia and Portugal enlisted the help of crusader Raymond of Burgundy, who sealed the alliance through marriage to the princess of Castile. Raymond and his cousin Henry were given Galicia and Portucale, with allegiance to Castile. From here Portugal's history diverges from Spain's.

Henry of Burgundy kept Portucale until he died in 1114, when his wife Tareja became regent for her son, Afonso Henriques. In 1128 Afonso's army defeated his mother's forces and he became Count of Portucale. By 1143 Afonso of Portucale, the first of the Burgundian line, was acknowledged by Castile as King of Portucale, after his defeat of a Moorish army at Ourém, a turning point in the Moorish wars. Portugal's formal allegiance to Castile lasted until the recognition of an independent Portuguese kingdom by Pope Alexander III in 1179.

Meanwhile Santarém was wrested from the Moors, and in 1147 Lisbon was taken with the help of English, Flemish and Burgundian crusaders. During the reigns of Sancho I, Afonso II and Sancho II the battle with the Moors continued, the lines of control sliding up and down the Alentejo until Afonso III finally pushed the Moors out of the Algarve in 1249. Castile, which took two centuries longer to drive out the Moors, recognised the new borders of Portugal in 1297.

The Burgundian kings fostered progressive agriculture, developed shipping and engaged in trade with England and the low countries. Dinis I, known as the Farmer King, promoted wheat, barley and millet production, expanded irrigation and mining and required that each tree cut be replaced by planting another. He planted a huge pine forest in the dunes of Leira, protecting the shoreline and creating lumber for shipbuilding. He is remembered by today's travellers as the Castle King, for the 50 castles he built along the eastern border, protecting Portugal from Castile. He married a Castilian princess, Isabel, who was so revered for her acts of kindness (including caring for his seven illegitimate children) that she became known as Santa Isabela. When the rest of Europe, with the blessing of the Pope, threw out the Knights Templars, Dinis remembered that these crusaders had freed Portugal from the Moors, and invited them to join the new Portuguese Order of Christ. His 45-year reign was followed by two more monarchs who expanded agriculture, shipping and trade.

Portugal, traditionally an ally of England, was forced into allegiance with Castile after a disastrous Castilian invasion. But the commercial and mercantile classes of Lisbon, who formed a body called the Cortes, selected João of Avis, the illegitimate son of a previous king, to be ruler, ousting an unpopular royal widow. The monarchy, now associated with the entrepreneurial class, became popular, gaining even more support when João defeated a Castilian invasion in 1385 at the Battle of Aljubarrota. The monastery of Batalha, erected close by, is a memorial to this victory which freed Portugal from forced allegiance to Castile. In 1386 a formal treaty between Portugal and England, the Treaty of Windsor, forged a bond which exists to this day, and which was used to permit British bases in the Azores during World War II, despite Portugal's neutrality.

Further sealing the bond, João I married Phillipa of Lancaster, daughter of John of Gaunt, Duke of Lancaster. João and Phillipa had six sons and one daughter. The eldest became Duarte I, the third an extraordinary diplomat referred to as Pedro the Traveller, and the fourth, Infante Henrique, became known as Prince Henry the Navigator for his drive to promote Portuguese exploration and maritime development. The Order of Christ, which Dinis I had founded, became central to this mission. João I and his sons captured Ceuta, in Morocco, but failed to take Tangiers, losing the younger son Fernando in the process.

The Infante Henrique established a school of navigation on the bleak shores of western Algarve at Cabo São Vicente, providing a safe haven for passing ships of all nations and using their sailors as a source of information. He sponsored explorations of the African coast and the southern Atlantic; his mariners discovered and settled Madeira, moving on to the Canaries. When Henrique died in 1460, Portugal was committed to the quest for India and the spice route,

Opposite
Rural Covelaes

Above
Monsanto

which led Bartolomeu Dias to round the cape of Good Hope in 1488.

The Avis dynasty reached its apogee under Manuel I. Under his leadership Vasco Da Gama reached the spice markets of Asia in 1497, establishing Portuguese dominance. In 1500 Manuel married Isabella of Castile and yielded to Castilian demands for the expulsion of Jews, which led to an Inquisition in 1535.

The Manueline period saw Portugal grow wealthy and influential, its vast empire including Brazil and colonies in Africa and Asia. This dependence on the sea inspired Portugal's unique style of architecture, the Manueline, a form of baroque incorporating maritime and nautical motifs.

The great Avis dynasty died with Sebastião I in an ill-conceived North African crusade at Alcacer-Quiber, and in 1581 Philip II of Spain became Philip I of Portugal. A disaster for Portugal, Spanish rule meant the end of important trading relationships with Britain and the Netherlands. The country was impoverished and increasingly harsh Spanish domination drained it further. It was 60 hard years before political problems inside Spain allowed Duke João of Bragança to claim the Portuguese throne as João IV.

Under Bragança rule trade was resumed, and the historic ties with Britain and the Netherlands re-established, to the benefit of the Port wine trade. During the first half of the 18th century, under João V, treasure pouring in from Brazil created seemingly endless wealth, resulting in wildly expensive buildings, including the Monastery of Mafra. When the weak José I ascended the throne in 1750 he chose the Marquês de Pombal as Prime Minister, then allowed him to become a dictator.

In 1755 a devastating earthquake rocked southern Portugal, virtually destroying Lisbon. Pombal, in one of the earliest examples of modern urban planning, rebuilt the city, much as it exists to this day. Fearful of the growing power of the Jesuits, he expelled them in 1759.

Portugal was invaded by Spain in 1801 and later by Napoleon, whose army was rebuffed by Lord Wellesly, later Duke of Wellington. King João VI escaped to Brazil, which became the seat of the Portuguese empire until the royal family's return in 1821. Prince Pedro, remaining in Brazil, declared that colony's independence, depriving Portugal of a major source of wealth. The century ended with Portugal's prosperity continuing its decline, as dissatisfaction rose. This lead to the assassination of King Carlos I and the Crown Prince in 1908. The younger son, Manuel III, ruled only two years, until a 1910 revolt led to his abdication and exile to England.

The republic that followed proved helpless. Joining the allies in World War I, Portugal suffered heavy casualties as discontent continued to rise. In 1928 the government called upon a professor of economics at the University of Coimbra, Dr António Salazar, to be Minister of Finance and two years later he became Prime Minister. As happened in Italy and Germany, and shortly thereafter in Spain, Salazar issued a new constitution in 1933, making him dictator of a police state. The dictatorship lasted four years after his death in 1970, until an armed forces coup ended it in the Carnation Revolution of April 24, 1974. After a dismal showing in 1975 elections, the Communist party attempted a coup, defeated by General António Eanes. A new constitution was adopted in 1976 and Eanes was elected President. Since then democracy has flourished and the economy has made slow, but steady advances. In 1986 Portugal became a member of the EEC and has benefitted from EU help, especially in building highways.

Architecture

Portugal's architectural largesse follows many of the same styles as the rest of Europe, but usually with a different flare. Local history, climate and building materials have shaped both domestic and monumental architecture. The early Celto-Lusitanian people built round houses of stone on their fortified hilltops. In the south the sun and the Moors strongly influenced building styles. Other influences came from occupying Romans and Visigoths.

Monumental architecture, the grand public buildings such as churches and monasteries, follow the same general trends as the rest of Europe,

Architectural and church terms

Ambulatory: the rounded corridor behind the main altar in some large churches, usually lined with small chapels.

Azulejos: decorative tiles; early ones were polychrome, later most often blue and white.

Below
A typical Manueline door

but somewhat later and with a local twist. The Roman-Visigothic experience, and the constant threat of war, shows in the fortress-like cathedrals of Guarda, Coimbra and Evora, bastions of faith in the face of the Muslim threat. Scattered about, especially north of Lisbon, are small jewels of Romanesque parish churches, like the Igreja Matriz in Bravães, just west of Ponte da Barca. The Roman Catholic Church played a significant role in the expanding kingdom, as did an awareness of trends elsewhere in Europe, so when a suitable offering was sought for the victory at Santarém it was a more sophisticated and graceful form of Gothic that came to Alcobaça, and later to Batalha.

The unique form of Portuguese architecture is the Manueline style, born during the reign of Manuel I, when Portugal's wealth and influence exploded. Late Gothic with marine-themed decorative elements, it uses ropes, cables, armillary spheres and shells carved in stone, often in complicated designs, as reminders of Portugal's maritime might. The unfinished chapels of Batalha, the castle at Tomar, the Tower of Belém and the Monastery of Jerónimos at Belém are some of the best examples, but you will find sudden bursts of this style everywhere.

The sea-borne adventures of the Infante Henrique's explorers brought incredible wealth just as the Renaissance flowered, and into the baroque period that followed. In Portugal, Renaissance architecture first appeared in the church of Nossa Senhora da Graça in Evora, a building of classical lines with somewhat awkwardly executed sculptural elements. One of the most powerful influences was Niccola Nasoni, an Italian who came to Portugal early in the 18th-century and inspired Portuguese architects with baroque and rococo styles.

Some of his works include the Solar de Mateus near Vila Real, and the Clérigos tower and Bishop's Palace in Porto, one of his earliest designs.

Chancel: the alcove containing the high, or main altar.

Coro Alto: upper choir, or choir loft, where you will often find beautifully carved stalls.

Igreza Matriz: parish church.

Misericórdias and Misericords are entirely different things, although both derived from the word 'mercy'. The first is a hospital and church owned by a private public welfare foundation, the second a merciful rest for choristers who had to stand during masses sometimes hours long.

Pelourinho: Granite posts, often carved, which were originally pilliories, but later symbols of municipal power.

Sacristy: a room used for robing and storage of vestments, usually just off the chancel or in the closest corner of the cloister, and often filled with art treasures.

Sé: cathedral.

Transepts: 'arms' in a church built in the shape of a cross.

Later influences show particularly in the major cities. French Empire style appears, for example, in the splendid Astoria Hotel in Coimbra. Art nouveau and art deco also live in these cities, good examples being the Orion-Eden Hotel on the Praça dos Restauradores in Lisbon and the outstanding Fundação de Serralves in Porto. Architectural design continues to evolve, as seen in the 1960 monument, Padrão dos Descobrimentos and the nearby Centro Cultural de Belém and its associated art buildings. Perhaps the two most strikingly original modern buildings are the Torres das Amoreiras, a post-modern shopping and office complex, and the beautiful Oriente train station at the Expo98 site, whose soaring steel arches recall the vaulting of the great Gothic cathedrals.

Domestic architecture varies from north to south. In the rocky north, stone predominates; many towns still have granite houses with exterior stairways and porticoes, often dating from the medieval period. Look in the Minho region for *espigueiros*, granite and wood granaries for maize. Toward the central regions many buildings are of limestone, often without stucco, but a bit more ornate, with more detail in the cornices and windows.

In the Alentejo and particularly in the Algarve, Moorish influence becomes more pronounced. Houses are single storey, with fewer windows, often painted white to reflect the sun. Chimneys become more obvious, huge shapes rising above the houses, usually topped by a pierced ceramic cap of fascinating and varied form.

Much of Portugal's greatest art is in its churches and monasteries, themselves architectural works of art. The Portuguese government sacked its monasteries much in the style of King Henry VIII, but much later, in 1834, rolling up the welcome mat that Dom Dinis had rolled out to the disbanded Knights Templar centuries earlier. Monastic churches usually continued as parish churches; conventual buildings fell to various fates. Some were sold to private owners who stripped them of everything saleable and let them crumble. The greatest of them came under public patrimony, in the hands of the Ancient Monuments Commission, which, in the guise of artistic cleansing, stripped them of everything, too. The difference was that the commission scraped centuries of artistic heritage from the very stones, reducing everything to naked 'purity'. Out went priceless and irreplaceable carved Renaissance choir stalls, altarpieces, *azulejos*, frescoes and stone painting that was often original medieval decoration. This accounts for the cold sterility of the monasteries that have undergone government restoration. After decades of outraged pleas from their own and the world art and historical circles, that seems to have stopped, and the government is now working to restore – or at least stabilise – some of the monasteries, such as Tibaes, that had languished in private hands for nearly two centuries.

Touring itineraries

Touring Portugal

Unless you have unlimited time, you will probably want to connect the loops described at the end of each chapter, travelling only one side of each and connecting them into a much larger loop. Choose which leg of the loop to follow by reading each and deciding which has the most attractions that interest you. As Portugal's new long-distance motorway system is completed, there will be more options to connect regions quickly.

The unexplored north

Expect mountain driving, with hairpin bends and steep gradients, but also expect to see a world you thought was long gone in Europe. Take the A4 east from Porto to Amarante, following the 'North of the Douro' route (see page 134) to explore the river valley where Port wine is produced. Leave Amarante on the IP9 for the charming small city of Guimarães, continuing north on the N101 to Braga, stopping to visit the Celtic hillfort of Citânia Briteiros. From Braga, take the IC14 to Barcelos, especially if you can plan your visit for its splendid Thursday market.

Follow the N103 north to Viana do Castelo, exploring the coastal villages and 'The Minho Region' (see page 158) to Ponte de Lima. Return to Ponte da Barca, then head south on the N101 to the N206, joining the route to 'Braga and the Gerês Mountains' (see page 170) as far as Venda Nova, then joining the northern leg of the 'Northern Mountains' route (see page 182) to Bragança.

'The Northeastern Borderlands' route (see page 192) links directly into the eastern 'Fortified Towns' (see page 200) via the N221, and to its base in Guarda. From Guarda, choose either the northern leg of the 'Serra da Estrela' route (see page 208) along the edge of the mountain range, or the route through Manteigas and over the spine of the range past its highest elevation, at Torre. Either leads to Seia where you can take the IC12 northwest to Viseu. From Viseu, follow the eastern leg of the 'South of the Douro' route (see page 114) to Lamego, continuing north on the N2 to Pêso da Régua and Vila Real, where the IP4 will take you back to Porto.

Left
São Lourenço, near Guimarães

Insider's Algarve

While Portugal's southern coast is justly famous for its beautiful beaches and magnificent sea cliffs, it would be a shame to miss its rarely visited inland attractions. Leave Lisbon via the A2 over the 25 de Abril bridge, following the 'South of Lisbon' route (*see page 274*) in reverse to explore the Setúbal peninsula and continuing south to Santiago do Cacém via the coastal N261. Continue south on the N120, meeting the 'Western Algarve' route (*see page 264*) at Aljezur. Follow it southward to Sagres and around the coast, turning inland at Portimão to explore the mountain scenery of Monchique. Backtrack briefly to the N124, following it to Silves. Follow the 'Central Algarve' (*see page 256*) itinerary along the N124, staying on this road to join the 'Eastern Algarve' route (*see page 246*) in reverse to Alcoutim, Vila Real and along the coast to Faro. After a detour to Milreu, head west on the N125 to the IP1, north of Albufeira. Follow that motorway north to Lisbon, perhaps with a detour to Beja, via the N123 from Ourique and returning to the IP1 on the N121 and IP8.

The mini Grand Tour

This tour of central Portugal hits many of its best-known highlights, packing a lot into a relatively short distance and covering all of Portugal's mainland World Heritage sites.

Leave Lisbon following the 'Lisbon's Coast' route (*see page 58*) to Queluz, Sintra and Mafra, continuing north on the suggested detour to Torres Vedras, where you leave the route and head north on the IC1 to Obidos, following the 'North of Lisbon' itinerary (*see page 70*) through Alcobaça and Batalha to Fátima.

Follow the N356 to Ourém, and the N113 to Tomar, taking the IC3 south to the N118 or the IP6 mototway east to the N246, which leads to Castelo de Vide and Marvão. Follow the 'Upper Alentejo' route (*see page 228*) south through Elvas and Vila Viçosa, leaving the route to continue on the IP7 to Estremoz.

Follow the N18 southward to visit Evora (*see page 220*), leaving via the N114 to the A6, which returns to Lisbon.

Below
The rooftops of Porto's
Ribeira district

Ratings

Architecture	●●●●●
Museums	●●●●●
Art and crafts	●●●○○
Children	●●●○○
Historical sights	●●●○○
Scenery	●●●○○
Walking	●●●○○
Castles	●●○○○

Lisbon

O ne of the world's most romantic cities, Lisbon lives in a happy semi-timewarp. Its 21st-century comforts and conveniences exist in a setting of belle époque buildings, broad tree-lined promenades, mirrored cafés and pushcarts selling hot chestnuts and nosegays of violets. The past is not re-created, it lives here. Creaky old trams with carefully polished wood interiors warn Volvos off their tracks with persistent little bells. Two modern bridges span the Tagus, but cars still queue up for the wheezy little ferry. Lisbon will warm the heart of anyone who loves fine architecture. The city has managed to build – and keep – the best from nearly every period of its history. All around there are extraordinary examples of medieval, Renaissance, Gothic, neoclassical, art nouveau, art deco and postmodern buildings. Plus the definitive example of Portugal's own style, called Manueline.

Getting there and getting around

ⓘ **Turismo** *Praça dos Restauradores; tel: (01) 346 63 07; Open daily 0900–2000.* It is crowded, friendly but not especially well-informed. Ask for *Lisboa Step by Step* for current information.

Turismo de Lisboa *R. Jardim do Regedor 50; tel: (01) 343 36 72; open daily 0900–1800.*

Arriving and departing
International flights arrive at Lisbon's one airport which is small, modern and easy to navigate. The bus to the hotels downtown is cheap and the ticket entitles you to a day's free travel. TAP Air Portugal passengers leaving Lisbon ride free. Taxis are inexpensive, drivers polite and usually honest, but get a fare estimate from the tourist

The **Lisboa Card** €€€ may not include the most useful tram routes or the museums you wish to see; read the details carefully before buying. If you plan to rush through a lot of sights, it could be worthwhile, but a **one-day ticket** (€) for buses, lifts and trams may be a better buy.

information desk at the airport before taking one into town. Drivers will tell you it's metered, but they can add charges, so be sure they know you're wise.

Getting around

Lisbon lies along the Tejo (Tagus) river, always a good point of reference. With it and Castelo de São Jorge, you can usually get your bearings. The city's heart is the Bairro Baixa, a flat grid of streets between the river and the Rossio, a broad square a few blocks inland. As you head towards the Rossio from Praça do Comércio, at the river, the steep streets and steps of the Alfama rise to your right, capped by the castle. To your left, the fashionable Chiado district leads up to the Bairro Alto.

Beyond the Rossio, bearing slightly left as traffic must, is the long Praça dos Restauradores which narrows only slightly to become Avenida da Liberdade, a tree-lined esplanade leading to Praça Pombal. Many major in-town hotels are in this area; a right turn at Praça Pombal leads to the airport.

Most sights are also in this central area or in Belém, a riverside neighbourhood some distance beyond the Bairro Alto reached on the old-fashioned tram (No.15) or buses (No.27, 28, 29, 43, 49 or 15) from Praça do Comércio. About halfway, the docks of Santo Amaro and Alcântara, reclaimed from warehouse wasteland, face the marina and cruise port with a lively quay of restaurants and nightspots.

Driving: Visitors claiming rental cars at the airport can drive into the city quickly, along some of Lisbon's loveliest avenues. Major access routes are surprisingly easy to navigate and well signposted, but leave the car parked while exploring the city. Follow signs for 'Rossio' to get to the heart of the Bairro Baixa and major in-town hotels.

Trams and buses: Trams and buses are easy to use; the free city map shows the lines, and drivers are very helpful. Fellow passengers are even more helpful; Lisbons love their city, and delight in sharing it. Lisbon's Metropolitano (tube) is designed for commuters, and most sightseeing areas are better served by surface transport, which has views better too.

Lifts and funicular: Two convenient transports ascend to the Bairro Alto. Below Rossio is the Elevador de Santa Justa, a lift with a connecting bridge (possibly closed for repairs) to Largo do Carmo. The funicular, Elevador da Glória, climbs from Praça dos Restauradores to just above Largo Trinidade.

Boats: One of the world's great port cities, Lisbon looks beautiful from the wide Tejo (Tagus), its old buildings rising in terraces to the castle. Cruzeiros do Tejo, Estação Fluvial, Terreiro Paço, tel: (01) 882 03 48, fax: 882 03 65; two-hour cruises daily Apr–Oct, 1100 and 1500.

Above
The Castelo de São Jorge

🏛 **Castelo de São Jorge** € *East of Barrio Baixa, No.37 bus; open daily 1000–1800.*

Sights

Castelo de São Jorge✦✦✦
The castle floats above Lisbon, a constant reminder of the city's history. First occupied by Phoenicians, later a stronghold of Romans, Visigoths and Moors, its walls are punctuated by ten tall square towers and contain the old *bairro* (neighbourhood) of Santa Cruz. Views from its crenellated walls and park-like belvederes are sweeping; from below the castle looks best when floodlit at night. In the vaulted interior, four multimedia exhibits detail the history of the city and fort.

Elevador de Santa Justa✦
The quickest way to get to the Igreja do Carmo and the Bairro Alto, this impressive cast iron lift (*R. Santa Justa, one block south of Rossio*) has great views of the Baixa and Castelo São Jorge. It was not designed by Eiffel, but by his student. The bridge from the top may be closed for reconstruction.

Igreja do Carmo✦✦
On November 1, 1755 this church (*Largo do Carmo at Calçada Sacramento, Bairro Alto*) was filled with worshippers at mass for All Saints when the earthquake brought the vaulted roof down on their heads. Today its Gothic arches and walls enclose a beautiful park commemorating the dead of the earthquake. Many artifacts of the church remain.

Above
Lisbon's waterside square, the
Praça do Comércio

🏛 **Igreja de São Roque** *Largo Trinidade Coelho, bus 58, 100, Elevador da Glória at Praça dos Restauradores; open Tue–Sun 1000–1700, closed holidays.*

Igreja de São Vicente de Fora € *Largo de São Vicente, tram 28, bus 12; open daily 0900–1230, 1500–1800.*

Jardim da Estrela *Largo da Estrela, off Calçada da Estrela west of Bairro Alta; tram 25, 28 bus 9, 20, 22, 27, 38; open 0700–2400.*

Igreja de São Roque❖❖
The interior of this atypical Portuguese church is open, almost airy, its altar uncluttered. The deep side altars are the highlight, especially the Capela de São João Baptista, built in Rome in 1742 of lapis lazuli, agate and marble. The Capela deNossa Senhora de Piedade is in gold intaglio and the Capela da Assunção has splendid polychrome reliquaries. The museum houses paintings, vestments and religious treasure.

Igreja de São Vicente de Fora❖
The 16th-century church and monastery's main features are a canopied baroque altar and the cloister which has good 18th-century *azulejos* depicting rural and court life. The monks' refectory is now a pantheon of the Bragança family, with tombs of kings and queens from Dom João IV, who died in 1656, to Dom Carlos, assassinated in 1908.

Jardim da Estrela❖
Located opposite the Basílica da Estrela, the exotic trees and plants make this one of the most beautiful gardens in the city. It is designed for leisurely strolls among its statues and along the shores of its lake, or for sipping coffee in its café.

Jardim Zoológico €
Estrada de Benfica, bus
16, 26, 31, 41, 46, 54, 58,
Metro to Jardim Zoológico;
tel: (01) 723 29 00; open
1000–2000 Apr–Sep,
1000–1800 Oct–Mar.

Museu Antoniano €
Largo de Santo António da
Sé; open Tue–Sun
1000–1300, 1400–1800,
closed holidays.

Museu do Azulejo € R.
da Madre de Deus, buses
18, 42, 104, 105; tel: (01)
814 77 47; open Wed–Sun
1000–1800, Tue 1400-
1800. The very pleasant
café (€–€€) fills a rear
courtyard.

**Museu Calouste
Gulbenkian €** Av. de
Berna, 45A; bus 16, 26, 31,
46, 56; Metro São Sebastião
or Praça de Espanha; open
Tue–Sun 1000–1700, closed
holidays. Garden open daily
0800–2000.

Museu da Cidade €
Campo Grande 245, bus 1,
3, 7, 33, 36, 47, 50, Metro
Campo Grande; open
Tue–Sun 1000–1300,
1400–1800, closed holidays.

Jardim Zoológico*

A pleasant blend of garden and zoo, Jardim Zoológico has 2 500 animals, including a pair of pandas and rare white rhinoceros. Grounds include displays of flowers and a rose garden. In addition to parrot and reptile performances, there are dolphin shows in the dolphinarium. However, children and adults may be unimpressed by its conditions.

Largo do Martim Moniz*

Exciting contemporary fountains and 46 kiosks make this plaza on Av. Almirante Reis, two blocks from Rossio, an interesting place to stroll. The kiosks (*open daily 1000–1900*), symbolising battlements (bring a good imagination) sell old books, antiques and handicrafts; one is a tourist information centre. Be wary of the fountains on windy days.

Museu Antoniano

If you think St Anthony of Padua was Italian, think again. The spot where he was born, opposite the Sé, is now a church and museum of icons, clothing and other memorabilia. Although St Vincent is the city's patron, the local boy made good is the clear favourite, especially in late June when his festival brings a week of merrymaking.

Museu do Azulejo***

The former Convento da Madre de Deus houses a definitive collection of the tiles that make Portugal's churches and other buildings unique. Arranged chronologically are the earliest known examples from Sevilla, in Spain, later ones from Italy and Holland and contemporary Portuguese *azulejos*. The rooms around the cloisters are perfect for displaying the tiles, and the museum opens into the richly decorated choir of one of Lisbon's most beautiful (and tile-lined) churches.

Museu Calouste Gulbenkian***

The Gulbenkian family, Portugal's major benefactors, donated this outstanding museum with extensive collections of Egyptian, Greco-Roman, Mesopotamian, Islamic and Oriental art, as well as European works from early medieval to the 19th century. A separate museum shows modern art. Surrounding these, the Jardim da Fundação Calouste Gulbenkian, filled with sculpture and plants, is a nice counterpoint to the intensity of the collections inside.

Museu da Cidade*

Lisbon's own story is told at the 17th-century Palácio da Pimenta in archaeological relics of its earliest years through the 19th century. Some of the fine collection of paintings of the city predate the 1755 earthquake; others include the original watercolour renditions of plans for its reconstruction. The palace itself is decorated in *azulejo* tiles.

Museu do Chiado € R. Serpa Pinto 4, tram 28, bus 58, 100, Metro Baixa Chiado; open Wed–Sun 1000–1800, Tue 1400–1800, closed holidays.

Museu-Escola de Artes Decorativas Portuguesas €€ Largo das Portas do Sol; tram 12, 28, bus 37; tel: (01) 886 19 91; open Sun–Fri 1000–1700.

Museu Nacional de Arte Antiga € R. das Janelas Verdes, tram 15, 18, buses 7, 40, 49, 51, 60; open Wed–Sun 1000–1800, Tue 1400–1800, closed holidays.

Museu Nacional do Traje € Largo Júlio Castilho, tel: (01) 759 03 18; open Tue–Sun 1000–1800, closed holidays.

Museu do Teatro € Estrada do Lumiar, tel: (01) 757 25 47. Open Wed–Sun 1000–1800, Tue 1400–1800, closed holidays, buses 1, 3, 4, 7, 36, 101, 108 to the northern outskirts.

Palácio dos Marquêses de Fronteira €€ Largo São Domingos de Benfica, north side of Parque Florestal de Monsanto, bus 72 or Metro to Sete Ríos then a 20-min. walk along R. das Furnas and R. São Domingos; tel: (01) 778 20 23 for hours and booking (bring ID). Prices vary by tour.

Museu do Chiado*

Following the disastrous 1988 Chiado fire, the museum has reopened, refurbished to show off the old structure as well as 19th- and 20th-century drawings, paintings and sculpture illustrating the development from Romanticism to Neo-Realism, mostly Portuguese.

Museu-Escola de Artes Decorativas Portuguesas **

Also known as the Fundação Ricardo Espírito Santo, the 17th-century *palácio* filled with exquisite furniture, paintings and decorative objects preserves the lifestyles of the 17th and 18th centuries. Preserving the artistry entailed in creating these works is also part of the museum's mission, and workshops teach such skills as bookbinding and gilding.

Museu Nacional de Arte Antiga***

Portuguese art and its influence on other artists is the focus of the collections covering the 12th–19th centuries. The best art from the monasteries – closed with the 1834 expulsion of religious orders – came here. A highlight is the *Adoration of St Vicent*, a six-panel polyptych by Nuno Gonçalves painted in 1460 and depicting contemporary society, literally a group portrait of everyone who was anyone. Among others represented are Frei Carlos, Grão Vasco, Hieronymus Bosch, Albrecht Dürer and Hans Holbein the elder. One fascinating exhibit documents the 16th-century Japanese encounter with Portuguese missionaries.

Museu Nacional do Traje, Museu do Teatro*

Separate museums in adjacent refurbished palaces, the first records national dress, the second the theatre. The Museu Nacional do Traje depicts professions, classes and periods through dress. The Museu do Teatro preserves theatrical costumes, set sketches, art, sets and memorabilia of theatres and performers.

Palácio dos Marquêses de Fronteira**

Difficult to get to, this 17th-century palace is worth the effort for anyone who likes *azulejos*. Used throughout the palace are the finest examples of early Portuguese tile work, and in the dining room are 17th-century Delft tiles, the first ever imported. Formal parterre gardens with box hedges have tiled panels; benches, walls, pools and other surfaces of the extensive gardens are also covered, in subjects ranging from historic to bucolic. Still occupied, the palace is open limited hours, by reservation.

Praça de Touros*

The neo-Moorish bullring dominates Campo Pequeno with its red brick arcades and round domes. *Tourados* (bullfights) are held *Thu 2000 May–Sep; tel: (01) 793 24 42.*

Right
The Sé (Cathedral) de Lisboa

Parque Eduardo VII*
This elegant formal park named after King Edward VII of England, commemorates his visit in 1902 to reaffirm the alliance between Britain and Portugal. From the upper end there is a good view over the city. Next to it, the Estufa Fria is a slat house where exotic plants grow amidst ponds and waterfalls.

Sé de Lisboa*
This imposing Romanesque cathedral was built by the first king of Portugal after he ousted the Moors, about 1150. Twice damaged by earthquakes, it acquired Gothic and later embellishments without losing its essential elements. St Anthony, whose own chapel stands nearby, was baptised here in 1195. Highlights are the Machado de Castro nativity scence sculpted in 1766 and the Gothic ambulatory, empty but for tombs.

ⓘ **Museu Nacional dos Coches** € *Praça Afonso de Albuquerque; tram 15, bus 14, 27, 28, 43, 49, 51; tel: (01) 361 08 50. Open Tue–Sun 1000–1730, closed holidays.*

Mosteiro dos Jerónimos (cloister €) *Praça do Império, tram 15 or buses 27, 28, 29, 43, 49 and 15; tel: (01) 362 00 34. Open Tue–Sun 1000–1700, closed holidays.*

Belém❖❖❖

Although some distance from the rest of the city, Belém's attractions are fairly close together, except for the Torre de Belém, a 15–20-minute walk down river. Avoid Monday, when nearly everything here is closed.

The **Museu Nacional dos Coches❖❖❖** is, without question, among the world's finest collection of coaches. Gilt-laden carriages in almost overwhelming numbers are exhibited in the 18th-century royal riding school, well worth seeing in its own right. Descriptive panels tell the stories, from grand coronation and ambassadorial coaches to the diminutive carriage of the king's illegitimate sons, conveyances designed for status as well as transport.

The **Mosteiro dos Jerónimos❖❖❖** is arguably the finest monastery in Portugal and has been declared a UNESCO World Heritage site. Building was begun after the 1499 discovery of the sea route to India and substantially finished by 1572. The nautical motifs are especially appropriate in this shrine to Portugal's maritime prowess, the definitive example of the unique Manueline style. In the church,

Padrão dos Descobrimentos *Av. de Brasilia, tram 15, bus 27, 28, 43, 49. Opposite the Mosteiro dos Jerónimos.*

Museu Nacional de Arqueologia € *Largo das Portas do Sol (Mosteiro dos Jerónimos), tram 15 bus 27, 28, 29, 43, 49, 51; tel: (01) 362 00 00 /22. Open Wed–Sun 1000–1800, Tue 1400–1800, closed holidays.*

Museu da Marinha €; *Praça do Império; tram 15, bus 27, 28, 29, 43, 49, 51; tel: (01) 362 00 19. Open Jun–Sep 1000–1800, Oct–May 1000–1700, closed holidays.*

which has soaring stone vaulting, is the tomb of explorer Vasco da Gama. The double cloister is outstanding, as are some of the surrounding rooms; the arches are filled with delicate carved tracery that hardly seems possible in stone.

Portugal's Age of Discovery was largely inspired by Prince Henry the Navigator, son of Dom João I and Philippa of Lancaster. The 500th anniversary of his death in 1460 was commemorated by the striking **Padrão dos Descobrimentos**✶✶ (Monument to the Discoveries) overlooking the Tagus. It stands like the prow and sails of a great ship thrusting forward, its rails lined with the discoverers and other Portuguese heroes.

The **Museu Nacional de Arqueologia**✶✶✶ serves as repository for some of the country's most ancient artifacts, from sites you will encounter throughout your travels. Collections include excavated pottery, stelae and household goods. Exhibits dramatise Portugal's development with menhirs, stone pigs, and classical art from Roman settlements. A separate gallery has a fine collection of rare gold jewellery.

Portugal's love affair with the sea is well demonstrated in the **Museu da Marinha**✶✶ an outstanding collection of ships and boats. The centrepiece is the *Bergantim Real*, a royal barge built in 1778, but equally interesting are small craft from around the country. Scale models include 15th–20th-century vessels: historic caravels, humble fishing boats, tankers and submarines. Displays on the explorers and discoverers go beyond the caravels, extending to early air pioneers, with a display of seaplanes including Cabral's plane from the 1922 crossing of the South Atlantic.

Right
The Museu Nacional dos Coches

Museu Nacional de Arte Popular € *Av. de Brasilia; tram 15 bus 9, 27, 28, 43, 49, 51; tel: (01) 301 12 82. Open Tue–Sun 1000–1230, 1400–1700 (free Sun am).*

Torre de Belém € *Av. de Brasilia, tram 15, bus 27, 28, 29, 43, 49, 51; open Tue–Sun 1000–1700, closed holidays. See it when the late-afternoon sun turns it gold.*

Palácio Nacional and Jardim Botânico da Ajuda € *Calçada de Ajuda, north from the Museu dos Coches; tram 18, bus 14, 32, 42, 60; tel: (01) 363 70 95; Thur–Tue 1000–1700, closed holidays.*

For the **Museu Nacional de Arte Popular**✦✦✦ 'popular' means 'of the people', not current kitsch, referring to traditional arts and crafts from all over Portugal. Painted wagons, fascinating variations of pottery from around the country, painted furniture, cork art, costumes and rugs, beautifully displayed and interpreted, offer a one-stop exposure to the best of Portuguese popular culture.

The impressive Manueline tower in the middle of the Tagus, **Torre de Belém**✦✦, was left high (but not entirely dry) after the 1755 earthquake changed the course of the river. Built in 1515 to protect the river and its shipping, it is now a museum of the Portuguese seafaring tradition.

Palácio Nacional da Ajuda✦✦, the royal residence from 1862 until the revolution in 1910, sits above Belém overlooking the river. Its elaborately over-decorated salons give an interesting insight into the private lives of the last of the Portuguese royals. Adjoining the palace, the **Jardim Botânico**✦✦ (botanical garden) was created in the 18th century as a place for the many new and strange plants brought home by Portuguese explorers. Look for the Jardim das Damas with waterfalls and ponds, where ladies-in-waiting once strolled.

Accommodation and food

Locations most convenient to sightseeing and restaurants are close to the Rossio or on Av. da Liberdade, which includes Praça dos Restauradores.

Orion-Eden €€ *Praça dos Restauradores 24; tel: (01) 321 66 00, fax: (01) 321 66 66.* A stunning renovation of an art deco building, the well-appointed mini-apartments are attractive and in the city centre. Parking available.

Hotel Americano €–€€ *Rua 1º de Dezembro 73; tel: (01) 347 49 76.* Just off the west side of the Rossio, this no-frills hotel was recently remodelled; private baths and air-conditioning.

Hotel Venezia €€ *Av. da Liberdade 189; tel: (01) 352 26 18, fax: (01) 352 66 78.* The 1886 building retains its original elegance but the transformation to modern hotel has brought wonderful modern touches, such as colourful murals of Lisbon Street scenes. Updated rooms have all the expected conveniences.

Hotel Avenida Palace €€€ *R. 1º de Dezembro 123; tel: (01) 346 01 51, fax: 342 28 84; e-mail: hotel.av.palace@mail.telepac.pt* Recent renovations have restored the brilliant 19th-century elegance of the public rooms; the service never lost its shine. Views over the busy Rossio or Praça dos Restauradores, in the heart of the city. Parking available.

Sancho €–€€ *Travessa da Glória 14.* An attractive stucco dining room, dark-beamed ceilings and uniformed waiters serving a standard menu of local dishes.

Above Right
The art-deco Orion-Eden Hotel

Left
The Torre de Belém

Alpendre €-€€ *R. Augusto Rosa 32, tel: (01) 886 24 21.* Across from the Cathedral, serving grilled meats and fresh seafood; roast sucking pig at midday.

Cafreal €-€€ *R. Portas de Santo Antão 71; tel: (01) 346 84 47,* in the tourist zone, but excellent grilled seafood and good, if pricey, wines.

Consenso €€€ *R. Academia das Ciências 1, tel: (01) 343 13 11.* Fine dining in elegant, contemporary style, in the former palace of the Marquês de Pombal. Traditional ingredients shine in updated treatments: monkfish in cream and tarragon sauce, or duck with chocolate and chestnuts.

Alecrim aos Malhos €€ *R. do Alecrim 47A. Open Mon–Fri 1200–1500, 2000–2400, Sat 2000–0200,* on the river side of the Bairro Alto, above Cais do Sodré station; fresh vegetables and home-made desserts.

O Nobre €€€ *R. das Merces 71-A-B, tel: (01) 362 21 06.* Another upscale restaurant, near Belém. In attractive traditional *azulejo*-panelled dining rooms, enjoy fish dishes and meat such as *duck magret.*

Hotel Mundial €€ *R. Dom Duarte 4 (Largo Martim Moniz); tel: (01) 886 31 01; fax: (01) 887 91 29, e-mail: mundialhot@.telepac.pt* Wonderfully comfortable and hospitable, two blocks east of Rossio, with all amenities and facilities, including restaurant with a bird's-eye view, exercise and sports at a nearby club. Ask for a room with balcony overlooking the Largo or stunningly floodlit Castelo São Jorge.

As in most Portuguese cities, restaurants tend to gather in groups. **Rua Portas de Santo Antão**, off Rossio behind the theatre, is lined with pricey eateries that draw tourists to their outdoor tables (Lisboans rarely dine on the street). Small restaurants (€) on the **Rua da Glória**, west of Av. Liberdade, cater mostly to locals. Tiny **Rua do Arco da Graça**, off Rossio to the right of the theatre, has several more. Of Lisbon's old cafés, see at least **Nicola** (€), facing Rossio, and **A Brasileira** (€) at the top of Rue Garrett, where the literati met.

Passejo d'Avenida €-€€ *Av. da Liberdade, Plaça Central near the Cinema Condes, tel: (01) 342 37 55.* On the esplanade in a belle époque cast-iron gazebo with art-deco interior, this excellent restaurant looks as if it could be touristy, but it is not; local specialities are well prepared and nicely served.

Entertainment

Several restaurants and clubs feature **Fado**, the most Portuguese of music. Food and drink tend to be pricey. Call for reservations and performance times, usually about 2300 to the wee hours. Most are in the Bairro Alto or Alfama:

Nono, *R. do Norte 47; tel: (01) 342 99 89.* **Fado Folclore**, *R. das Gaveas 51; tel: (01) 346 12 04, (01) 342 83 14.* **Faia**, *R. da Barroca 54; tel: (01) 342 67 42.* **Café Luso**, *Travessa da Queimada 10; tel: (01) 342 22 81.* **Canto de Camões**, *Travessa da Espera 38, tel: (01) 346 54 64.*

Shopping

Feira da Ladra (*Campo Santa Clara; Tue 0700–1300, Sat 0700–1800*), is the big flea market, where you may find treasures among the chipped *azulejos* and rows of not-so-old-school ties.

Right
The Elevador de Santa Justa

For more fashionable shops, go to the Chiado (R. Garrett) or Bairro Baixa, where **Madeira House** on R. Augusta sells pricey, but high quality hand-embroidered linens, porcelain and *azulejos*. The best place to find traditional crafts is at the shop in the **Museu Nacional de Arte Popular**, where quality and selection are high, prices low. Or see the excellent choices at **Artesanato Santos Oficios** on Largo Madalena, just below the Sé.

The central **Mercado** (market) is opposite Cais do Sodré train station, west of Praça do Comércio. **Celeiro** sells groceries and a wide range of farm cheeses, just off Rossio on R. 1º de Dezembro; next door is a health-food store with good grainy breads.

Suggested tour

Start at the **ROSSIO ❶**, whose long oval shape reveals its Roman origins as a hippodrome. From its south (river) end walk east, toward the castle, through **Praça da Figueira** to R. Madalena. Turn right and follow it to **Rua das Pedras Negras**, where a left takes you to the 12th-century fortress-like **SE ❷** (cathedral) and the church of **Santo António** and **Museu Antoniano**, birthsite of the saint.

Rua Augusto Rosa leads uphill, becoming **Rua do Limoeiro**, and passing an astonishing tree with 2-metre roots, before reaching **LARGO SANTA LUZIA ❸**. This garden belvedere has *azulejo* panels and views out over the Alfama to the river.

Shortly beyond is the **Largo das Portas do Sol**, another vantage point, and the **MUSEU DAS ARTES DECORATIVAS ❹**. Backtrack to **Largo Santa Luzia** and turn right, climbing through the sloping **Largo Contador-Mor** to **Rua Chão da Feira**. Turn left, along the **castle walls** and into **CASTELO SAO JORGE ❺** for splendid views over the city and river.

After exploring the castle, return to **Largo das Portas do Sol** and take one of the stairways leading down into the heart of the old **ALFAMA ❻**, a warren of steep streets that are delightful to explore (but only by daylight). When you are ready to leave the Alfama, continue downhill to **Rua João da Praça** which becomes **Rua São Pedro**. Follow it westwards (the river downhill to your left) to **Cruzes da Sé**. Continue past the **SE ❷** on R. Santo António into **Largo Madalena** where the **Artesanato Santos Oficios**, carries fine Portuguese handicrafts. From Largo Madalena, follow **Rua da Madalena** left to **Rua Alfândega** and **IGREJA CONCEICAO VELHA ❼**, a church partially destroyed in the 1755 earthquake. A right turn takes you into the arcaded **PRACA DO COMÉRCIO ❽**, known as **Black Horse Square** to British merchants who landed at the busy docks once located here. Go through the **Arco da Rua Augusta** and follow this fashionable shopping street to **ROSSIO ❶**, where you began. Notice the fine shop fronts behind the commercial signs, and the old store names in the mosaic pavement in front.

R Santo António dos Capuchos

Campo dos Mártires da Pátria

Rua do Saco

Rua A Vidal

Rua Maria da Fonte

Av Almmirante Reis

Rua Damasceno Monteiro

Rua da Graça

de São José

Rua do Telha

Rua Instituto Bacteriológico

Rua de S Lázaro

Rua da Palma

Rua Bombarda

Trav do Monte

Avenida da Liberdade

Elevador do Lavra

Calç de Santana

Miradouro da Senhora do Monte

Largo da Graça

Glória

Rua Portas de Santo Antão

Largo do Martim Moniz

Rua dos Cavaleiros

Rua Lagares

Convento N S da Graça

Rua Voz do Operario

evador Glória

Palácio Foz

i

Calç Sto André

Calç da Graça

Rua S Vicente

Railway Station

Largo de S Domingos

Castelo de São Jorge

Costa do Castelo

R das Escolas Gerais

São Roque

Rossio Dom Pedro IV (Pr)

1

5

Elevador de Sta Justa

Museu Arqueológico

Rua da Misericórdia

Calç do Sacramento

Rua do Carmo

Rua Nova do Almada

Rua de Santa Justa

Rua dos Sapateiros

Rua dos Fanqueiros

Rua dos Correeiros

Rua da Madalena

R do Chão da Feira

4 Alfama **6**

Chiado

Rua Garrett

Rua Ivens

Rua do Ouro

Rua Augusta

Rua da Prata

Largo dos Lóios

R de S Tiago

3

Praça Luis de Camões

Baixa

Rua Saudade

Largo do Limoeiro

S Miguel

Teatro Nacional

2 Sé

Rua do Alecrim

Rua António Maria Cardoso

Museu do Chiado

Rua da Alfândega **7**

Rua Cais de Santarém

o Paulo

Rua V Cordon

✉

Campo das Cebolas

Avenida Infante D Henrique

Doca da Marinha

Praça Duque de Terceira

Rua do Arsenal

8 Praça do Comércio

Estação do Sul e Sueste

ay on

Avenida Ribeira das Naus

Tejo

0 ———— 200 metres

0 ———— 150 yards

Lisbon's coast

Ratings

Architecture	●●●●
Beaches	●●●
Castles	●●●
Children	●●●
Food and drink	●●●
Scenery	●●●
Historical sights	●●
Walking	●●

An almost fairy-tale sense of unreality pervades Sintra, Cascais and Estoril, as though they were waiting patiently for the royal family to return. Tiaras do not seem out of place at the Palácio Estoril, where the world's dwindling supply of royals are still greeted with bows. The Portuguese royal family built residences at Sintra and Queluz, and took the sea at Cascais. Foreign and exiled royalty chose Estoril. English poets favoured Sintra's lush green hillsides, covered in rainforest-like vegetation. At the continent's westernmost point, Cabo da Roca's cliffs face the Atlantic like the prow of a caravel. The entire coast is an alternating series of these sheer headlands and beaches in the coves between them. Winter is hardly in the vocabulary of Estoril and Cascais. Water temperatures are warm; people swim almost year-round at Tamariz in Estoril.

CASCAIS✧✧

ℹ Tourist Information R. Visconde de Luz 14; tel: (01) 486 82 04, open daily 0900–2000 Jun–Sep, 0900–1900 Oct–May.

⇄ A 30-minute train to Cascais and Estoril leaves Lisbon's Cais do Sodré station every 15 minutes; tel: (01) 888 40 25.

⊙ Fish auctions are Mon–Sat 1800 at the market; on Wed and Sat mornings there's a **craft market**.

No longer just a quaint fishing village, Cascais balances its boutiques, restaurants and hotels with its colourful fishing harbour so well that neither seems incongruous. Tourists buy ice cream beside stacks of traps and piles of fishing nets and buoys, while fishermen drag boats onto the beach between toddlers' sand castles. In a surprisingly untouristy old neighbourhood, tile panels and a richly carved and gilded high altar make the **Igreja Matriz**✧ worth seeing. Cascais also has the the largest Praça de Touros (bullring) in Portugal.

It seems fitting that Cascais should have a **Museu do Mar**✧ (Av.da República, open Tue–Sun 1000–1700), since its history has always been entwined with the sea. From a rare 16th-century map and shipwreck salvage to the watery world of fish and molluscs, if it's in the sea, it's in this museum.

It is easy to spot the **Museu Condes de Castro Guimarães**✧ (Estrada da Boca do Inferno, open Tue–Sun 1000–1700) as its turreted and

balconied tower rises out of the opposite side of the park, near Praia de Santa Marta. The interior is no less fanciful, with Persian-rug patterned tiles on its walls and swirled carvings over arched doorways. Guided tours in English are available.

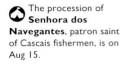

The procession of **Senhora dos Navegantes**, patron saint of Cascais fishermen, is on Aug 15.

Some distance further along the cliffs a pathway leads to Boca do Inferno, 'Mouth of Hell', where waves pound through an arch into a large collapsed sea cave, to even greater effect during heavy seas.

To ride through Cascais in style, *charrettes* can be hired (€€) at the Visconde da Luz gardens; to view the town from the sea, there are sailing-boats for rent at the harbour.

Accommodation and food in Cascais

Hotel Albatroz €€€ *R. Frederico Arouca; tel: (01) 483 28 21, fax: (01) 484 48 27.* Built for the Portuguese royal family in mid-1800s, overlooking water with sea views from most rooms.

Hotel Baia €€ *Av. Marginal; tel: (01) 483 10 33, fax: (01) 483 10 95.* Facing the fishing harbour, with balconies overlooking the heart of town.

Camping Praia da Guincha €; *tel: (01) 487 10 14.* Pitches among the coastal pines and dunes.

Beira Mar €€–€€€ *R. das Flores 6; tel: (01) 482 73 40.* Closed Tue. If you splurge on prawns only once, do it in this cosy restaurant with attentive service. The shellfish is so succulent it stands out even in a town known for fine seafood restaurants.

Restaurante Mare Alta €€–€€€ *R. do Cobre, Largo dos Tanque; tel: (01) 482 22 68.* In the Cobre neighbourhood, off the N9-1, near the A5 highway. Their speciality is *arroz de mariscos* for two, a paella-like dish full of shellfish. Closed Mon.

Below
The beach at Ericeira

Ericeira✢

ⓘ Tourist information R. Dr Eduardo Burnay 33; tel: (061) 631 22, open 0900–2400 Jul–Aug, 0900–2000 Oct–Apr, 0900–2200 spring and autumn. Handy telephones require neither card nor coin; pay afterwards at desk.

A relaxed seaside resort perched on a cliff with views south to Cabo da Roca, Ericeira has long beaches on either side and a fishing harbour under the cliffs in the middle. Above, streets of whitewashed houses wind upwards to the wide, tree-shaded Praça da República, with mosaic pavement.

The scenic Esplanada Furnas runs south from the fishing harbour, along the sea past a section of spongy black rock filled with caves and sink-holes. Explore these from paths and stairways off the esplanade. The colourful harbour is busiest in the late afternoon. The Igreja Matriz has very good *azulejos* and a coffered ceiling.

Two surfing beaches offer varying degrees of challenge in Ericeira, and boards can be rented from Ultimar (*R. 5 de Outubro; tel: (061) 623 71, closed Sun*).

Accommodation and food in Ericeira

Lodging and dining in Ericeira is less expensive than Estoril or Cascais.

Hotel Turismo €€ *Centro; tel: (061) 868 02 00, fax: (061) 86 31 46.* Refurbished without losing its wonderful aura of belle-époque grandeur, has smallish, spotless rooms, expansive sea views and a friendly staff. Its dining room (€€) has a nice way with grilled fish and meats.

Parque Campismo Municipal € *Praia São Sebastião, N247; tel: (061) 627 06.* Pleasant campsite with caravan hookups and a swimming pool. Walk to the beach or catch a bus into town.

Marisqueira Gairota €€ *R. Capitão João Lopez 18; tel (061) 86 61 00.* Open *Fri–Wed 0900–2400*, overlooking the fishing harbour, specialises in shellfish, especially shrimp, which you order by weight.

Grill Pinta €–€€ *R. Dr Eduardo Burnay*, serves a traditional menu.

Café Central and other sidewalk cafés and bakeries cluster in *Praça da República*. Leading out of the lower end of the square, *R. Dr Eduardo Burnay* is lined with restaurants and more cafés.

Estoril✢

ⓘ Turismo da Costa Estoril Arcadas do Parque; tel: (01) 466 38 13, fax: (01) 467 22 80. Regional information.

As World War II engulfed Europe, the royal families of invaded countries moved to the safety of their earlier summer playground at Estoril. Many built villas, others made the Hotel Palácio their temporary palace. Nobility that had escaped with only what they could carry paid for their rooms with jewels. Many stayed on after the war: Umberto of Italy and Don Juan of Spain have firmly established

Find riding lessons and horses for hire at **Centro Hípico da Costa do Estoril**, *Charnica; tel: (01) 487 20 64.*

Estoril as the Coast of Kings. Look in the telephone book to find who's who – listed by title instead of surname.

Although it may still be filled with royalty, Estoril is not filled with tourist sights. People come to play, to swim or sun on the beach, to tee-off at the Hotel Palácio's golf course (or any of five other top-rated courses in town), to sip wine or coffee in cafés or to tempt luck at the casino. People-watching is as popular as lying by the pool.

Estoril enjoys its own micro-climate, sunny even when Lisbon is wrapped in winter mists. Jan–Mar temperatures hover around 13ºC, Apr–Jun 18ºC , Jul–Sep 21ºC and Oct–Dec 15ºC. Each summer, a handicraft fair brings craftsmen from all over the country to demonstrate pottery, carving, weaving and other skills.

Accommodation and food in Estoril

Hotel Palácio €€€ *tel: (01) 468 04 00, fax: (01) 468 48 67.* This hotel isn't just located in the centre, it IS the centre of Estoril. Rooms are elegant and tasteful, with marble baths, some with balconies overlooking the large pool and grassy terrace. **Four Seasons** dining room (€€€) is among the highest rated in Portugal.

Hotel Paris €–€€ *Av. Marginal; tel: (01) 467 03 22, fax: (01) 467 11 71, e-mail: www.estorilcoast.com/hotelparis* Rooms with balconies overlooking the shore, steps from beach and centre.

Cozinha do Mar €–€€ *Av. S. Pedro, Monte Estoril; tel: (01) 468 93 17; Wed–Mon 1200–1500, 1900–2300.* Midday specials on weekdays at particularly reasonable prices.

Below
Estoril's beach

Frolic €–€€ *Av. Clothilde; tel: (01) 468 12 19, open daily 1200–1600, 1930–2300.* Outdoor dining in the heart of town.

MAFRA*

Hotel Castelão €
*Av. 25 de Abril; tel:
(061) 81 20 50, fax: (061)
81 16 98.* Opposite the
monastery, in the centre of
town, with a good
restaurant (€–€€).

The yellow, stone-towered façade of the Palácio de Mafra is 220 metres long. It is not by accident that it outmeasures Spain's Escorial by 12 metres. Its 154 full flights of stairs connect corridors so wide that the army, which uses much of its sprawling central grid as barracks, drives jeeps along them. The great carillon can be heard for miles and from May to October there are bell-ringing concerts on Sundays (*1600–1700*).

An interminable tour is highlighted occasionally by royal apartments, a Balmoral-style dining room completely out of character with the rest, an apothecary and a florid throne room. But it is the only way to see one of Europe's most magnificent libraries, the tour-de-force of the entire palace-monastery, an 83-metre room with barrel-vaulted ceiling and floors of coloured marble.

The **basílica***, not part of the tour, is unlike most Portuguese churches, tall and resplendent in marble inlay and Bernini-style sculpture. The smaller 13th-century **Igreja de Santo André***, in the village below, is a Romanesque-Gothic church with two fine Gothic tombs. For a key, ask at the tourist office.

Just outside Mafra, toward Ericeira, the **Aldeia Típica José Franco*** is identifiable by its windmill and clutch of tiny white buildings with blue-trim. Don't let the theme-park appearance scare you away from this delightful work of a talented potter, around whose studio it stands. The bakery, mill, chapel and shops showing traditional trades hover between naf and cute, but carry it off well. Children will especially like the miniature village, with tiny homes and working windmills. An *adega* serves wine with bread and local sausage. There is an excellent selection of pottery from all over Portugal, at reasonable prices, and a tiny farmers' market selling home-cured olives, honey and dried fruits. José Franco's atelier features his whimsical terracotta sculptures. Expect crowds at weekends in the summer. The town of **Malveira***, 8km to the east, holds a traditional country market every Thursday.

King João V built the monastery at Mafra to fulfill a 1711 vow of thanks for an heir to the throne. No detail was spared, no expense too great. When the Belgian firm from which he ordered the great carillon asked if he realised the cost, he doubled the order. The project grew more grandiose as it progressed, until it became one of the largest palaces in Europe, financed by gold that was pouring in from Brazilian mines.

QUELUZ✧✧✧

ℹ **Tourist Information** *Largo do Palácio; tel: (01) 435 00 39, fax: (01) 435 25 75.*

🏛 **Palácio National de Queluz** €; *tel: (01) 924 16 23, open Wed–Mon 1000–1300, 1400–1700.*

🎵 Concerts of Romantic Period music are held in the palace; get schedules at the TIC here or in Lisbon.

Right
The Palácio Naçional de Queluz

A yellow confection of a summer palace, set in beautiful formal gardens, is the beginning and end of this town between Lisbon and Sintra. A nice *pousada* adjoins, with one of Portugal's best-known restaurants.

It's not hard to imagine lines of gilded carriages pulling up at Palácio Naçional de Queluz, designed for parties, for balmy summer evenings and long languid summer days. Unlike most, it is built in a single style (although not a copy of Versailles, as is often suggested). It is pure 18th-century baroque, on one level with spacious bright rooms. Even its frescoes are light-hearted, especially those in the queen's dressing-room, showing children dressing up in adult finery. Architectural details and furnishings make it a museum of decorative arts.

The gardens give the palace an appropriate setting, combining the formal parterre beds and fountains of the upper terrace with the pure romantic frivolity of the lower reaches. Royal guests once cruised in little boats along the canal lined with colourful *azulejos*. These lower gardens are filled with pools, allegorical statues and fountains, all slightly unkempt and thoroughly charming. On most days adults and children in period costume frolic in the gardens, inviting visitors to join their games.

Accommodation and food in Queluz

Pousada de Dona Maria I €€–€€€ *Largo do Palácio; tel: (01) 435 61 58, fax: (01) 435 61 89.* Beautifully appointed rooms in a former palace outbuilding.

Cozinha Velha €–€€€ *Largo do Pálacio; tel: (01) 435 61 58.* The restaurant transforms the palace's old kitchen, with the giant free-standing fireplace as its centrepiece. Specialities include roast kid, *cataplana* of pork with clams (steamed in a special covered pan; from which the dish takes its name) and poached sole.

SINTRA✦✦✦

ⓘ Tourist Information *Praça da República; tel: (01) 923 11 57.*

Below
Sintra

Wedding-cake villas poke their candy-coloured turrets from the lush green that cascades down the steep hillsides. Buildings seem glued to the sheer slopes, as though the bottoms of the turrets were as sharply pointed as their tops, holding them in place like giant hatpins thrust into the rock.

Parque da Liberdade begins just past Volta do Duche, a lopsided square where incoming streets form a V below the palace. Paths wind along the steep bank through exotic trees and dense foliage, ferns grow from tree trunks. The park drops to a vale of giant plants and rock formations. At the base, people line up to fill jugs with Sintra's famously clear spring water from an elaborately tiled fountain in an Moorish arched alcove.

Sintra is 45 minutes by train from Lisbon's Rossio Station; it's a 15 minute walk along the park to the old town, but you need a car to visit attractions on the N375 or in the village of S. Pedro, both a bit of a hike.

Horse-drawn carriages await passengers in the lane below the Palácio National.

Palácio Nacional € *open Thu–Tue 1000–1230, 1400–1630 (free Sun am).*

Quinta da Regaleira €€ *N375 1 km from centre, open daily 1000–1800 Oct–May, tours 1000, 1030, 1330, 1500, 1530; 1000–1930 Jun–Sep, tours every half-hour.*

Shop in Sintra's many boutiques, antique and craft shops, but don't expect any bargains. The combined craft, flea and farmers' market on the second and fourth Sundays of the month at **San Pedro de Sintra** is of 14th-century origin.

The **Palácio Nacional***, whose two giant chimneys give it the silhouette of an oversized oast-house, is a conglomeration of overlayed styles; the final neo-Moorish layer has an astonishing variety of tiles. Some are set in *trompe-l'oeil* patterns, others are cut in unusual shapes, set in basket-weave or coloured like cloisonné inside relief designs. When it seems too much, a window or door will give on to an open courtyard with a fountain. In the kitchen a tiled stove takes up one entire wall under a ceiling that ends inside the giant chimneys.

If you think the Palácio Nacional is a tutti-frutti of styles, try the **Palácio da Pena*** (*€ open Tue–Sun 1000–1700*). It's a three-dimensional reference guide to every architectural style from medieval onwards: crenellated walls, parapets, Renaissance cupolas, Gothic towers, Moorish arches and tiles, onion domes, Manueline stone carving, all trimmed up like Hansel and Gretel's gingerbread cottage. No one takes it seriously; it's an architectural lark that puts into perspective all the other mini-castles dotting the hillsides. Inside is just as eclectic, a pastiche of Victorian excesses. Children love Pena, with its small rooms and something new to discover round every corner. The older chapel has a lovely delicate cloister.

The castle rises at the edge of Parque da Pena, a walled hilltop planted with exotic trees, camellias and rare plants from all over the world, studded with pools, bridges and formal flower-beds. Below are walls of the ruined **Castelo dos Mouros*** (*open 1000–1700, later in summer*), overlooking town. A trail leads from Sintra to the Moorish castle, taking about 55 minutes, and a steeper path goes on to Palácio da Pena. Keep going for spectacular vistas from the peninsula's highest point, Cruz Alta.

The late 18th-century Palácio de Seteais sits in manicured grounds, with formal boxwood parterre and terraced gardens. Look inside to see beautiful frescoed walls in the bright, airy public rooms. In one parlour, fresco trees grow up a wall and spread branches across the ceiling.

A relatively new addition to Sintra's roster of palatial residences to visit is the **Quinta da Regaleira***, a complex of fanciful buildings set in landscaped gardens. The ornate palace combines Gothic revival with Renaissance and Manueline; the garden and its grottoes are replete with Knights Templar symbolism (although there is no historic connection). Descend into the warren of underground passages via a spiral staircase into a 60-metre-deep dry well.

If you search Sintra's crowded streets in vain for the "glorious Eden" described by Byron, try **Monserrate***, a steep hillside transformed a century ago into a botanical garden and arboretum of rare plants. Sintra's unique microclimate is hospitable to plants far out of their usual range. This garden, wild and overgrown with giant trees, is quiet and usually deserted. Above is a sadly empty neo-Moorish palace, hardly larger than a pavilion; look through the doors to imagine what it must have been like.

Accommodation and food in Sintra

Seteais Palace €€€ *N375; tel: (01) 923 32 00, fax: (01) 923 42 77*. Some frescoed and antique-furnished guest rooms have balconies overlooking the gardens, also enjoyed from the terrace café, lined with red geraniums. The outstanding dining room (€€–€€€) serves French-inspired local specialities, such as Sintra trout with shrimp sauce.

Sapa € *Volta do Duche 12; tel: (01) 923 04 9*. This café is home to the best *Queijadas de Sintra*, delectable bite-sized cheese tarts.

Dos Arcos €€ *R. Serpa Pinto 4, São Pedro de Sintra; tel: (01) 923 02 64, closed Thu and Jun 15–30, Oct 1–15*. Atmospheric surroundings and market-fresh local ingredients.

Suggested tour

Total distance: 95km; 159km with detours.

Below
Costumed guides play cards in the grounds of Queluz palace

Time: Two hours driving, more on summer weekends. Allow 2 or 3 days with or without detour. Those with limited time should concentrate on Queluz and Sintra.

For a scenic ride through the Serra de Sintra to a beach north of Cabo da Roca, catch the **Eléctricos de Sintra** (€ tel: (01) 929 11 66), a century-old tram line that passes through the wine-producing town of Colares en route.

Farol do Cabo da Roca (Lighthouse); tel: (01) 929 09 81. Stop here for a certificate (€) proving that you have been to the continent's westernmost point.

Restaurante Furnas do Guincho €€–€€€ Estrada do Guincho; tel: (01) 486 92 43, open daily 1230–2300. Fish and shellfish, within sight of the sea, in summer from an open terrace.

Hotel do Guincho €€€ Estrada do Guincho; tel: (01) 487 04 91, fax: (01) 487 04 31. Perched on a rock above a beach, this reincarnation of a 17th-century fort is decorated to that period.

Links: Direct from CASCAIS to LISBON (*see page 58*) on the A5, or northward to Peniche via Lourinhã.

Route: Leave **LISBON ❶** on the IC19 through **QUELUZ ❷** and **San Pedro de Sintra** to **SINTRA ❸**. Follow the N9 north over steeply rolling terrain to **MAFRA ❹**, turning left (west) past the monastery and village, on to the N116, signposted to **ERICEIRA ❺**. Shortly, on the right is the **Aldeia Típica José Franco**.

Detour: Instead of turning left to Ericeira, go east on the N116 through Malveira, turning north (left) on the N8 to **Torres Vedras**. Students of the Peninsular Wars will recognise this name from Wellington's defensive walls, which prevented the French army from taking Lisbon.

From Torres Vedras, turn west on the N9. On the left, just after a signpost to Gibraltar, take a road sometimes marked with a yellow arrow, continuing to the left at the fork in a little cluster of houses. This lane ends at some farm buildings and the iron-age hillfort of **Castro de Zambujal**. Carbon-dating shows it to be from 2 500 BC, among Iberia's oldest; you can trace its three sets of defensive lines and the foundations of its round buildings.

Follow the N9 west to the N247, turning left (south) to follow the scenic cliff-lined coast and rejoin the main route in Ericeira.

From Ericeira go south onto the N247, returning to Sintra and climbing into the **Serra de Sintra** via the N247-3, which travels along a rocky ridge through the forests of **Parque Natural Sintra-Cascais** to the **Miradouro da Urca**. When the road meets the N247, turn right to the wine-producing town of **Colares**. Several roads lead northwest from Colares to cliff-guarded beaches. Backtrack on the N247, turning right (west) onto the N247-4, signposted **Cabo da Roca❖❖**. **Praia do Guincho**'s wild dunes and beach curve to the tall cliffs of Cabo da Roca, under constant attack from the Atlantic. Breakers and steady winds make the beaches near Cabo da Roca a favourite of surfers and windsurfers. In the spring, the wild lands around it are covered in white tufts of an *Armeria* (the wildflower known as sweet-william) unique to this cape.

Return to the N247 and continue east, following the coast around one of Europe's largest dunes at **Oitavos**, past the lighthouse at **Cabo Raso** and another, Farol da Guia, just before entering CASCAIS ❻. Between the two, look for signs to sea caves with thundering surf and, just before entering town, to the even more impressive **Boca do Inferno**.

Cascais blends almost imperceptibly into **ESTORIL ❼**, where the shore route becomes (just as imperceptibly) the N6. This leads past beaches, the large **Forte de São Julião da Barra** and lesser forts into the Belém district of Lisbon.

Also worth exploring

Southeast of Mafra, near the village of Negrais, is an area of strange giant weather-worn rocks called **Campo de Lapias**, some of which appear to have been also carved by prehistoric peoples. Also east of Mafra, near Vila Franca do Rosario, is a large circular Neolithic tomb from the 11th century BC, at **Monte da Pena**.

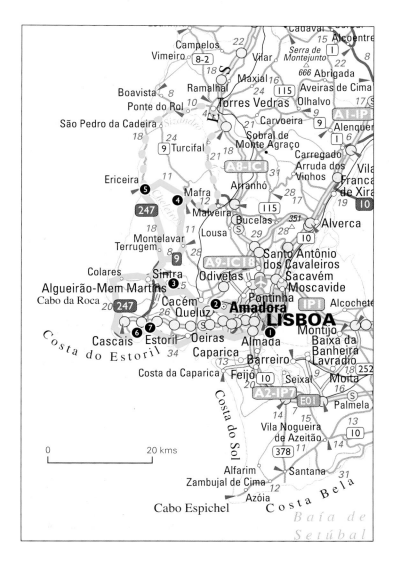

North of Lisbon

Ratings

Architecture	●●●●●
Art	●●●●○
Castles	●●●●○
Beaches	●●●○○
Geology	●●●○○
Scenery	●●●○○
Children	●●○○○
Museums	●○○○○

Two of Portugal's three great monasteries, one of Europe's most perfect walled towns and a major religious pilgrimage site all cluster in this region within easy reach of Lisbon. The third point for a neat triangular route is the riverside city of Santarém, with its pleasant old streets and Gothic churches. The shoreline to the west alternates between ragged rock formations and wide Atlantic beaches. In the 15th century, King Dinis ordered that the entire coast be planted with trees to stabilise the sand dunes and provide timber for shipbuilding. This royal forest still lines parts of the coastal road. Although the region's undoubted highlights are the magnificent stone-carvings of the two monasteries and Obidos's narrow streets and whitewashed homes inside a band of tall walls, it would be a shame to miss the coast and countryside that lie to either side.

ALCOBAÇA✦✦✦

ℹ Tourist Information
Praça 25 de Abril; tel: (062) 423 77, open daily 1000–1330, 1400–1730 Apr–Oct, 1400–1900 Nov–Mar.

🅿 Pay and Display Parking (€) in front of monastery in Praça 25 de Abril.

The great monastery, **Mosteiro de Santa Maria✦** (€ *open daily 0900–1900 Apr–Oct, 1000–1700 Nov–Mar*) at Alcobaça, combines splendid architecture and art with a love story that touches even today's traveller (*see box*). The church's long nave of clustered columns leads to the transept and the tombs of Dom Pedro and Inês de Castro, so delicately carved that in places they appear too fragile to support themselves. Pedro's tomb rests on stone lions; that of Inês is on the grotesque figures of her murderers. In the ambulatory, a fine Manueline doorway is surrounded by stone trees, their branches twining to form the arch.

In the adjoining **cloister** (€), a formal garden is surrounded by delicate Manueline columns, with a graceful lavabo in one corner. Off the far end a gargantuan kitchen has tiled walls, a six-ox roasting spit and a stream flowing through, so the monks would have fresh water.

Outside from the south (left) transept is an overgrown cemetery and little stone chapel with twined columns and a Renaissance façade.

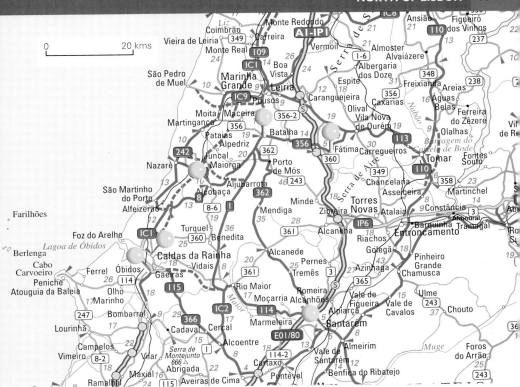

Museu da Vinha e do Vinho *Olival Fechado (N8, 1km north of town). Open Mon–Fri 0830–1230, 1400–1730, Sat–Sun 1000–1230, 1400–1800.*

St Bernard's Fair *(Aug 20)* and **St Simon's Fair** *(last week Oct)* include processions, markets and music.

To best appreciate the magnificent façade of the monastery, view it from one of the sidewalk cafés along the square, preferably as the late afternoon sun bathes it in honey shades and its bells ring out in deep, satisfying tones.

For a bird's-eye view of the whole monastery, follow R. Castelo past the 16th-century Misericórdia, climbing to the ruins of a Moorish castle. An interesting **Museu da Vinha e do Vinho**✝ traces viticulture and winemaking, a regional speciality.

Alcobaça is home to a brightly painted style of blue-glazed pottery, which you will see displayed in front of shops but is not common elsewhere. Market days are Mon and Wed.

Prince Dom Pedro married his true love, Inês de Castro, in secret because his father feared the influence of her Spanish family. The king found out about the marriage and had Inês murdered. Broken-hearted, Pedro bided his time. When he ascended the throne at his father's death, he had Inês's body exhumed and crowned, then buried at Alcobaça. He designed her tomb himself, and his own, facing it, so that they would rise to view each other on Judgement Day.

Accommodation and food in Alcobaça

Challet Fonta Nova €€ *R da Fonta Nova; tel: (062) 59 83 00, fax: (062) 59 84 30*. Only 200 metres from the monastery, this 1861 manor house retains the charm of antiquity, but with modern amenities.

Pensão Coracões Unidos € *R Frei António Brandão 39 (N8); tel: (062) 58 21 42*. Simple lodgings within steps of the monastery in town centre. Restaurant (€) serves standard menu.

Parque Municipal de Campismo € *Av. Prof Vieira Natividade; tel: (062) 58 22 65*. Town campsite.

Café Trinidad €–€€ *Praça D Alfonso Henriques 22; tel: (062) 50 82 72, closed Sat in winter*. A pleasant dining room and cheerful outdoor café next to monastery; great *frango na pucara*, a popular local chicken dish; good also are grilled sardines and roasted rabbit.

BATALHA✛✛✛

Turismo Regional *Directly behind the unfinished chapels; enter door facing the abbey; tel: 044 968 06, open daily 1000–1300, 1400–1800.*

Mosteiro de Batalha (€ cloister) *open daily 0900–1700.*

Market day is Monday at Batalha and 4th and 20th of each month at São Mamede, between Batalha and Fátima.

Procession of the Holy Trinity, *late May or early Jun, next to the monastery.* Procession of decorated offerings, traditional cakes.

The English influence of Philippa of Lancaster, wife of King João I, is immediately felt in the soaring perpendicular lines of the nave in the Dominican Abbey at Batalha . These cool, crisp columns and arches, however, are surrounded by some of the finest examples of Portuguese architecture and intricate Manueline stone carving you will see anywhere.

Immediately to the right as you enter the **Mosteiro da Batalha✛**, is the **Capela do Fundador✛**, rising to a dome whose vaulting joins at celestial stone snowflakes. Around the central tombs of the royal couple in their finely carved crowns are tombs of four of their sons, including Prince Henry the Navigator. At any time of day, the stonework is dappled with colours from the stained glass windows.

The abbey, which was begun by a young João in thanks for the victory that freed Portugal from Spanish rule, continues with an exquisite cloister, its delicate Manueline pillars supporting arches filled with lace-like stone filigree. The fountain is at the far corner of the boxwood garden, in a delicately carved pavilion.

Off the cloister, in the Chapter House, is the tomb of the Unknown Soldier, beneath an unsupported dome of such daring design that its architect slept a night under it when the last underpinning was removed, in order to prove its safety.

Beyond is another, simpler cloister and a door leading outside. Follow the building around to the right to enter the abbey's pièce de résistance, the **Capelas Imperfeitas✛**, or unfinished chapels. King João III, two centuries later, abandoned work on his ancestor's abbey to build his own at Belém, leaving this circular series of chapels unfinished. But enough was completed to see what this would have been, and only the final arches and dome are missing, allowing the sun to stream in and light every detail of its indescribably detailed stonecarving.

Although it was designed to be a royal pantheon, only one king is buried here, Duarte I, eldest son of João I and Philippa. The huge doorway, with eight layers of carved columns, is one of the earliest in the Manueline style.

Concerts of sacred and secular music are held frequently in the monastery (the tourist office has schedules). On the north side, a school of stonecarving has an open studio outside the abbey, providing a fascinating view of how these carved stone decorations are created.

Accommodation and food in Batalha

Pousada Mestre Alfonso Domingues €€ *Largo Mestre Alfonso Domingues; tel: (044) 962 61, fax: (044) 962 47.* A modern *pousada* directly opposite the monastery.

A Cava €–€€ *Largo Papa Paulo VI; tel: (044) 96 68 88, open daily 1000–2400.* Traditional food, with a sidewalk café, located behind the *pousada.* Try the *espetada mista,* a mixed grill.

Café-Restaurante Stop € *N356, 4km east of Batalha.* Friendly people, simple good food served in or outside.

Below
The Mosteiro de Batalha

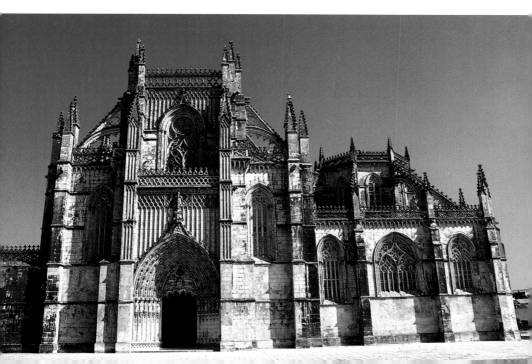

CALDAS DA RAINHA❖❖

Unlike most Portuguese towns, which have their colourful street markets only once a week, the stately old spa town of Caldas da Rainha has one every morning. So, for the traveller who seems to miss each market day in turn, this one is a sure bet. And it's a lively one, too.

Stalls of bright fruit and vegetables fill the long Praça da República, and others sell home-cured olives and mountain cheeses at unbelievably low prices. At the lower end look for baskets and woodenware. In the street, you may meet a donkey patiently awaiting the trip back to the farm.

Near the bottom of the sloping square, follow the pedestrianised R. do Almirante Candidos Reis, lined with pottery and ceramic shops, to the Largo da Rainha Donna Leonor. Ahead is the low Termas, a once-grand spa building now under reconstruction. Behind the large hospital to the left is the **Igreja de Nossa Senhora do Populo**❖. The church walls are covered in 17th-century blue tiles and it has a most unusual belltower, whose gargoyles you can face eye-to-eye from the street above.

Beyond the Termas is the lovely Parque Dom Carlos I, its meandering walks and swan-filled pools shaded in willows. At the far end, the **Museu de Cerâmica**❖ (€ *R. Visconde de Sacavem, open Tue–Sun 1000–1200, 1400–1700; free Sun am*) features the unique pottery and ceramic styles Caldas is known for.

ℹ Posto do Turismo
R. Duarte Pacheco; tel: (062) 83 10 03, open all year, and Praça da República; tel: (062) 345 11, open June–Aug only.

🅿 A large car park is located above the municipal fish market, two blocks from Praça da República, off R.Diario de Noticias. Metered parking is adjacent to Parque Dom Carlos I, near spa.

Accommodation and food in Caldas da Rainha

Hotel Internacional € *R. Dr Figueiroa Rego 45; tel: (062) 83 23 07, fax: (062) 84 44 82.* Bright modern hotel just north of centre on N8. Balconies, pool and two restaurants (€ and €€).

Festa Brava II €€ *R. Dr Figueiroa Rego 45; tel: (062) 83 23 07.* A class act with *adega* décor and updated traditional cuisine. Wide variety of fresh fish carefully described in English, expertly cooked and served. Roast spring lamb is excellent.

Above
Caldas da Rainha's
Praça da República

Fatima*

Posto de Turismo
Av. José Alves Correia da Silva; tel: (049) 53 11 39.

Restaurants abound, offering inexpensive, well-prepared traditional food.

Pensão Floresta
€–€€ Estrada da Batalha; tel: (049) 53 14 66, fax: (049) 53 31 38. Modern rooms, some with balconies. Few frills, but a reliable restaurant.

Even for those sceptical of miraculous appearances leave Fátima with the feeling that something significant happened here. For the faithful, this plain little village filled with pilgrim accommodations is a lifetime goal, especially during its holiest occasions, the 13th of each month, particularly May and Oct when as many as 100,000 may gather here.

The story is a well-known one, of three shepherd children meeting the Virgin Mary, who appeared five more times as promised, each time with a plea for peace in war-torn Europe. Although seen only by the children, her last visit on October 13, 1917 was accompanied by a celestial phenomenon witnessed by 70,000, many of them sceptics from the world press who had come to debunk the whole thing.

The 60-metre white tower of the Basílica do Santuario, begun in 1928, stands above a huge open square, filled during pilgrimage days. At night, pilgrims light the entire sanctuary with hundreds of thousands of candles and torches. But the heart of the sanctuary is the small Capela das Aparições on the site of the apparition. Many pilgrims approach in prayer, on their knees, a most touching sight.

Fátima is a matter of faith; there is little here for the casually curious. Most attractions relate to the shrine including the **Museu de Cera*** (*€ R. Jacinta Marto; open Mon–Fri 1000–1700 Nov–Mar, 0930–1830 Apr–Oct, Sat–Sun 0900–1830 year-round*) which tells the story of Fátima in 30 scenes with wax figures, and the **Museu de Arte Sacra e Etnologia*** (*€ R. Francisco Marto 52; open Tue–Sun 1200–1700 Nov–Mar, Apr–Oct 1000–1900*), a small collection of arts from around the world representing the Christian faith.

Below
The Capela das Apariçoes, in Fatima

Right
The walls of Obidos

In **São Mamede**, 8km west of Fátima, are the **Grutas da Moeda**✦ (€ *open daily 0900–1700 Oct–Mar, 0900–1800 Apr–Jun, 0900–1900 Jul–Sep*), a series of limestone caves with chambers of different coloured stalagmites and stalactites. Tours are every half-hour. In a separate cavern, you can enjoy a drink at an underground bar, refreshingly cool on a summer day.

Obidos✦✦✦

Tourist Office R. Direita; tel: (062) 95 92 31, open Mon–Fri 0930–1800, Sat–Sun 1000–1300, 1400–1800.

Park outside the gates unless you are staying overnight, in which case your lodging will have a parking space designated for you.

WCs are under the little belvedere just inside Porta da Vila, opposite the grocery shop.

Semana Santa (Holy Week) is observed with masses and processions of statues through the streets.

The story goes that King Dinis honeymooned in Obidos, and the beauty of this white town wrapped in stone walls so enthralled his new bride that he gave it to her as a wedding gift. Later kings kept up the tradition.

Entered via two right-angle turns inside the tile-lined Porta da Vila, the town itself is the attraction, and although you may find less tidied-up versions, you won't find a more picturesque walled village. The first thing to do is walk the ramparts that surround Obidos, and survey the town from above its red-tiled rooftops. Access the walls from stairs just inside the gate or from the castle at the opposite end of town, a former royal palace with a good Manueline window in the courtyard. The two sections of town walls do not connect.

The narrow streets run in layers, one often even with the rooftops of the next. Occasional small shops on R. Direita show some very good handicrafts, but do not dominate or make Obidos into a giant souvenir kiosk. Flowers are everywhere, especially pots of geraniums, and the air is heady with the wisteria that climbs the walls.

The interior of **Igreja Santa Maria✦** (*open Tue–Sun 0930–1230, 1430–1900, 1430–1700 in winter*) is lined in blue *azulejos* in floral designs, topped by an unusual painted ceiling. The **Museu Municipal✦** (€ *open 0900–1230, 1400–1800*) has art by Josefa de Obidos, Roman artifacts and relics of the area's involvement in the Napoleonic wars.

The hexagonal **Santuário do Senhor da Pedra✦** (*open 0930–1230, 1430–1900 Apr –Sep*), below the walls, houses a 3rd-century stone figure with arms raised in the shape of a cross, and the carriage used to transport a statue of the Virgin from Obidos to Nazaré during festivals. Also outside the walls is a 3km stone aqueduct from the 1500s.

Tour buses begin to arrive in Obidos about 1000 so visitors staying overnight will have the town to themselves early in the morning and in the evening.

Right
The Pousada do Castelo, Obidos

Accommodation and food in Obidos

Above
Santa Clara

Opposite
Detail from Santarém's tiled market building

**Albergaria Rainha Santa Isabel € ** *R. Direita; tel: (062) 95 93 23, fax: (062) 95 91 15.* Attractive, well-furnished rooms and friendly, hospitable management make this a preferable alternative to the pricey *pousada*.

Casa de Santiago do Castelo €€ *Largo de Santiago; tel: (062) 95 95 87, fax: (062) 95 95 87.* Directly under the castle in the centre of town, a tiny cottage in the *Turismo de Habitação* programme.

Pousada do Castelo €€€ *tel: (062) 95 91 05, fax: (062) 95 91 48.* Antique-furnished rooms in a Moorish fort transformed into a royal residence, then a *pousada*. Most atmospheric is room 203, in its own tower with a separate steep stone stairway. The restaurant (€€€) serves regional specialities: roast suckling pig on Saturday, kid on Thursday.

Conquistadores €-€€ *near Porta da Vila*, serves some unusual dishes, including eel and pigeon, along with traditional fare.

1º Dezembro Restaurante-Café € *Praça da Sta Maria; tel: (062) 95 92 98, closed Thu.* Tiny café beside the church, serving grilled sardines, veal and other local dishes.

Bar Ibn Errik Rey € *R. Direita.* Cosy wine shop serving light meals or a pre-dinner snack of bread, Azorian cheese and savoury *chorizo* sausage grilled at the table in terracotta dishes.

Pastelaria da Moura € *Porta da Vila*, serves snacks and lunches and also has a few rooms.

A small grocery store at *Porta da Vila* sells bread, local cheese, fruit and drinks for picnics. A gate in the high town wall on the left, reached through the arch at the end of R. Direita, leads to a quiet picnic site with a view over the valley.

SANTAREM**❖❖**

ⓘ Turismo de Santarém *R. Capelo Ivens 63; tel: (043) 231 40, open 0900–1230, 1400–1730.*

Overlooking the River Tagus from a hilltop perch, Santarém has figured prominently in Portuguese history as one of the last Moorish strongholds and home to several kings. Today it is a pleasant town usually bypassed by tourists, but with enough artistic treasures hidden in its churches to keep a traveller busy for a day. The day should not be Monday, however, when all is closed.

The city was a religious centre in the Middle Ages, and even today, because of its churches, it is often referred to as the Gothic Capital. Igreja de Santa Clara has a long nave with two side aisles, lit from a stone-carved rose window at one end; but for a church of such imposing size, it is oddly lacking the expected grand portal. The even larger Convento de São Francisco across the street was once magnificent, but was used to stable cavalry and is now empty and likely to be closed.

The old city begins at a small square faced by two 17th-century churches: the small cross-shaped Igreja de Nossa Senhora da Piedade, and the baroque façade of the Igreja do Seminário, with a painted ceiling and marble altar. *Azulejos* line the corridors of the vestibule to the right of the main church entrance.

Follow R. Serpa Pinto from this plaza to find the Torre das Cabaças and Igreja de São João de Alporão, which contains the **Museu Arqueológico***. This 13th-century Romanesque-Gothic church holds, along with an interesting jumble of carved stone work from Roman, Arabic and later times, a 15th-century carved tomb considered by some to be the finest in Portugal. Nearby, Santarém's other 'best in Portugal' is the rose window at the 14th-century Gothic **Igreja da Graça***, carved from a single piece of stone. The doorway beneath is intricately carved, and inside are tombs, including that of Pedro Alvares Cabral, the 'discoverer' of Brazil. The 12th-century Igreja Marvila shows the evolution of churches, with a Manueline doorway and a lining of 17th-century *azulejos*.

On the far end of town, overlooking the Tagus, is Portas do Sol, a garden inside the old Moorish walls (and a good picnic site).

The market building facing the café-filled **Jardim da República*** is an outdoor art gallery of 20th-century *azulejos*. Between each of its many doors is a panel depicting local farming activities, landscapes or folk life. By all means see the market in the morning when it is filled with colourful activity, but also go later when the panels are not covered by stacks of fruit.

The National Agricultural Fair, which takes place in early June, is one of Europe's foremost fairs. It includes an international folklore festival, bullfights, and traditional herdsmen's races and contests. In late October, Santarém is the venue for the National Gastronomy Festival, a celebration of food, crafts and traditions.

ⓘ Turismo do Ribatejo R. Pedro de Santarém 102; tel: (043) 33 33 18. Regional tourist office.

ⓗ Churches open Tue–Wed 0930–1230, 1400–1800, Thu–Sun 0930–1230, 1400–1730, except **Santa Clara**, closed Tue morning. Note that these times are 'official' but may vary in practice.

Museu Arqueológico € R. Conselheiro Figueiredo Leal. Open Tue–Wed 0930–1230, 1400–1800, Thur–Sun 0930–1230, 1400–1730.

(P) To park, leave the main square from the side opposite the market building, passing the large Santa Clara church on the right, to Praça Egas Montiz.

Accommodation and food in Santarém

Casa da Alcacova €€ *Largo da Alcacova 3, Portas do Sol; tel (043) 388 01 00, fax: (043) 388 01 05, e-mail: casa@mail.telepac.pt, internet: www.alcacova.com* Inside the walled terrace of Portas do Sol, with views over the Tagus Valley, a noble estate where travellers can sample the good life of past centuries. Monumental carved and curtained beds from one era, jacuzzi from another.

Quinta de Vale de Lobos €€ *Azóia de Baixo; tel: (043) 42 92 64, fax: (043) 42 93 13.* An old farm on a hunting estate 6km north on the N3. Pool, gardens and woodlands surround.

Hotel Alfageme € *Av. Bernardo Santareno 38; tel: (043) 37 08 70, fax: (043) 37 08 50.* Functional modern rooms, with buffet breakfast, parking.

Pigalle € *R. Capelo Ivens 15; tel: (043) 242 05, closed Sun.* Friendly family-run restaurant serving local specialities in prodigious quantities or generous half-portions; the squid is tender, the veal excellent. Sandwiches and snacks served at counter.

Taverna Raphael €€ *Travessa das Borras 10; tel: (043) 265 17, open Mon–Sat 0900–2400.* Daily dishes are well prepared and good value.

Suggested tour

Total distance: 206km; 321km with detours.

Time: 4 hours driving. Allow 2 days for the main route, 3 days with detours. Those with limited time should concentrate on Obidos, Alcobaça and Batalha.

Links: From Mafra and Ericeira (*see page 63*) via the N247 through Lourinha. To Leiria (*see page 85*) via the N1 from Batalha.

Route: Leave **OBIDOS ❶** (*see page 83*) on the N114, following signs to **Rio Maior** – note that the new IP6 is slowly replacing this route; use it as far as it goes, then rejoin. Turn right at the unmarked T-junction in Rio Maior, then left at signpost to centre, following signs to **SANTAREM ❷** from the central roundabout. Signage is equally deficient on approaching Santarém. Follow 'Santarém-Almeirim' signs to reach the centre; when in doubt, head uphill. From Santarém, head north on the A1 51km to **FATIMA ❸**.

Detour: For a slower, but more interesting ride, go north from Santarém on the N3. Just after crossing the IP6, turn left on the N243 to **Minde**, following the N360 to Fátima, a journey of 75km. This route travels alongside two natural parks and reaches a particularly scenic viewpoint just south of Minde.

Leave Fátima travelling west on the N356, 18km to **BATALHA ❹**.

Head north from Batalha on the N1, quickly taking the exit signposted Nazaré. Follow the N356 to **Martingança**, over a road which some maps erroneously label 'scenic'. Turn left (south) on the N242 into **NAZARE** ❺. Traffic snarls Nazaré's beachside streets even off-season, so unless you're keen to see the local women's unusual clothing (shawls and petticoated short skirts), stick to the high road through town. With the building of a new marina to the south, the once-colourful fishing beach is now sun-worshipper domain and the bright boats no longer haul up there. To see the beach, and perhaps to lunch

Right
Monastery cloister in Batalha

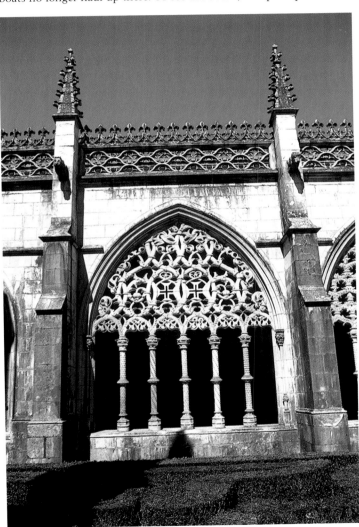

Ilha da Berlenga Ferry €€€ *ViaMar, Pensão Residencial Avis, Praça Jacob Pereira; tel: (062) 78 95 71, Jun–mid-Sep.*

Estrela do Mar *€–€€ Av. Marginal, São Pedro de Muel; tel: (044) 59 92 45, open Thu–Tue 1200–1600, 1900–2300. Fresh fish and a sea view.*

Right
Belfry in Caldas da Rainha

at one of the restaurants facing it, and avoid the traffic, follow signs from the N242 to **Sitio**, just before entering Nazaré. A funicular (€ *daily 0700–0100)* descends to the beachfront.

Detour: Beach-lovers should turn north instead of south on the N242 in Martingança, to **Marinha Grande**, going 3/4 way around the roundabout and following the N242-2 to **São Pedro de Muel**. A fortress-like lighthouse north of town overlooks ragged cliffs and pounding surf; beyond is a sandy beach. Follow the unnumbered road south along the shore through low open forests. Take any of the side roads labeled *praia* to beaches, the most scenic of which is **Paredes de Vitória**, with a rock outcrop at one end. The road rejoins the N242 at Nazaré.

Leave Nazaré, following signs to **ALCOBAÇA** ❻. The N8 heads south from the front of the monastery, to **CALDAS DA RAINHA** ❼ and on to Obidos.

Detour: From the N8 just south of Obidos, follow the N114 west through small farming villages to **Peniche**, where a Vauban fortress overlooks the busy and colourful commercial fishing harbour. Peniche is a centre of lacemaking, which you can see demonstrated at the school on R. do Calvario. Return to the N114 and continue to its end, along the precipitous coastline to **Cabo Carvoeiro**. Here, a 45-minute walk leads to a promontory of unusual layered rock formations. A boat trip to **Ilha da Berlenga**, a nature reserve on a tiny barren island 10km off the cape, is good way to see the rock formations. The island also has caves and colonies of sea birds, but choose a calm day as the crossing can be rough.

Also worth exploring

The **Serras de Aire e Candeeiros** is a natural reserve that includes two mountain ranges, both lying within the circle route of this tour. The most scenic road through the area is the N362, from **Santarém** to **Batalha**, through **Porto de Mos**, which has an interesting castle; side roads lead to little villages and to **grutas** (caves), which are common in this region of eroded limestone.

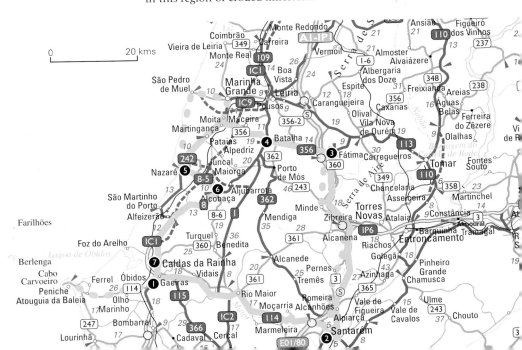

South of Coimbra

Ratings

Castles	●●●●●
Architecture	●●●●
Historical sights	●●●●
Scenery	●●●●
Mountains	●●●○○
Villages	●●●○○
Children	●●○○○
Nature	●●○○○

The precipitous slopes of the Serra da Lousã provide a dramatic backdrop for an area rich in the history of the Knights Templar. Their citadel at Tomar is among the country's architectural highlights, and other nearby fortresses were also Templar strongholds. Romantic castles crown hillocks, crags and entire cities, most with ramparts to walk and buildings to explore – some restored, some in ruin. Whatever the condition, the views are always extensive. Conimbriga takes history back before the Templars and before the Moors they vanquished, with an excavated Roman city about 2 000 years old. Older still are the footprints giant dinosaurs left as they walked near Ourém in prehistoric times. To the west, the region is bounded by the vast waters of the dammed River Zêzere, which flows from the snow-covered Serra da Estrela into the River Tagus, south of Tomar.

CONIMBRIGA✦✦✦

ⓘ **Ruinas de Conimbriga €**
Condeixa-a-Nova. Open 0900–1300, 1400–2000.

Museu de Conimbriga €
Open 1000–1300, 1400–1800. A pleasant café adjoins the museum.

◐ **Pousada de Santa Cristina €€** *Condeixa-a-Nova; tel: (039) 94 12 86, fax: (039) 94 30 97.* A modern *pousada* close to the ruins.

The finest Roman site in Portugal, Conimbriga is best known for its extensive, finely detailed mosaic floors. The thermal baths are well preserved, as are the details of some of the villas, with atrium pools and fountains. Most graphic and poignant is the enormous wall thrown up through the city's centre to protect it from Suevi invasions. The rough fortification is built of whatever was quickly available, including pieces of homes, columns, even statuary. Another wall, from the 1st century AD, is currently under excavation.

Before exploring the site, visit the adjoining **museum**✦, which arranges artefacts to show how Roman colonials lived and to interpret the history of Conimbriga.

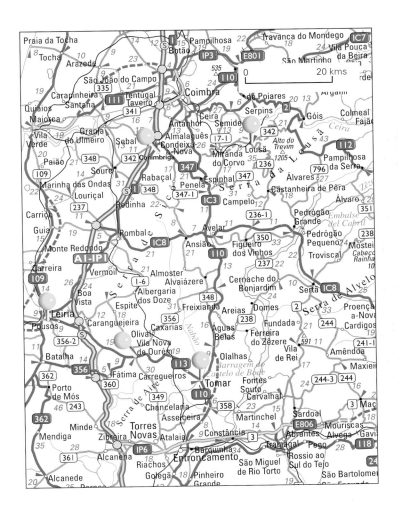

LEIRIA*

Turismo Região
Jardim Luís de Camões;
tel: (044) 82 37 73, e-mail:
rtleiria.fatima@mail.telepac.
pt

Market days are Tue
and Sat.

The large **Castelo de Leiria*** (*open Mon–Fri 0900–1830, Sat–Sun 1000–1830 Apr–Sept, until 1730 Oct–Mar*), with arcaded loggias and impressive outer walls, was begun in 1135 and twice occupied by Moors. It forms a stunning backdrop to the city, especially floodlit at night. Inside are a royal palace and semi-ruined chapel.

On the edge of town, the Sanctuário de Nossa Senhora da Encarnação is reached by a monumental baroque staircase decorated with small religious statuary. A sweeping view over pine forests rewards the climb.

Feiras de Artesanato, Antiguidades e Lelharias *Praça Rodrigues Lobo, 2nd Sat each month, 1000–1700.* Crafts, antiques and jumble.

In the **Museu Escolar**∗ (*Largo da Feira 18, open Fri–Sun 1400–1800*), in neighbouring Marrazes, rooms 2 and 5 are of interest, with traditional crafts and toys.

Leiria makes a pleasant base for exploring the area, especially during the Leiria Exposition which culminates in the festivities of May 22, with folk dancing and music, or during the Leiria Music Festival, in June and July, when there are concerts in the castle and elsewhere.

Accommodation and food in Leiria

Pensão Ramalhete € *R. Dr Correia Mateus 30; tel: (044) 81 28 02, fax: (044) 81 50 99.* A four-star hotel with comfortable rooms and pleasant staff.

O Fausto € *R. do Beirão 4; tel: (044) 83 35 58, closed Sun.* Specialises in *leitão* (roast suckling pig).

Casinha Velha €€ *R. Professores Portelas 23, Marrazes; tel: (044) 85 53 55, closed Tue.* Just to the north of Leiria, in Marrazes, featuring roast kid.

Lousao∗∗

Right
Pilgrimage chapel
in Lousão

Restaurante Burgo
€€–€€€ *Nossa Senhora da Piedade.* Overlooking the gorge, chapels and castle, the views are as attention-getting as the fine food. A terrace café overlooks the pool.

Although it is a pleasant town with old streets and patrician houses, Lousão's main attraction is outside the centre; follow signs to *castelo* and Nossa Senhora da Piedade. The mimosa-lined road continues upward until it ends at **Castelo da Lousão**, an atmospheric stacked-shale fortification on a crag overlooking a deep ravine. The whole scene is at the bottom of a much larger steep ravine.

Perched on another narrow crag below, a series of tiny white chapels are connected by steep stone stairs. To reach them walk downhill through a near-jungle of trees growing from the vertical slope. Along the stairs to the chapels are stone benches and tables built into tiny viewpoints overhanging the river at dizzying heights. Weekend **Romarias** (processions) are held at the chapels mid-April and mid-May.

Follow the riverside path into the moss-covered gorge. At a small pool, miniature shale houses surround a fountain. The river is enclosed above a waterfall to create a stone-lined swimming pool.

OUREM***

Praça do Municipio; tel: (049) 421 94, e-mail: c,ourem@mail.telepac.pt web: www.cm-ourem.pt Very helpful office, with open racks of brochures. Ask here for the key to the small ethnographic museum.

Parking for castle is at the top, inside the gate.

Medieval €€ *R. S. José; tel: (049) 54 48 08, open daily 1000–2400.* Pricier than restaurants in the new town, but excellent for veal; choose *Vitela a Paço Ducal.*

Market day is Thu.

The walled old town of Ourém stands between the newer town below and two castles above. Inside the gates, stairs beside a fountain lead up to a small tree-shaded square. Only the crypt remains of the original 15th-century Colegiada church, its arches framing a fine effigy tomb of the Count of Ourém, fashionably turned out in a beret.

Narrow streets of whitewashed houses wind to a garden, surrounded by noble homes, one of which is now the Museu de Etnografia e Arqueologia, with tools and implements for traditional crafts.

The older of the two castles is 12th-century, its three towers guarding a triangular enclosure with an unusual 9th-century Moorish cistern. It is spring fed, which may explain why this castle was never taken by siege. The commanding site overlooks 360 degrees of wooded hills, red-roofed villages, olive groves and farms.

The lower **Palácio de Conte Afonso** (*open Mon–Fri 0900–1730*), connected by a now-roofless passageway, has rooms overgrown with wild flowers and views of the countryside from its remaining stone windowseats. Two towers of this 15th-century palace remain intact, surrounded by brick arched balconies of strong Venetian influence. On Palm Sunday and Good Friday there are processions with statues through the old winding streets.

Accommodation and food in Ourém

Quinta da Alcaidaria-Mor €€ *off N113; tel: (049) 422 31, fax: (049) 422 31.* Family estate since the 1600s, 2.5km from Ourém, with gardens and chapel. English is spoken.

TOMAR❖❖

ℹ Turismo de Tomar
*Av. Candido Madureira;
tel: (049) 32 24 27, open
Mon–Fri 0930–1230,
1400–1800, Sat–Sun
1000–1300, 1500–1800,
Oct–May closed Sat pm and
Sun.* At the west end,
under the castle walls.

Turismo Regional *R.
Serpa Pinto 1; tel: (049) 32
90 00, fax (049) 32 43 22.*
Near the river.

ℙ Park on Av. Marquês
de Tomar, along the
river adjacent to the old
town, in the small lot
opposite the water wheel.

Aloof from the old city, separated by a national forest, is the 12th-century castle and subsequent monastery of the Order of the Knights Templar, the **Convento de Cristo**❖ (€ *open daily 0915–1230, 1400–1700*). Building continued until the 17th century, spanning all the great ages of Portuguese architecture.

The original church is the 12th-century octagonal Charola, modelled on the Holy Sepulchre in Jerusalem. Eight graceful pillars separate the centre from an ambulatory, which opens to a later nave and choir. The Manueline window at its end can be seen only from the main cloister outside. The window combines every maritime and nautical motif known to the Manueline style: ropes, shells, coral, fishing floats, seaweed, even an anchor chain.

The conventual buildings surround a series of cloisters, the largest in double-storey Renaissance style, hiding another remarkable Manueline window. Two 15th-century Gothic cloisters were built when Prince Henry the Navigator was Grand Master of the Order of Christ.

The Convento parking terrace overlooks **Nossa Senhora da Conceição**❖ (*open daily 1100–1215, or ask at Convento de Cristo*), perhaps Portugal's finest early-Renaissance church. While the outside is plain, the beautifully proportioned interior has finely carved Corinthian columns and faces with acanthus-leaf beards flanking the sanctuary arch.

Above
Tomar's Convento
de Cristo

Sinagoga and Museu Luso-Hebraico R. Dr Joachim Jacinto 73. Open Thur–Tue 0930–1230, 1400–1800 (1700 winter). Ask English-speaking guides to point out acoustic jugs in upper walls.

Friday is market day, but the municipal market is open every morning.

Concerts are held frequently in the Biblioteca Municipal (library) and the Convento de Cristo.

Old Tomar lies between the river and the wooded hill topped by the Convento's outer walls. Narrow streets run straight between the hill and river, with few cross streets. At the centre is the **Igreja de São João Baptista**, with two fine Manueline doorways and a richly carved altar covered in gold.

South of its 17th-century square, along a narrow stone-paved lane, is the **Sinagoga***, built in the 1400s and now housing the **Museu Luso-Hebraico***, a museum of Portuguese Judaism. Inside are 14th-century cemetery stones and Mizrah plaques; the women's ritual baths next door have been excavated.

Tomar's most famous festival, which takes place every two or three years, is the Cortejo dos Tabuleiros, a grand procession of girls balancing huge trays of decorated breads on their heads.

Accommodation and food in Tomar

Casa dos Pinheiros € R. de Capela, Chão de Maçãs; tel: (049) 461 06, fax: (049) 461 06. Five rooms, one with private terrace, in vineyard-surrounded farmhouse; meals on request.

Residencial Luz € R. Serpa Pinta 144; tel: (049) 31 23 17. On the main walking street in the centre of the old town.

Pensão União € R. Serpa Pinta 92; tel: (049) 32 31 61, fax: (049) 32 12 99. Plain but hospitable rooms, behind an azulejo façade.

Restaurant Beira Rio € R. Alexandre Herculano, nothing fancy, but good traditional food.

A Bella Vista €–€€ R. Fonte do Choupo, off R. Marquês de Pombal; tel: (049) 31 28 70. Closed Mon. Indoor or outdoor dining overlooking the river.

The Knights Templar

Begun as a military-religious order to guard pilgrim routes to the Holy Land, the Knights Templar had its own rules, its own confessors, and its own sizable wealth. Known for their military skill, if not piety (vows of chastity were not required), they were especially successful in driving Moorish conquerors from Iberia.

The king of France, badly in need of money, coveted the order's wealth and convinced the Pope that they were not only too worldly, but dangerous. The order was abolished and Templar properties were distributed to the kings in whose countries they had holdings. But King Dinis remembered their bravery in ridding Portugal of the Moors and, with the Pope's approval, established a new Order of Christ. Without the Pope's blessing, he invited all former Templars to join, in effect restoring to them all their properties in Portugal.

Suggested tour

ℹ️ **Turismo de Pombal** *Largo do Cardal; tel: (036) 232 30.*

🌙 **Estalagem Vale da Ursa** €–€€ *N238, Cernache do Bonjardim; tel: (074) 909 81, fax: (074) 909 82. e-mail: hotelvaledaursa@mail.telepac.pt A modern resort with swimming, tennis, and other sports, plus a good restaurant, overlooking the water.*

Total distance: 265km, 341km with detours.

Time: 5-6 hours driving. Allow 3 days for the main route, 4 days with detours. Those with limited time should concentrate on Tomar and Conimbriga.

Links: The N1 connects Leiria to Batalha, 11km south (*see page 72*); Conimbriga is 11km south of Coimbra (*see page 92*).

Route: From **LEIRIA ❶**, follow the N113 through the pleasant town of **Pinhel**, amid groves of olives and oranges, to **OUREM ❷**, high up on its castellated hill. Turn right on to R. 5 de Outubro. A series of right turns, following *castelo* signs lead ever upward until you can go no further.

Detour: Drive south from Ourém to **Bairro** (10km) and follow signs to **Pegadas Dinossaurios Serra de Aire**⁕ to see a large stone surface covered in dinosaur tracks (€ *open Tue–Sun 1000–1230, 1400–2000 mid-Mar–mid-Sep; closes at 1800 in winter*).

From Ourém, continue through olive orchards to **TOMAR ❸**. Look out for sign with a binocular symbol, signalling a lookout with fine views of the Templar's castle. Follow **Convento de Cristo** signs right to visit the headquarters of the Knights Templar before visiting the old town.

Detour: Take the N10 south from Tomar, crossing the dammed Zêzere river at **Castelo de Bode** via the N358-2, to **Constancia**. Go west on an unnumbered road along the River Tagus to see the island castle of **Almoural**. Continue through **Vila Nova da Barquinha** to the IC3 and the N110 north and back to Tomar.

Cross the river and leave Tomar on the N10 to the N238, heading northeast on a winding, but very scenic, climb. Just past **Aguas Belas**, follow signs left through plantations of fragrant eucalyptus to the beautifully situated **Dornes**, with a medieval tower and an outstanding pulpit in its 14th-century church. Rejoin the N238, dropping to cross the impounded River Zêzere. In **Cernache do Bonjardim**, follow the N237 north (left) towards **Figueira dos Vinhos** – look out for the tiny signpost at the roundabout. After descending 7km of rough road, cross below the Zêzere dam and turn left on to a much better road to Figueira dos Vinhos.

Follow the N236-1 north through **Castanheira de Pera**, then the N236 across the **Serra da Lousã** winding and climbing through breathtaking wild landscapes, to **LOUSA ❹**. The N342 heads west through **Miranda do Corvo** and over the ridge to **Condeixa**, past **CONIMBRIGA ❺**. Return to **LEIRIA**, either on the N1 or the high-speed A1, with a short diversion to Pombal.

The town of **Pombal*** is topped by a 12th-century Knights Templar **castle*** (*open Mon–Fri 0800–1700, Sat–Sun 0800–1200, 1300–1700*) with crenellations and wide arches inside. The area has a number of sites connected with the Templars and their successor Order of Christ.

Also worth exploring

The **Zêzere River**, impounded to form a meandering lake, is surrounded by low, steep mountains. Crossing its eastern watershed, the N2 heads north from **Abrantes**, where a splendid castle overlooks the River Tagus. Rejoin the main route via the N348 from **Vila de Rei** to **Ferreira do Zêzere**, or continue to **Serta** and rejoin at **Cernache do Bonjardim**.

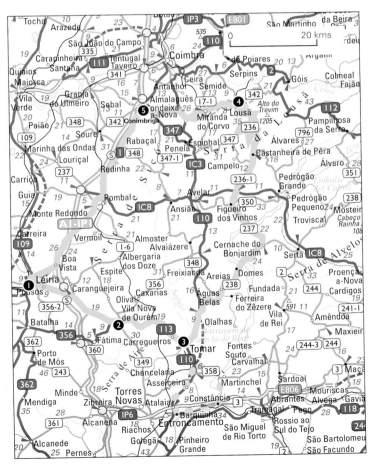

Coimbra

Ratings

Architecture	●●●● ○
Art	●●●●
Children	●●●● ○
Museums	●●●● ○
Historical sights	●●● ○○
Walking	●●● ○○
Food and drink	●● ○○○
Outdoor activities	● ○○○○

Despite its size, Coimbra has not lost its small-town feeling. Students in black capes rush between classes or loll dashingly in cafés. Streets twist and turn through tiny largos as they climb the hill, where remnants of Moorish encircling walls still stand. Between the old stones of its streets and buildings are welcome swaths of green gardens, and sudden vistas over the red rooftops. It is a city to savour, with cafés and *pastelarias* conveniently spaced. Above all, it is a city meant for walking, the only way to see its narrow old streets, where the turn of a corner may bring you face to face with a stunningly carved Manueline doorway – or a cat sunning on a windowsill. Its two major influences – the church and the university – have given it an artistic legacy few small cities can match.

Getting there and getting around

ℹ Turismo Regional *R. Emídio Navarro (south side of Largo da Portagem); tel: (01) 330 19, open weekdays 0900–1800, weekends 1000–1300 and 1500–1730, good for brochures, but not much else.*

The Ponte de Santa Clara, the bridge from the motorway exit, ends at the Largo da Portagem. Most of the old city is within walking distance of this square, at the intersection of Avenida Emídio Navarro (which runs along the River Mondego) and Rua Ferreiora Borges, the main commercial street that leads right through the old city.

Parking
It is best to park your car and then visit the sights of Coimbra on foot. Metered parking is along the river at the end of Ponte de Santa Clara, next to the Hotel Astoria.

Buses
In-town buses leave from Coimbra A train station on Rua Emídio Navarro, and from Coimbra-Parque station south of the Largo at the

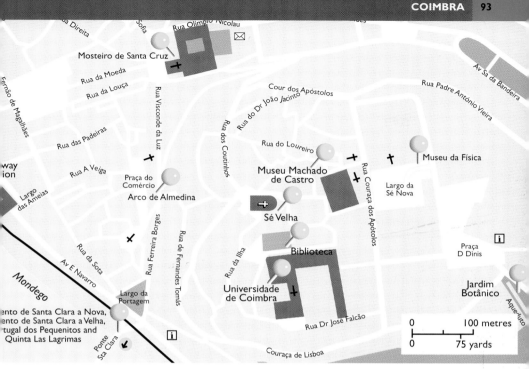

Map labels:

Rua Direita · Sofia · Rua Olimpio Nicolau · Mosteiro de Santa Cruz · Rua da Moeda · Rua da Louça · Fernão de Magalhães · Rua das Padeiras · Rua Visconde da Luz · Rua A Veiga · Largo das Amieas · way ion · Praça do Comércio · Arco de Almedina · Rua Ferreira Borges · Rua de Fernandes Tomás · Rua da Sota · Av E Navarro · Mondego · Largo da Portagem · Ponte Sta Clara · ento de Santa Clara a Nova, ento de Santa Clara a Velha, tugal dos Pequenitos and Quinta Las Lagrimas · Rua dos Coutinhos · Cour dos Apóstolos · Rua do Dr João Jacinto · Rua do Loureiro · Museu Machado de Castro · Sé Velha · Rua da Ilha · Biblioteca · Universidade de Coimbra · Couraça de Lisboa · Rua Dr José Falcão · Rua Couraça dos Apóstolos · Largo da Sé Nova · Av Sa da Bandeira · Rua Padre António Vieira · Museu da Física · Praça D Dinis · Jardim Botânico · Aqueduto

0   100 metres
0   75 yards

---

*Praça Dom Dinis, close
to the University, tel: (01) 83
25 91, open Mon–Fri
0900–1800, Sat–Sun
0900–1230 and
1400–1730, is much more
cordial.*

Turismo Municipal
*Praça da República; tel: (01)
332 02, open Mon–Fri
1000–1830, east of city
centre at the intersection
of Av. Sá da Bandiera and
R. Olivo Matos.*

Right
The old city, Coimbra

🛈 Convento de Santa Clara a Nova
Calçada de Santa Isabel, south of the Ponte Santa Clara, tel: (039) 44 16 74, open Tue–Sun. 0900–1200 and 1400–1700.

intersection with Rua do Brasil. From Coimbra A take bus No.1 to the University. Buses also stop at the Largo da Portagem.

Telephone numbers
Coimbra is changing from five- to six-digit numbers, so if you try a five-digit that does not work, try adding 8 before numbers beginning in 2 or 3, and 4 before numbers beginning 1 or 2.

Sights

Convento de Santa Clara a Nova◦
When the Poor Clares moved to their new Baroque convent they carried Saint Isabel's remains in procession to the new church, where you can see her silver tomb today. Her old painted stone tomb is also there showing her dressed in a nun's habit and staring into eternity. The convent sits high (and dry, this time) on the south side of the river, with good views back to Coimbra.

Convento de Santa Clara a Velha *Av. do Covento Velho, at the south end of the Ponte Santa Clara, opposite Portugal dos Pequenitos.*

Jardim Botânico *Calçada Martim de Freitas, tel: (039) 82 28 97, open daily, in winter 0900–1730 and summer 0900–2000.*

Mosteiro de Santa Cruz € *Praça 8 de Maio. Open Mon–Sat 0930–1215 and 1400–1800, Sat 1600–1800.*

Museo da Física *Largo Marquês de Pombal, tel: (039) 41 06 00, open Tue–Sun 1430–1730.*

Museu Nacional Machado de Castro € *Largo Dr. José Rodrigues; tel: (039) 82 37 27; open Tue–Sun 0930–1230, 1400–1730, closed holidays.*

Convento de Santa Clara a Velha✦✦

When this Gothic convent was built in the 14th century by Santa Isabel, the widow of King Dinis, it was beside the river. It was finally abandoned in the 18th century when constant flooding left it uninhabitable. Isabel was buried here as was Inês de Castro, the murdered mistress (or wife) of Pedro I, who was grandson of Isabel. Isabel's tomb is now in Santa Clara a Nova on the hill and Inês is at Alcobaça (*see page 70*) with Pedro. The graceful old ruin retains much of its fine stonework.

Jardim Botânico✦

The city's large gardens were laid out by the ever-busy Marquês de Pombal. The design is circular with fountains and formal flower beds and paths leading through avenues of tall trees.

Mosteiro de Santa Cruz✦✦

The façade, a mass of carved stone figures, begins beneath the present street level, just below the Arco de Almedina. The nave of the 16th-century church is lined with *azulejos* set in sections and capped with a cut-out baroque scroll. To the left of the altar is the tomb of Afonso Henriques, first king of Portugal, and across from it is that of his son Sancho I. Other highlights are a fine pulpit by Nicolas Chanterène carved in Renaissance high relief, and the carved wooden choir stalls depicting the travels of Vasco da Gama. The ceiling is Manueline, as are the cloisters, designed in 1524 and decorated with *azulejos* depicting scenes from the parables.

Museu da Física✦

Those interested in the sciences will enjoy this wide-ranging collection of scientific instruments from the 18th and 19th centuries, located in two period rooms of the old College of Jesus.

Museu Nacional Machado de Castro✦✦

The old episcopal palace, noted for its fine Renaissance porch and loggia, was the birthplace of the Portuguese sculptor Joaquim Machado de Castro. Among its fine collection of Renaissance sculpture look for works by Master Pero, Houdart, Jean de Rouen and Charterène. Paintings represent Flemish and Portuguese artists from the 15th–17th centuries. Below, the Crytoporticus is the base from the forum of the Roman town of Aeminium.

Arco de Almedina✦

On the Rua Ferreira Borges, opposite stairs leading down to the Praça do Comércio, a narrow street leads uphill to the Arco de Almedina, one of the last remaining gates in the medieval walls. The name is a reminder of the city's Moorish past. This is the best route to the Sé Velha (old cathedral) and the old University.

Opposite
Coimbra's Convento de Santa Clara a Velha

Portugal dos Pequenitos € *Santa Clara, on the south side of the Mondego near Santa Clara a Velha; tel: (039) 44 12 25; open all year, summer 1000–1900, winter 1000–1730, closed Christmas.*

Quinta Las Lagrimas *Estrada das Lages, Santa Clara; tel: (039) 44 16 15; open daily 0900–1700.*

Sé Velha (cloisters €) *Largo da Sé Velha, generally open Sat–Thur 1000–1230 and 1400–1730.*

Universidade de Coimbra *Paços de Escolas. Generally open daily 0930–1230 and 1400–1730.*

Portugal dos Pequenitos***

Child-scale models of Portuguese architectural highlights are a perfect way to introduce children to Portugal. Buildings from around the country and from Portuguese colonies in Brazil, Angola, Goa and Macao fascinate children while they learn about the nation and its explorations and former empire. A children's museum, the Museu da Criança, is also there.

Nearby, the **Quinta las Lagrimas*** is where King Pedro I and his mistress Inês de Castro met in secret. Today visitors can see the garden and fountain where Inês was assassinated (*see Alcobaça, page 70*).

Sé Velha*

On a slanting plaza below the University, the fortress-like Romanesque Old Cathedral was built in the 12th century, over the remains of a mosque. Tiles that once lined the columns were stripped by restorers, but the gilt and polychrome high altar remains.

Universidade de Coimbra**

Until the 15th century this ensemble of buildings high on the hill overlooking the city was a royal palace. Stairs in the Paços da Universidade lead to the loggia and the Sala das Capelas, where doctoral theses are defended, rectors are installed and graduations held.

The crowning glory of the university, and of Coimbra, is the **Biblioteca***, the library, built in 1724 and considered among the finest baroque rooms in the world. Its 30,000 books and 5,000 manuscripts are housed in a setting of red, green and gold, under *trompe-l'oeil* ceilings whose pillars seem to move as you walk beneath.

Fado, the soul of Portugal

Roughly translated as 'fate', fado is peculiar to Portugal, its wry, often sad tones rising and falling as it speaks of love, passion and misfortune, in free four-line stanzas or a sung poem.

Fado has two distinct styles. In Lisbon it is the personal and deeply emotional song of individuals. In Coimbra, the province of black-caped University students, the style is that of the troubadour. One of the best known *fadistas* in recent years is Amália Rodrigues whose recordings are readily available.

Opposite
The Universidade
de Coimbra

After this visual overload, rest your eyes on the view of the city from the University plaza.

The Capela, opposite, behind an impressive portal, is no less interesting inside, with a painted ceiling, 17th-century *azulejos*, a splendid organ and a tiny museum of ecclesiastical art.

Accommodation and food

Astoria €€ *Av. Emídio Navarro 21, tel: (039) 82 20 55 or 56, fax: 82 20 57, e-mail: almeida.hotels.pt* Recently restored to its former elegance, the Astoria is a landmark, its flat-iron shape greeting everyone who enters via the Santa Clara bridge. Ask for a room with a balcony on the 'prow' overlooking the Largo da Portagem and the bridge. Rooms are tasteful and bright. In addition to a fine dining room, the **Amphitryon €–€€**, and a café, the Astoria has an attractive art deco lounge.

Hotel Dom Luis €€ *Quinta da Varzea, Santa Clara, tel: (039) 44 25 10 and 22, fax: 44 51 96, e-mail: hoteld.luis@mail.telepac.pt* Built in the 1980s, the Dom Luis is an attractive and comfortable modern hotel across the river in the Santa Clara section. Large comfortable rooms have modern amenities. The hotel also has an excellent restaurant, the **Panorama €–€€**, with a view of the city.

Casa Alda Martha € *Av. Marnoco e Sousa 38, tel: (039) 71 86 87.* This attractive Turihab property in a private home is opposite the wooded gardens of the Penedo da Saude. The three rooms are large, furnished with antiques and have private baths. It is also close to the Jardim Botânico and on a bus line.

Dom Pedro €€ *R. Emídio Navarro 58, tel: (039) 82 91 08.* On the main street along the Mondego, the Dom Pedro serves Portuguese specialities.

Taberna €€ *R. dos Combatentes da Grande Guerra 86, tel: (039) 71 62 65.* Very pleasant dining room with polished red tile floors and stone walls. They offer wood-fired regional specialities.

Trouvador €€ *Largo da Sé Velha 17, tel: (039) 82 54 75.* The food is good, especially the kid, and they are one of the more popular places for *fado*. Closed Sun.

Praça Velha € *Praça do Comércio 69, tel: (039) 83 67 04.* Situated right on the plaza, it is a good spot for breakfast and lunch. Seating inside is limited but tables spread on to the square on fine days.

One can search here for hours looking for a restaurant, then come upon a street lined with them. The narrow R. Azeiteiras, which runs from the west end of Praça do Comércio to the R. da Sota behind the Astoria, is one of these. Walk the street, peer in and read the posted menus at these and others:

Left
The Astoria Hotel

Torre de Anto, part of the old city walls, is an *artesanato*, with crafts from all over the Coimbra region.

Viela € *R. Azeiteiras 3, tel: (039) 83 26 25, closed Sat.* Specialities are *bacalhau* (salted cod), *porco alentejo* (pork with clams) and *leitão* (roast suckling pig).

Ze Neto € *R. Azeiteiras 8, tel: (039) 82 67 86.* The first restaurant off Praça do Comércio, and always busy.

Giro € *R. Azeiteiras 39, (039) 83 30 20, closed Sun.* This *churrasqueira* restaurant is decorated in blue and white *azulejos*.

Calado & Calado € *R. da Sota 14, (039) 82 73 48.* On the corner of R. Azeiteiras and close to the Astoria. Specialities are *arroz de mariscos* (a seafood paella) and mixed grill Brazilian style.

O Serenata € *Largo da Sota, just behind the Astoria.* A pleasant small place with red check tablecloths, serving local dishes in full and half portions.

Shopping

The main shopping street is Rua Ferreira Borges, a mélange of small shops which use every centimetre of their limited frontage by arranging displays on the floor behind their glass doors for window-shoppers to see in the evening. A bookstore with English titles, a camera shop and other travellers' necessities, including banks, are found here.

Walking tour

The old city was built on a steep hillside, first by the Romans and then by Moors and Christians in turn. Begin exploring it at **LARGO DA PORTAGEM ❶** at the north end of the Ponte de Santa Clara. Behind the large monument to Joaquin António de Aguiar Ferreira Borges, follow the street named after him, lined on either side by shops. A short distance beyond, bear right up the hill, opposite a stair that descends to the Praça do Comércio.

Detour: Instead of turning right to the Arco de Almedina, go straight on to R. Visconde da Luz to the **Câmara Municipal.** Turn right to the **MOSTEIRO DE SANTA CRUZ ❷**, behind the Câmara Municipal. Retrace your steps to the main route.

You will soon come to the **ARCO DE ALMEDINA ❸**, with escutcheons and a statue of the Virgin and Child. Beyond the gate turn left to the Escadas (stairs) de Quebra-Costas, which will take you into the end of the Largo da Se (a left-hand turn here would take you to the Torre de Anto, a craft centre in a medieval tower). The **SE VELHA ❹** (old cathedral) is at the end of the *largo*. Continue past the Sé on R. de Borges Carmeiro past the **MUSEU NACIONAL MACHADO**

DE CASTRO ❺. The **Sé Nova** is directly ahead. Turn right (south) onto R. Couraça dos Apóstolos to Praça Dom Dinis and right through Praça da Porta Férrea to the **UNIVERSIDADE ❻**.

After visiting the university, turn right from its gate, to R. Dr José Falcão, turning right again along the south side of the University along R. Dr G. Moreira to a stair leading to Couraça de Lisboa. Follow it downhill to R. da Alegria and right into **Largo da Portagem**.

Also worth exploring

The scenic river between Coimbra and Penacova is good for kayaking. Hire a kayak through the regional tourist office (*Praça da República; tel: (039) 83 32 02*); travel upstream by minibus and paddle back to Coimbra.

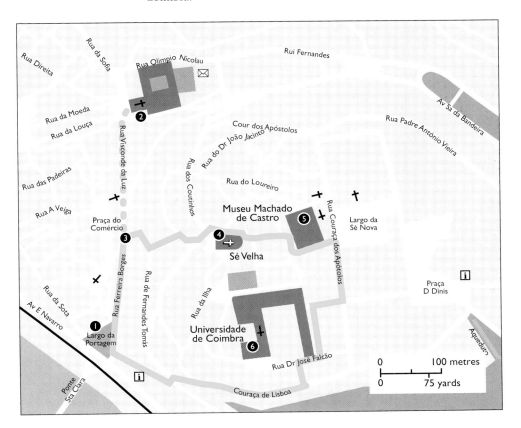

North of Coimbra

Ratings

Azulejos	●●●●●
Beaches	●●●●○
Art and crafts	●●●○○
Nature	●●●○○
Coastal villages	●●○○○
Museums	●●○○○
Walking	●●○○○
Scenery	●○○○○

An extraordinarily ornate royal palace, now a worth-the-splurge hotel, is set inside a forest of exotic trees so precious that the pope once threatened to excommunicate anyone who disturbed it. The Duke of Wellington prepared for his most stunning victory of the Peninsular Wars here, and the area is known for its mineral springs and the once-fashionable (and still very pleasant) spa resorts of Luso and Curia. Broad sand beaches backed by dunes stretch along the Atlantic coast; to the south is the wide Mondego River and to the north, the meandering estuaries, or *rias*, of the Vouga River which surround the attractive town of Aveiro. The water has been diverted into canals, spanned by graceful bridges and flanked by houses which look almost Dutch, giving Aveiro an appearance unlike anywhere else in Portugal.

ATLANTIC COAST*

ℹ Posto de Turismo *Largo do Municipal, Ilhavo, tel: (034) 36 95 60.*

🏛 Museu Marítimo e Regional € *R. Vasco da Gama, Ilhavo, open Wed–Sat 0900–1200, 1400–1730, Sun and Tue 1400–1730.*

Museu Histórico da Vista Alegre € *Vista Alegre, off N109, open Mon–Fri 0900–1230, 1400–1730.*

South of Aveiro, beach towns dot the coast and former ports strung along the N109, face now-silted-up estuaries. Between the shore and the N109 is a maze of local roads that often lead to beaches, but the route is not always direct and it is easy to get lost; the best routes to the shore are from Aveiro, Vagos and Mira.

Throughout the area, streets are lined by building after building faced in tiles. Art deco styles are common and some buildings, such as Vila Africano, in **Ilhavo◊** are fancifully decorated with both tiles and architectural frou-frou. Ilhavo was once a busy fishing port, as recorded in its **Museu Marítimo e Regional◊**, easily identified by the boats in front. Inside are ship models, typical fishing boats and an ancient binnacle, along with a shell collection and displays showing local customs and arts. The **Museu Histórico da Vista Alegre◊** illustrates the development of this well-known porcelain from its

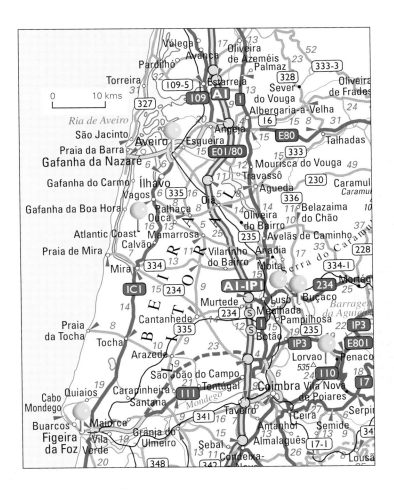

primitive beginnings in the early 1800s, and displays some of its finest examples. Opposite the museum, in the church of Nossa Senhora da Penha is the elaborate tomb of a bishop.

The beach towns are best known for their brightly painted, often striped façades. **Costa Nova***, on the Atlantic, is lined with houses painted in stripes, as are other towns further south, particularly **Palheiros da Tocha***. Just north of **Praia de Mira***, a tidy beach town with a promenade and several restaurants, brightly painted boats with tall sweeping bows line up on the beach.

The town of Vagos, south of Ilhavo is the site of an annual pilgrimage which brings thousands of pilgrims to the church of Nossa Senhora de Vagos on the Monday following Pentecost.

Accommodation and food on the Atlantic Coast

Parque de Campismo de Vagueira € *Praia de Vagueira; tel: (034) 79 76 18, fax: (034) 79 70 93.* Caravan sites and tent pitches in a family-friendly park with cafeteria, market and sports facilities. Half-price Nov–Mar.

O Infante €–€€ *Praça Infante (N109), Mira,* serves seafood and other local dishes.

Sal e Mar €–€€ *Av. João Corte Real, Barra (Ilhavo); tel: (034) 36 01 41.* Specialises in seafood.

AVEIRO✧✧✧

ⓘ Região de Turismo da Rota da Luz *R. João Mendonça 8, tel: (034) 42 07 60, fax: (034) 42 83 26.* Helpful staff; ask for brochures on surrounding towns and especially on *azulejos.*

Aveiro stands out in every visitor's memory for its canals and brightly painted boats. Canal Central is the largest, bordered by some fine old buildings that provide a backdrop for the tall painted prows that curve up from the water.

A block from the large bridge that forms a plaza over the canal, is the Misericórdia church, with a carved 17th-century doorway and *azulejo* walls in carpet pattern above the richly carved gold choir stalls. Beyond, the church of the former **Convento de Jesus**✧ (**€** *Praça do Milenario, open Tue–Sun 1000–1750, occasionally closed midday*) is completely decorated in baroque gilt carvings, with ceiling panels framed in gold and *azulejo* walls. In the adjoining room, the exquisite marble inlaid walls with carved wood panels and painted ceiling are overshadowed by the large, intricately inlaid tomb of Santa Joana, a princess who retired here. Above, accessed through the Museu de Aveiro, is an ornate choir decorated in Chinese style, with a fine painted ceiling. Look at the 15th-century wooden crucifix from different angles to see the change of expression. The nuns' workroom beyond is octagonal, decorated in carved and polychrome panelling.

The museum is extensive, filled with baroque art, both secular and religious, including excellent polychrome statues and a colourful nativity by Machado de Castro. The

You may still find printed material with five-digit telephone numbers; add the number 4 to the beginning of these.

Aveiro is a hard town to leave, not only because it is so pleasant, but because signage is virtually non-existent. Getting out at all is difficult; getting out in the direction of your choice almost impossible.

Lavandro Room is richly ornate, while in the cloisters is a fine 15th-century tomb and a refectory lined with floral tiles.

A colourful time to visit Aveiro is during the Ria Festival, in July or August, when brightly painted boats compete on the central canal. Boats are, in fact, the only way to see some of the areas along the web of *rias* (estuaries) that surround the town. Some launches provide fixed itineraries with point-to-point service; others offer a full circuit tour which makes a good day's excursion, with time for lunch at the Pousada da Ria. The tourist office will provide information.

North of the city itself, accessed by bridges over the wide Vouga estuary, is an area of marshes, saltpans and wandering waterways separated from the open ocean by a long barrier. This is the **Reserva Natural das Dunas de São Jacinto***, where tidal banks and wetlands attract thousands of wading birds in the winter and the reeds provide them with nesting places. Other species, including large birds of prey, nest in the pines and other trees in the dune forests.

Accommodation and food in Aveiro

Hotel Pomba Branca € *R. Luís Gomes de Carvalho 23; tel: (034) 42 25 29.* Traditional whitewashed walls and red tiled roof permit only a glimpse from the street of the lush courtyard contained within. Interior features include some of the finest of Portuguese architectural details, especially ornate wooden panelling and tasteful use of painted tiles.

Hotel Arcada € *R. de Viana do Castelo 4; tel: (034) 42 30 01, fax: (034) 42 18 86.* Pastel exterior evokes 19th-century gentility, and guests can enjoy excellent views of the bustling canal traffic from simple, serviceable rooms.

Left
Aveiro's canals

Above right
Tiled refectory in the
Convento de Jesus, Aveiro

Azulejos in the Ria Towns

The Aveiro region is especially rich in decorated tiles. Although common throughout Portugal, tiles decorate more buildings here than anywhere else, in styles spanning several eras. Some of the oldest are in the sanctuary of the **Sé** (cathedral), and the neighbouring convent. Traditional blue panels decorate the **Estação**, Aveiro's railway station, at the end of Av. Dr Lourenço Peixinho. In Ovar, to the north, and Ilhavo to the south, it is hard to find a building that is not decorated in *azulejos*.

Parque Campismo 'Orbitur' € *São Jacinto; tel: (034) 44 82 84, fax: (034) 44 81 22.* Campsite adjacent to the dunes and beaches of the São Jacinto reserve.

Restaurante Café Caneção €–€€ *R. Aires Barbosa 38; tel: (034) 42 51 10.* A favourite among locals for catered events, their specialities include *cataplana* of seafood and many grilled meats and fish.

O Telheiro Adega Típica € *Largo da Praça do Peixe 20-21; tel: (034) 42 94 73.* Casual eatery on the fishermen's wharf is especially proud of its eel, in addition to the seafood dishes you'd expect.

BUÇACO AND LUSO✶✶

ⓘ Turismo de Luso-Buçaco, *R. Emídio Navarro; tel: (031) 93 91 33.* Ask for the excellent walking maps showing trails through the forest, complete with plant lists and historical sites connected with Wellington's victory.

Manueline architecture is found throughout Portugal, in palaces, churches and monasteries, but rarely can one spend the night amid its marine rococo swirls and flourishes. But the **Buçaco Palace✶✶**, built as a hunting lodge for the last Portuguese kings before the royal family went into exile in Britain, has become a hotel. Even the turrets, towers and abundance of exuberant Neo-Manueline decoration on the outside do not prepare guests for the knockout entrance into a foyer so encrusted with stone carving that it stops them dead in their tracks. It is as though a wedding dress had seen Medusa and all its lace had turned to stone.

Around this fanciful froth of a building are formal gardens, and the whole estate is inside the **Mata do Buçaco✶**, a forest of native and exotic trees planted and tended by monks since at least the 11th century. So unique was this forest that it was protected by a 1643 papal bull which can be seen, carved in stone, at the Porta de Coimbra. The gate opens on to a viewpoint overlooking the Mondego Valley.

Most people begin their visit at the upper end of the forest, eye-to-eye with the treetops, and descend the winding paths. We prefer the lower approach, which begins from the N235, at Portas das Lapas, just

Above opposite
Buçaco Palace

To visit the palace in style, or to make a kingly excursion through the park if you are already a guest, go by **horse-drawn carriage** *(€€ Pensão Alegre; tel: 031 93 02 56)*. One-hour tours of Luso are less expensive.

The municipal park, opposite Grand Hotel de Termas, is a good place to picnic, with a children's playground and pond.

east of Portas das Ameias, which leads from Luso to the palace. Walk through the crumbling gatehouse and up the trail to find yourself in almost magical surroundings. The first clue that this is no typical Portuguese hillside is the moss-green fountain, then the giant ferns growing amongst the trees as you climb through the Vale dos Fetos (Valley of Ferns). Further up are the first of the towering trees, some of 5-metre girth, and a lake surrounded by camellias. This route gives more of a sense of having discovered the forest yourself; it's easy to spend a day wandering along the paths among the rhododendron and 700 other species of plant life inside its walls.

In the midst of the forest are several architectural surprises. At the elegant Fonte Fria, a double staircase flanks a tumbling cascade; chapels and hermitages are tucked under the towering trees. The Via Sacra, Stations of the Cross with terracotta figures, are connected by steps near the Cruz Alta viewpoint.

Little remains of the Carmelite Monastery, only a chapel and cloister with a few simple cork-lined cells, one of which housed Wellington the night before the decisive battle.

The town of Luso still keeps its graceful aura although the waters are not as popular as they once were. There are plenty of hotels, a

garden esplanade to stroll around, and cafés to linger in. The spa is open to everyone for soothing soaks, saunas and swims at quite reasonable prices.

Those interested in military matters should visit the Monumento a Batalha, commemorating Wellington's victory over the French here in 1810, with views over the valley. The nearby **Museu Militar da Guerra Peninsular**✣ has uniforms, weapons and maps so you can trace the routes of advance.

Accommodation and food in Buçaco and Luso

Palace Hotel €€–€€€ *Mata de Buçaco; tel: (031) 93 01 01, fax: (031) 93 05 09, e-mail: almeida.hotels@ip.pt* The palace does not rest on its architectural laurels, but is a well-managed property with spacious, elegant rooms overlooking gardens. The dining room (€€€), more restrained in its décor than the rest of the ground floor, serves a set-price dinner that combines the best of Portuguese and continental styles. In summer it extends on to a terrace, under a riot of carved stonework. The staff behaves as though their guests were still royalty.

Vila Aurora €€ *R. Barbosa Colen; tel: (031) 93 01 93, fax (031) 93 01 93*, a castellated villa overlooking the park, with its own swimming pool.

Pensão Alegre € *R. Emídio Navarro; tel: (031) 93 02 56, fax: (031) 93 02 56*. A conveniently located grand manor, offering its guests discounts on horse-drawn carriage rides. It has a reliable restaurant.

Left
Buçaco palace portico

FIGEIRA DA FOZ✣

At the mouth (*foz*) of the Mondego, Figueira da Foz is a fishing and resort town with a large beach, the attendant watersports (especially surfing and sailing) and ample cafés and restaurants. Few foreign tourists make their way here, however, so expect a Portuguese, not international holiday atmosphere. The beach, and beachfront tourist amenities, lies north of the Forte de Santa Catarina, a 16th-century fortress behind which lies the largely pedestrianised town centre .

The **Museu Municipal do Dr Santos Rocha**✣ (*R. Calouste Gulbenkian, open Tue–Sun 0900–1230, 1400–1730*) has a notable archaeological collection with artifacts found in nearby dolmens, as well as others from the Algarve.

At the northern end of the wide beach is the more colourful fishing village of **Buarcos**, popular with surfers, and beyond that is **Praia Quiaos**, less crowded than either of the beaches further south. Inland from Buarcos rises the **Serra do Boa Viagem**, with wooded walking trails, picnic sites, playgrounds and extensive seaward views.

Accommodation and food in Figueira da Foz

Casa da Azenha Velha €€ *Caseira de Cima, N111; tel: (033) 250 41, fax: (033) 297 04.* Country estate where wild boar are raised, but only 4km from Figueira's beaches; walking distance to restaurant. Landscaped grounds with swimming pool and tennis.

Dory Negro € *Largo Caras Diretas, Buarcos; tel (033) 213 33.* Seafood and other dishes, at less than the resort-driven prices in Figueira.

LORVAO❖❖

Several small cafés face the square in front of the convent, including the very plain **Café Lorvãoense** (**€**) which serves simple local dishes.

Tucked away at the bottom of a steep valley, Lorvão is the kind of town that, even though someone has told you about it, makes you feel you're the first to discover it. Women sit in the shade of trees in front of the convent carving toothpicks, the town's main cottage industry. They begin with what looks like a split fireplace log, chopping it into ever-smaller segments which they whittle into toothpicks with unbelievable speed. You'll find these sold in stores all over Portugal for a few escudos a box.

The **Convento de Santa Maria**✲, under whose wall they sit, seems much too big for the narrow little town with its one-way main street. A fine rococo arch stands alone in the square, all that remains of a wall that once enclosed the town. The chief attractions of the church are in the choir, which has a lovely iron grille studded with bronze medallions. The carvings on and above the choir stalls are especially good; be sure to tip up the seats to see the misericords, each a caricature, looking like fat-cheeked little gargoyles. The chests in the sacristy are false-grained with primitive paintings and the ceiling is painted, as well. The small cloister has box hedges and orange trees, as well as the original tombs of the two princesses who retired here.

Wander up the hill on narrow streets to look down on the convent and into the little gardens that drape over the walls between layers of houses. Porches and balconies intrude into what little space is available for streets.

Suggested tour

Total distance: 222km; 271km with detours.

Time: 5 hours driving. Allow 2 or 3 days for the main route, with or without detours. Those with limited time should concentrate on Aveiro, stopping at Buçaco en route.

Links: Coimbra is connected to Conimbriga and Leiria (*see page 84–85*) via the A1 and N1, which also connect it to Porto (*see pages 136–145*), to the north.

Leave **COIMBRA** ❶ on the N110 following the north shore of the river through the green terraced Mondego Valley for about 14km, turning left and sharply uphill at signposts to **LORVAO** ❷.

Detour: Instead of following the Mondego, leave Coimbra on the N17 through a succession of roundabouts, following signs to 'Estrada de Beira'. Tiny villages seem glued to the steep valley walls and laundry is spread to dry on the sandy banks of the River Ceira below. Turn left (north) on the N2 after about 27km, signposted

Arrifana. After a steep climb out of the valley, the road drops just as steeply down to the Mondego, crossing at Penacova. An immediate left turn along the river meets the main route at the right turn, signposted Lorvão.

Either backtrack to **Penacova** and take the N235 north to **BUÇACO ❸** and **LUSO ❹**, or climb out of Lorvão on unnumbered roads heading north to **Figueira de Lorvão**, then joining the N235 to head north.

The river is a favourite place for kayaking, with steep sides and gorges between Penacova and Coimbra. Hire a kayak in Coimbra (*see tourist information centre, page 92*) with baggage transport or travel upstream by minibus from Coimbra.

Leave **LUSO** on the N234 west, to **Mealhada**, stopping to enjoy the town's culinary speciality, *leitão*, or roast suckling pig, served at midday by any of a dozen roadside restaurants. Head north on the N1, making a brief sidetrack into the old spa town of **Curia**. No matter which of four roads you choose at the roundabout, you'll find hotels (and little else). The Palace stands in its solitary grandeur, the Hotel Termas, beautifully set in lush gardens, is straight ahead, and to the right is a well-kept pink confection, Vila Rosa.

Continue north on the N1, turning left on the N253 to **Oliveira da Beirro**, stopping at the interesting **Museu São Pedro da Palhaça***. The N235 continues into **AVEIRO ❺**.

Detour: Museum aficionados or train buffs should make a side-trip to the industrial city of **Agueda*** to see the ethnographic museum of the Vouga region, the house-museum of the Pinheiro Foundation, and Portugal's railway museum, which has steam locomotives dating back to 1886. (Note that Tue and Thur are the only days when all three museums are open.)

Leave Aveiro heading south along the **ATLANTIC COAST ❻** on the N109 through **Ilhavo**. The Vista Alegre Museum is signposted 2km south of the Maritime Museum. At **Vagos**, turn right to meet the beach road, exploring colourful **Costa Nova** to the north, along with Portugal's highest lighthouse at **Praia de Barra**. Backtrack south to **Praia de Mira**, rejoining the N109 in **Mira** or continuing along the shore through the **Dunas de Cantanhede** (sand dunes).

Praia da Tosha*, accessed from this road or from the N109 in **Tosha**, has particularly photogenic *palheiros*, colourfully painted wooden houses. Both the shore road and the N109 continue south into **FIGUEIRA DA FOZ ❼** (65km from Aveiro by the N109).

Follow the north bank of the wide Mondego River on the IP3 or the slower N111 to **Montemor-o-Velho****, a tiny medieval town whose

---

ⓘ **Museu São Pedro da Palhaça** *São Pedro da Palhaça, open Mon–Sat 0900–1230, 1400–1700, Sun 1430–1830.* Regional costumes, utensils and replica rooms illustrate rural life.

Casa Museu de Etnografia *Mourisca do Vouga, open Tue–Sat 1000–1200, 1400–1700.* Costumes, crafts and decorative arts.

Casa Museu da Fundação Dionisio Pinheiro, *Praça Dr Antonio Breda, open Tue, Thu, Sat, Sun 1500–1800.* House built in 1920s furnished with Portuguese and French antiques and art.

Seccão Museológica da C.P. *Estação Ferroviaria, Macinhata do Vouga. Open Mon–Fri 0900–1200, 1400–1700.* Rolling stock and memorabilia from the steam era.

Above
Curia's Hotel Termas

Pousada da Ria €€
*Torreira, Murtosa; tel:
(034) 44 83 32, fax: (034)
44 83 33.* A bright modern
pousada overlooking the
water of the estuary, near
the São Jacinto dunes.

Estalagem da Pateira
€–€€ *Fermentelos; tel:
(034) 72 12 19, fax: (034)
72 21 81.* Resort hotel
from a time only recently
gone by; guests can relax
on orange vinyl and regard
the locals harvesting
seaweed in the lagoon
below.

Hotel Termas da Curia
€€ *Curia; tel: (031) 51 21
85, fax: (031) 51 58 38.*
Gardens surround this
belle époque spa hotel
designed for relaxation.
Restaurante Dom Carlos
(€€–€€€) adjoins and a
café fills the great leafy
plaza in front of the bath
house.

narrow stone streets lead to an 11th-century castle. Inside is a chapel
with spiral columns. The N111 continues into Coimbra.

Also worth exploring

Wide lagoons bordered by marshes, dunes and pine forests continue
north of Aveiro to the *azulejo*-decked town of Ovar. Windsurfers and
canoeists share the waters with colourful *moliceiros*, brightly painted
boats that gather seaweed. Inland, hills rise to viewpoints over
farmland dotted with villages. Migratory birds stop at the **Barrinha da
Esmoriz** in autumn and winter, protected by the reeds and
surrounding trees.

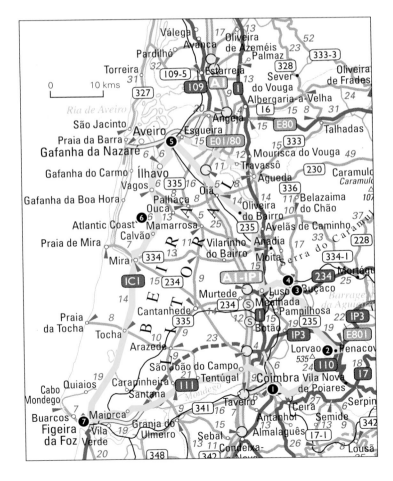

South of the Douro

Ratings

Historical sights	●●●●
Scenery	●●●●
Architecture	●●●
Mountains	●●●
Museums	●●●
Vineyards	●●●
Villages	●●●
Art	●●

Mountain driving, and a lot of it, characterises this route, but at the same time makes it one of the most appealing and beautiful in all Portugal. Four mountain ranges lie in the way, rising between the Vouga and the Douro valleys. Mountainsides are carved into green terraces covered with some of the country's finest vineyards. At upper reaches roads cover long stretches of almost barren land decorated with huge boulders and strange rock formations. The entire region abounds in prehistoric sites. Wine villages, some clearly showing their medieval origins, dot the slopes, crown the hills and are tucked into the deep valleys. Viseu and Lamego lie in an almost direct north–south line, forming halfway stopping places, whichever one you choose as a starting point. Both are pleasant cities to explore and each offers good tourist amenities.

AGUIAR DA BEIRA AND THE SERRA DA LAPA✤✤

ⓘ Tourist Information
Câmara Municipal; tel: (032) 42 20 14.

🍽 Look for restaurants on Av. da Liberdade, which include **Pardal** *(tel: 032 581 15)*, **Cabicança** *(tel: 032 584 15)*, and **Brasil** *(tel: 032 581 17)*, all € and serving local dishes.

The aptly named Serra da Lapa (Mountains of Stone) appears to be made of solid purple-grey rock. Village homes and lone farmhouses built of this stone seem to have grown out of the landscape. In March the hilltops turn solid pink with heather. The approach to Aguiar da Beira is over moss-covered rock punctuated by stone towns and pine forests.

The sloping cobbled Largo dos Monumentos that formed Aguiar's old centre is an unusually perfect assemblage of medieval buildings. Overlooked by a square tower topped with picket-fence merlons is a short square structure, the Fonte Ameada, also crenellated. Its top is open with stone benches around its walls, probably an early council chamber. The town spring is underneath, as was the custom.

Facing the square are buildings of hewn stone, one with a classic medieval stone stairway and porch (*Casa dos Magistrados – see page 115*). In the centre is a tall, slim *pelourinho* pillar with a delicate lantern.

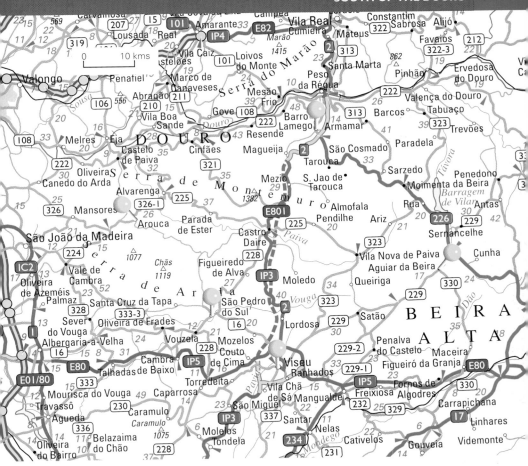

Market day in Aguiar da Beira is every other Monday. The best local product, other than Dão wines, is the mountain cheese sold in markets and at farms.

There are festivities in Aguiar da Beira on St John's Day, June 24, and the town celebrates its annual wine harvest on the first Sunday of October.

In Carapito, 12km south of Aguiar, is the region's largest Megalithic structure, **Anta do Carapito°**, from the fourth millennium BC. On the way, follow signs to the necropolis in Regada, where seven graves carved into solid rock date from the Christian Reconquest.

Accommodation and food in Aguiar da Beira

Casa dos Magistrados € *Largo dos Monumentos 4; tel: (032) 68 82 37, fax: (032) 68 89 13.* Rarely is there a chance to stay in a setting as perfect as Aguiar's medieval square. Four nicely furnished rooms, a sitting room and meals on request.

AROUCA*

ℹ Posto de Turismo de Arouca *Praça Brandão de Vasconcelos; tel: (056) 94 35 75.*

ⓒ Pensão São Pedro *€ Av. Reinaldo Noronha 24; tel: (056) 94 45 80, fax: (056) 94 30 54.* Simple, clean lodgings with spacious public areas.

A zigzag mosaic of paving stones form a foreground for the granite-bordered white baroque buildings facing the main square.

Set deep in a valley, Arouca seems almost hidden, and is rarely visited by tourists. Its claim to fame is the restored convent, **Santa Maria de Arouca***, upon which Queen Malfada lavished her attention – and fortune – when she retired there in the 13th century.

Portugal dissolved its holy orders (much as King Henry VIII had turned out the friars of England) taking over all monastic property in 1834. But government officials didn't reach remote Arouca before townspeople had carried away all the treasures they could hide. Years later, descendants returned them to the conventual church, which had since become the parish church, and they are now beautifully displayed in the **Museu de Arte Sacra*** (*€ Praça Central, open Tue–Sun 1000–1200, 1400–1700*), housed in the restored convent. The collection includes 15th- and 16th-century paintings of the Viseu school, 15th-century statuary, tapestries, jewellery, some exquisite reliquaries and a charming miniature of St Ambrose's cell, which looks far too worldly for a monk.

The **Igreja do Mosteiro*** (*Praça Central, open 0800–1700*) is also filled with art, including the silver and ebony casket of the mummified queen, Santa Malfada, carved and gilded altars, more than 100 richly carved choir stalls, and an elevated gallery of oversized nun statues with painted habits and saintly expressions.

Below
Harvest Festival in Arouca

Ask locally for exact directions to Frecha da Mizarela, a waterfall dropping in long ribbons over several stages of a rock face.

Locally adored Queen Malfada is celebrated on May 1, leading into the Festa das Cruzes the following day, when pilgrims hike into the hills of Serra da Freita to the chapel of the Senhora da Lage. The nearby town of Alvarenga, northeast of Arouca, hosts a colourful pageant, the Festa da Senhora do Monte, at their local shrine on September 8. And the last week of September sees the Feira das Colheitas, the biggest and most secular of Arouca's festivals, featuring folk-costumed dancers, street decorations, and crowds celebrating the year's harvest.

LAMEGO**

It is rare for a city in Portugal (or anywhere) to be all of one architectural style, but Lamego is almost pure baroque. The refined granite swirls and flourishes set against smooth white spaces of its façades give the city an air of grace and elegance.

Hills rise on either side of the city centre, one to a **castle ruin** (interesting mainly for the views from its walls), the other to the baroque **Nossa Senhora dos Remédios***, a pilgrimage church. The graceful double staircase to the sanctuary lead from Av. Dr Alfredo de Sousa, and are decorated with fountains, gazebos and *azulejos*. Pilgrims climb them on their knees. The plaza at the top has more statues, this time of royalty, in the Pátio dos Reis. The view from the top, down the symmetrical stairscase and across the city, is worth the climb.

The **Sé***, Lamego's cathedral, is primarily from the 16th and 18th centuries and has an excellent Renaissance portal carved with plant and animal motifs. The carved choir stalls are also outstanding, as is the cloister. The decoration in the Capela do Sacramento looks like tapestry translated into silver.

The grand Episcopal Palace now houses the **Museu de Lamego***, one of the best regional museums in Portugal. Along with medieval and baroque statuary and noble escutcheons which once marked mansions throughout the Lamego area, it has striking painted-wood panels from the altarpiece of the cathedral before its 18th-century renovations. When the Chagas convent was torn down, one of its ornate gilded chapels was saved and is installed here, along with two other superb baroque chapels. *Azulejos* (some very interesting polychrome ones) and other examples of Portuguese and foreign art complete the collections.

Lamego's vineyards yield a sparkling wine, one of two produced in Portugal. Tours of the winemaking process at **Caves da Raposeira*** (*Mon–Fri 1000, 1100, 1200, 1400, 1500, 1600*) on the N2, 2km west of city centre, include tastings.

Accommodation and food in Lamego

Hotel do Parque €€ *Parque Nossa Senhora dos Remédios; tel: (054) 621 05, fax: (054) 652 03.* Next to the sanctuary church, the hotel overlooks bosky slopes and a garden. Church bells can be startling, but the same is true for most Lamego lodgings.

Casa de Santo António de Britiande €€ *Britiande; tel: (054) 69 93 46, fax: (054) 69 93 46.* Unlike many historic manor houses, this one is bright, spacious and almost modern in its feel, never over-decorated. Priceless antiques furnish rooms with floor-to-ceiling windows. The chapel is brilliant, with *azulejos* and gilded carving throughout.

Restaurante Avenida €–€€ *Av. Dr Alfredo de Sousa; tel: (054) 623 44,* serves the usual suspects with a little more finesse than most.

Tas de Sé € *R. Tas de Sé; tel: (054) 624 68,* is good for hearty, cheap dishes like *feijoada*, the local bean stew.

SÃO PEDRO DO SUL AND THE VOUGA VALLEY⁕

ℹ️ **Turismo Dão Lafões** *Largo dos Correios, Termas de São Pedro do Sul; tel: (032) 71 13 20.*

🛒 Market day in **Vouzela** is the first Wednesday each month; in **Oliveira de Frades** it's alternate Mondays; **São Pedro** is more complicated as its market is held on the first Thursday and second Monday between the 16th and 22nd of each month.

🎉 **São Pedro do Sul** celebrates its festival on June 29; **Vouzela** on the first Sunday of August, and **Oliveira de Frades** during the second two weeks of August.

The towns of São Pedro do Sul, Termas, Vouzela and Oliveira de Frades lie companionably close in the Vouga valley. São Pedro's thermal springs were a favourite of weary Romans who bathed in a now ruined spa near the modern one. The sulfurous waters bubble out of the ground at **Termas⁕**, 3km south of São Pedro. Of the Roman baths, built in the 1st century AD, columns, capitals and a swimming pool survive. The medieval chapel of São Martinho is there, as well.

Vouzela⁕ lies right on the river, its 13th-century Romanesque Igreja Matriz decorated with corbels carved in grotesque faces. On Praça da República, the Misericórdia church is completely encased in bright blue *azulejos* and, inside, a fine Renaissance retable is carved in polychrome relief. In Cambarinho, south of the IP5, 12km southwest of Vouzela, the Reserva Botânica de Loendros protects a hillside of rare rhododendron that bloom from April to June, and are at their best in May.

About 7km east, signposted from the road through Fatauncos to Figueiredo das Donas, is one of the steepest sections of Roman road yet found, and also one of the best preserved, its worn stones still perfectly in place. About 6km south of Oliveira de Frades, past São Vicente Lafões, is another segment of the same road, also in good condition. Follow the footpath from the church of São Tiaguinho.

Accommodation and food in São Pedro do Sul and the Vouga Valley

Quinta do Pendão € *Santa Cruz da Trapa; tel: (032) 71 99 16, fax: (032) 29 95 40.* A farm in the foothills, 8km from Termas, with a well-preserved stretch of Roman road at its gates. Meals on request.

Quinta da Comenda €€ *N16, São Pedro do Sul; tel: (032) 71 11 01, fax: (032) 71 11 01.* Ecologically responsible farm selling wine, fruit and vegetables. Guest-rooms are in nicely modernised building adjacent to the 12th-century *quinta*.

Do Parque €–€€ *Termas; tel: (032) 72 64 61, fax: (032) 72 30 47,* one of several large hotels at the spa, with a restaurant and full facilities.

Restaurante Estrela da Manha € *Av. António Correira, São Pedro do Sul; tel: (032) 71 16 69,* a good place to try the famous local veal.

O Solar € *R. Dr Rameiro Ferreira, Oliveira de Frades; tel: (032) 76 13 82,* also serves locally raised meats.

Cambra, just north of the IP5 has several restaurants, including **Taverna Lavrador** (*tel: 032 77 81 11*), all serving typical regional dishes.

VISEU❖❖

ℹ **Região de Turismo Dão-Lafões** *Av. Calouste Gulbenkian; tel: (032) 42 20 14, website: www.autonet.pt/rt-dao-lafoes open 0900–1230, 1430–1800, longer in summer.* Excellent guides to walking and archaeological sites are available, very inexpensively, as is a small guide to the city. The free regional booklet is one of the best in Portugal, with abundant labelled illustrations.

Below
Misericórdia church, Viseu

The streets of Viseu's old centre wind from the gracious squares and gardens below past old granite buildings and baroque mansions to the great stone **Sé**❖ at the very top. This 13th-century cathedral faces a fine square (which would seem finer were it not used as a car park), bordered by the white baroque façade of the Misericórdia church and the former bishop's palace, now the **Grão Vasco Museum**❖ of Portuguese painting and sculpture. In the 16th century, Viseu was home to one of Portugal's two great schools of painting, and some of its finest examples are displayed here. Ceramics and furniture are among the other arts displayed.

Enter the Sé from the lovely *azulejo*-lined Renaissance cloister to the right, through a Romanesque-Gothic portal. The Cathedral's most remarkable features are the knotted ribs of the ceiling, the enormous gilded altar and the carved choir stalls and painted ceiling of the sanctuary, which you can observe up-close if a service is not in progress. A chapel to the left is lined with *azulejos*, as is the adjoining corridor, which leads to a sacristy with an exuberant painted ceiling. The treasury, upstairs, has two fine Limoges reliquary cases and a

P There is metered parking on R. 25 de Abril, near the tourist office, and carparks west of the centre near the Rossio. Avoid driving into the winding narrow streets of the old city.

Sé (Treasury €)
Andro da Sé, open Mon–Tue, Thu–Fri 0900–1200, 1400–1700, Sat–Sun 1400–1700, closed two weeks early July. Cathedral open longer hours.

Grão Vasco Museum €
Andro da Sé, open Tue–Sun 0930–1230, 1400–1730. Free Sun am.

nativity scene (and often a very amusing guide who'll make the children remember this place).

It would be appropriate if Viseu's cathedral were dedicated to St Peter, since it is built on a solid rock outcrop. In the street behind, under the imposing round walls of its sanctuary, paving stones give way to hummocks of an undulating rock surface that drop off into the warren of steep streets, all leading to Rua Direita. This is the central commercial street of the old city, narrow and lined with shops, restaurants and even narrower side alleys.

Look up to notice Renaissance and baroque buildings with finely detailed windows and carved crests. R. Senhora da Piedade has several 16th-century windows and on R. Dom Duarte is a particularly good Manueline window. R. Formosa, with several art nouveau buildings, leads down to the **Rossio** (officially Praça da República), a large shaded square bounded by a wall of *azulejos* showing regional scenes.

Facing one end of the plaza is the Igreja São Francisco, more often called Terceiros, with *azulejos* and a gilded altar. At the opposite side of the old centre, the Igreja São Bento has outstanding 17th-century *azulejos*.

Viseu's main annual festivals are the colourful Cavalhadas parade, on June 24, with large papier-mâché heads and costumed riders on horseback, and the Feira de São Mateus (*mid-Aug–mid-Sept*), an old-fashioned fair with wines, agriculture, crafts, music, food and fireworks.

A Roman road connecting Ranhaldos (just off the N116, 1km east of the ring-road) and São João de Lourosa, a grey stone town to the south, has two well-preserved segments. Ask the tourist office to draw precise directions on a local map. A unique 6-metre press for oil or

Left
The Sé (Cathedral), Viseu

Right
The cathedral cloister at Viseu

Market day is Tue, with stalls filling a large area northeast of the historic centre. In the streets dropping from the back of the cathedral to R. Direita are tiny workshops of tin and brass-smiths.

Casa da Ribeira *R. do Coval (near Cava de Viriato),* sells regional handcrafts, including black pottery, tinware, lace and embroidery.

possibly wine, Lagareta da Corga, probably medieval, is carved into a stone outcrop under trees on the west side of the N2, at Vila Chã de Sá, next to the turn-off for Soutulho and Aral.

Accommodation and food in Viseu

Hotel Avenida € *Av. Alberto Sampaio 1, tel: (032) 42 34 32, fax: (032) 256 43.* Pretty hotel on a corner, it faces gardens within walking distance of the historical area.

Quinta de São Caetano €–€€ *R. Poça das Feiticeiras 38; tel: (032) 42 39 84, fax: (032) 42 39 84.* Former manor house of a Viscountess, it has a lovely 17th-century chapel, gardens and views. Simple, tasteful interior maintains a folkloric feel.

Quinta Basteira € *Lugar da Igreja-Povolide; tel: (032) 93 17 84, fax: (032) 93 21 55.* Hospitable lodgings in farm country, rooms are linked to an internal patio with gardens and a pool.

Casa dos Queijos € *Trav. Escadinhas da Sé 7; tel: (032) 42 26 43.* Hidden upstairs over a shop selling delicious mountain cheeses, this simple tiny restaurant is filled with local people who know its ample portions of *arroz valenciana* (rice with shrimp, pork, clams, mussels, sausage, squid and chicken) and *frango na pucara* (savoury chicken stewed in local black pottery). Begin with a thick, satisfying *caldo verde*, Portugal's famous green soup.

Restaurant-Café O Patria € *R. Direita. Cataplana* and good mixed grill with freshwater clams. Very inexpensive daily specials.

Suggested tour

Total distance: 401km; 501km with detours.

Time: 8 hours driving. Allow 3 days for the main route, with or without detours. Those with limited time should concentrate on Viseu and Lamego.

Links: The east–west highway, IP5, connects Viseu to Aveiro (*see page 104*). The N2 and the more direct IP3 connect Lamego and Pêso da Régua (*see page 116*). You can join this route at Vale de Cambra from the coastal corridor between Aveiro and Porto via the N224 through Oliveira de Azemeis. The IP5 also connects Viseu to Guarda and the northern Serra da Estrela (*see page 208*) and the fortified hill towns (*see page 200*).

Route: Leave **VISEU** ❶ on the N229 to **Satão**, where the main road is paved in stone.

Detour: The N329 leads north on a twisting, turning road to **Queriga**, where women still wear traditional black-fringed shawls. Outside of town, in the middle of a rocky moor coloured by broom and heather, is **Orca dos Juncais**, a large dolmen with hard-to-distinguish paintings on its supporting slabs. To find the dolmen, follow faded signs to the right at Queriga school, left at the fork and left on to a dirt lane, bordered by a moss-covered stone fence. Turn right and follow the rough, rocky lane about 1.5km to a rise, where the dolmen, protected by a tin roof, is on the right. Backtrack to the N229 just east of Satão.

From Satão, continue east on the N229 to **AGUIAR DA BEIRA ❷**, turning left (north) at the later intersection with N226. Make a quick 4km sidetrack on the N229 to **Sernancelhe** and its Igrega Matriz, continuing on the N226 through **Moimenta de Beira** to **LAMEGO ❸**.

Detour: To shorten the route, or to divide it into two loops, return to the starting point in Viseu via the north–south N2, and/or the faster IP3 as it is completed. About half-way through these wild highlands is

Below
The Orcas dos Juncais
dolmen at Queriga

Restaurante O Tosco € *Av. Marechal Gomes da Costa, Castro Daire; tel: (032) 326 93.* Pretty standard offerings, but well prepared.

Dão wines

The river Dão gives its name to wines from grapes grown on the terraced plots along its banks. Although both reds and whites are produced, the red is by far the better. By law, Dão is matured in casks for a minimum of 18 months. Most of the casks are of oak from Buçaco or the Serra da Estrela. Dão reds are full-bodied wines, smooth, aromatic and the colour of garnets.

Castro Daire, where the **Igreja da Ermida do Paiva** is considered one of the most beautiful Romanesque churches in Portugal, with a rare Romanesque cloister and medieval burial chamber in its churchyard. For a more modern artifact, stop in the **Jardim Municipal** (gardens) in the town centre, to see the huge machine, built in 1912, used until 1978 by a local sawmill.

Leave Lamego on the N226, past stunning views into the valley ahead, turning left (west) to follow the south bank of the Douro on the N222. The route through **Resende** and **Cinfaes** to **Castelo de Paiva** is winding and hilly, but the scenery is splendid. From the junction in Castelo de Paiva, more mountain driving awaits to the south on the N224, through rocky landscapes to a left turning on the N326 into the lush valley of **AROUCA** ❹.

Back on the N224 the route continues south to **Vale de Cambra**, where the N227 leads east through **Junqueira** to SAO PEDRO DO SUL ❺ and the Vouga valley. Return to Viseu on the N16.

Also worth exploring

Mangualde lies in wine country east of Viseu, south of the IP5, a small town with two manor houses, one of which you can visit. Also in town, the **Citânia da Raposeira**, an excavated Roman villa, is reached by a footpath, signposted from Quinta da Raposeira. Another signpost from the centre leads to the **Igreja São Julião**, older than Portugal itself, with a medieval cemetery of graves carved from bedrock. The area around it is filled with megalithic monuments, including fine chambered tombs at **Cunha Baixa**. Almost directly to the north, in the area around **Penalva do Castelo**, are more dolmens and medieval tombs and a pre-Roman *castro*.

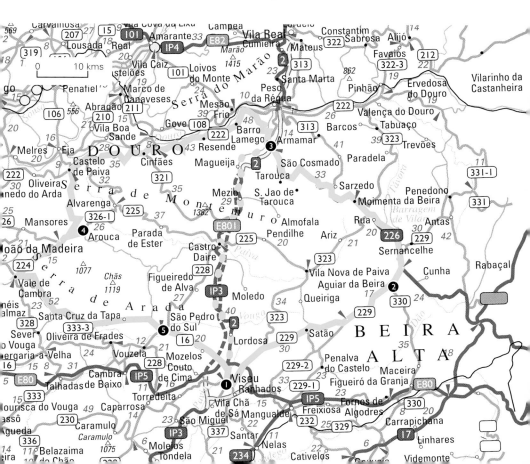

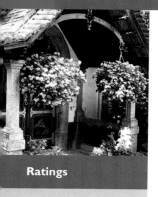

North of the Douro

Ratings

Vineyards and wine	●●●●●
Mountains	●●●●○
Scenery	●●●●○
Nature	●●●○○
Villages	●●●○○
Walking	●●●○○
Historical sights	●●○○○
Trains and boats	●●○○○

Asmall area with big scenery, this land north of the famous wine river packs a lot into limited space. Here travellers will find one of the country's most endearing small cities with an equally endearing saint, a dramatically beautiful mountain range and a river that once literally flowed with Port wine. Near the river are two foremost solares, each set in gardens, both romantic, but in very different ways. Perhaps more than anywhere else in Portugal, you will find here a microcosm of what makes this such a delightful country to visit. It is Portugal at its most Portuguese. Take advantage of this by staying in some of the many manor houses and quintas that welcome guests. It is a unique opportunity to step inside the region, as well as to see places not otherwise open to the public.

AMARANTE✦✦

ℹ Tourist Information
R. Cândido dos Reis, Alameda Teixeira de Pascoaes; tel: (055) 43 22 59, open daily 0930–1230, 1400–1900, 0930–1900 summer.

⊕ Rent rowing boats along the riverside, near the bridge.

The deep arches of Amarante's bridge reflect in the Tâmega to form a pair of perfect circles, beneath the tower and honey-coloured walls of the **Igreja de São Gonçalo✦** (*Alameda Teixeira de Pascoaes, open daily, daylight hours*). This lovely and memorable scene sets the tone for a delightful town. Inside, the church is soaring and cheerful, with angels and curly-haired cherubs, a two-tailed merman that opens his mouth when the organ plays, and the tomb of São Gonçalo, where unmarried women pray and married ones offer little nosegays in thanks.

The first of the two adjoining cloisters retains its monastic air, the second is now the **Museu Amadeo de Sousa Cardoso✦** (€ *Alameda Teixeira de Pascoaes; tel: (055) 43 26 63*). This locally born artist who became the most famous Portuguese painter of the 20th century, is known for his Cubist-influenced experimentation with colour and shape. Along with his works, the museum has works by some of his

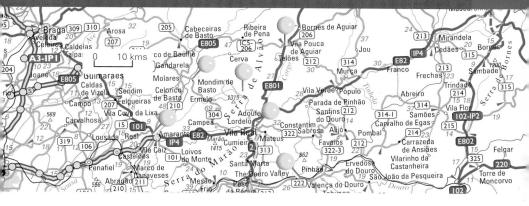

The Mercado Municipal is on the east side of the Alameda Teixeira de Pascoaes, near the church. Main market days are Saturday and Wednesday; otherwise buy picnic makings at the little shops and bakery on R. 31 de Janeiro, across the bridge.

contemporaries, as well as local historical artifacts.

Above, the round Igreja São Domingos has large windows which show off the rich gold interior. Beyond, and up a second hill, is the Igreja São Pedro whose grey-green interior is decorated in white relief designs, like a Wedgewood box. Colourful wooden balconies, several of which are cafés or restaurants, overhang the river, and stone carvings, wrought ironwork and other flourishes decorate the buildings. As the town's brochure so charmingly promises, 'Amarante rewards princely those who walk slowly along its streets'.

The Festas de Junho, in honour of São Gonçalo, take place on the first weekend in June. Celebrations begin the week before with concerts and decorations, progressing to an all-night drumming competition, the exchange of phallic-shaped São Gonçalo pastries and a colourful procession.

East of the city, visible from the IP4, is the granite town of Abondela, whose moss-covered Roman bridge with four arches is still in everyday use. Leading to the bridge is a street of medieval stone houses with granite stairs rising to pillared porches. Under a granite cross at one end is a stone fountain and laundry basin. The bridge looks down on scenes that have changed very little in the last centuries: hay ricks above riverside gardens where women gather greens for dinner.

Accommodation and food in Amarante

Hotel Navarras € *R. António Carneiro; tel: (055) 43 10 36, fax: (055) 43 29 91.* Nothing fancy, but balconied rooms are plain and comfortable. In the town centre, with parking, good breakfast buffet and most accommodating staff.

Pousada São Gonçalo €–€€ *IP4; tel: (055) 46 11 13, fax: (055) 46 13 53.* Don't be put off by maps that show this on a mountain road; it's literally at the end of the slip road off the IP4. Warm and exceptionally welcoming staff, smallish rooms, cosy atmosphere and an excellent dining room.

Casal de Aboadela € *Aboadela (9km east of Amarante); tel: (055) 44 11 41*. Picturesque lodgings in a granite farmhouse are for the more rurally inclined travellers. Simple, attractive rooms overlook a gorgeous mountain view across the valley.

Casa de Pascoaes €€ *São João de Gatão (1.5km north of Amarante); tel: (055) 42 25 95*. A stonework and stucco gate and richly tiled courtyard greet visitors to this manor house, also a museum of a local poet. Elegantly but comfortably furnished rooms, dark wood detail and ceilings brightened by ivory-coloured walls and bedspreads.

Retaurante Ze da Calçada €€€ *R. 31 de Janeiro; tel: (055) 42 20 23*. The best restaurant in town, with a glorious view of the river, bridge and church. It is, frankly, overpriced and a bit pretentious, but sometimes atmosphere is worth paying extra for.

Restaurante Lusitana €–€€ *R. 31 de Janeiro; tel: (055) 42 67 20*. A hospitable and down-to-earth restaurant also overlooking the river and bridge. They serve simple food, like their specialities of roasted kid and tripe Porto-style.

Tasquinha da Ponte €–€€ *R. 31 de Janeiro; tel: (055) 43 37 15*. Cosy winecellar atmosphere, where they serve local specialities like lamb chops, roast kid, and *petiscos* – small, inexpensive servings similar to tapas that make good lunches and snacks.

THE DOURO VALLEY❖❖❖

ⓘ **Turismo do Douro**
R. de Ferreirinha 505, Pêso da Régua; tel: (054) 238 46, fax: (054) 32 22 71, open Jun–Sep 0900–1230, 1400–1830.

Ⓒ **Companhia Turística do Douro**
€€–€€€ tel: (054) 628 11. Call ahead to reserve seats for a 90-minute jaunt by boat from Cais da Barragem de Bagauste (just up from Régua) to Pinhão.

For more than two thousand years man has sculpted the steep hillsides overlooking the Douro and its tributaries, planting the flat terraces, carefully tending the vines and making wine from the harvest. The resulting landscape is indescribably beautiful especially in autumn when the green vines turn shades of ochre and deep red.

Old boats with long prows, which once filled the river carrying wine to Porto, still float in its waters, but are a rarer sight. The N222 hugs the south shore of the river, the railway line the north; there is barely room for either. Bridges cross at Pêso da Régua and Pinhão. Exhibits at Régua's **Instituto do Vinho do Porto**❖ (Port Wine Institute; *R. dos Camilos 90; tel: 054 32 11 75, open Mon–Fri 0900–1230, 1400–1630*) introduce the history and process of port production, a more colourful tale than one might expect.

In the mountains north of the river, Sabrosa is the birthplace of the explorer Magellan. An uphill turn past the Café Vesuvio leads to Castro de Sabrosa, an Iron-Age hill-fort in a wild setting, with walls and foundations intact. Park at the quarry and follow the trail to the right.

Several trains leave Porto daily, following the Douro River to Pêso da Régua; some change direction in Livração, 60km out, to climb over the Alto do Espinho to Vila Real, via Amarante. Either route is filled with stunning scenery and, if travelled in the opposite direction, makes a nice way to spend time in Porto without having to deal with a car in the city.

Accommodation and food in the Douro Valley

Port wine

Port is made from grapes of high sugar content grown in the Douro Valley, and fortified with brandy to stop its fermentation. The finest Ports are aged for 10 to 20 years, or even longer.

The British are thought to have invented the process in the late 17th century when their supply of French wine was cut off, and they added brandy to Portuguese wine to preserve it during shipping. All true ports come from Porto, at the mouth of the Douro.

Quinta de la Rosa €€ *Quinta da Rosa Vinhos do Porto, Lda. (2km east of Sabrosa); tel: (054) 722 54.* Live on a major port-producing estate, perched overlooking the River Douro. Simple, comfortable bedroom has natural wood walls and ceiling.

Quinta do Paço €–€€ *Vila Marim (4km north of Mesão Frio); tel: (054) 69 93 46, fax: (054) 69 93 46.* Moss-encrusted granite gates welcome you as they did the Marquis of Nisa, a commander of the Battle of Trafalgar. His home has undergone a few changes – big windows with calico drapes let the light into spacious, simply arranged rooms.

Pousada de Mesão Frio €€ *Mesão Frio (10km west of Régua); tel: (054) 89 01 30, fax: (054) 89 01 39.* A stately baroque estate house, all granite, red tile, whitewash, and iron, Mesão Frio is meant for slowing down the pace of life; the rooms match the façade in elaborate luxury. A good place to stop and ponder the greatness of port.

Quintas do Douro (Turihab Booking Agency) will book rooms in the *quintas* (wine estates) and houses of the area from their office in Pêso da Régua; *tel: (054) 32 27 88, fax: (054) 32 27 88.*

Restaurante Cacho d'Oiro €€ *R. Branca de Martinho, Pêso da Régua; tel: (054) 32 14 55.* Serving local specialities with forays into haute cuisine, this is one of the nicer dining rooms in town.

Restaurante Papa Leguas € *N322, Sabrosa,* a handy lunch stop *en route.*

Right
Douro Valley farmhouse

MONDIM DE BASTO AND SERRA DE ALVAO❖❖

ⓘ Turismo *Praça 9 de Abril; tel: (055) 38 14 79. Open Oct–Jun Mon–Fri 0930–1230, 1400–1730; Jul–Sep open weekends as well.* Has maps for local hikes.

ⓘ Parque Natural do Alvão Information Centre *Zona do Barrio, Sitio de Retiro. Open Mon–Fri 0900–1230, 1400–1730.* Some laybys at viewpoints in the Parque Natural have picnic tables.

Right
Roman road

Mondim de Basto, an attractive town in a beautiful setting, is a good stopping-off point or a base for hiking rather than a destination in itself. The surrounding scenery is literally breathtaking, since Mondim lies in the deep, precipitous valley of the River Tâmega. At the southern edge, below a little chapel, is a stretch of Roman road and a Roman bridge.

The town is hemmed in on the south and west by the Serra de Alvão, and carved into a corniche, the N304 is suspended above plunging drops. The scenery is outstanding, with layers of blue mountains behind an alternately forested and rocky foreground. The well-surfaced and relatively level road is not for acrophobics. In the centre of the **Parque Natural do Alvão❖**, close to the N304, is Fisgas de Ermelo, a 550-metre waterfall.

Romarigues❖ (*Av. Bombeiros, Mondim de Basto; tel/fax: (055) 38 25 24*), is a rare *artesanato* that encourages the preservation of authentic local crafts. A big floor loom is often at work amid shelves of fragrant local honey, embroidery and other products of the long mountain winters. English-speaking owners are a good source of information on the area.

Accommodation and food in Mondim de Basto and Serra de Alvão

Casa das Mouroas € *R. José de Carvalho Camões, Mondim de Basto; tel: (055) 38 13 94.* Grey stone house in typical regional style with inviting, but not *folclórico* interior. Right in town, walking distance to restaurants.

Quinta do Fundo € *Vilar de Viando (1.5km south of Mondim de Basto); tel: (055) 38 12 91, fax: (055) 38 20 17.* Buildings of the *quinta* are dotted among neat terraces of grapevines clinging to the hillside. Large airy rooms have dark wood and stone walls and big windows overlooking the rivers in the valley below.

Casa da Cruz € *Campeã (12km northwest of Vila Real); tel: (059) 97 94 22, fax: (059) 729 95.* Very homey lodgings in the striking rural style with corner supports and window frames of huge cut blocks of stone, and walls of thousands of small flat fieldstones. Decorated in a quiet way, with simple wooden furniture and woven rugs.

Adega São Tiago € *R. Velha, Mondim de Basto; tel: (055) 38 22 69.* Closed Sun. Cheerful atmosphere and a mostly local crowd fill this small *adega*, serving local cuisine at terrific value.

VILA POUCA DE AGUIAR✤

ⓘ Tourist Information *Largo Camilo Castelo Branco, Vila Pouca de Aguiar.*

◉ The Corgo River is renowned for its trout; fishing licences are easy to get from the Forest Institute, Parque Florestal, in Vila Pouca de Aguiar.

There is not much left of the pre-medieval Castelo Roqueiro de Aguiar, off the N2, south near Pontido, but the tiny village on the connected hill is almost pristine. Were it not for a small sign for the town telephone, it would be hard to tell what century you were in. In summer the rough stone streets are arcaded in grape vines, and new community washing tubs sit beneath fine stone corncribs. The setting of Vila Pouca de Aguiar is as interesting as its medieval stone houses, which are dwarfed by the huge boulders covering the hilltop.

For sweeping views, drive up to the chapel of Nossa Senhora da Conceição. At Povoação, the medieval cemetery has 11, 7th-century graves carved into the granite bedrock.

The mountains south and west of Aguiar are scattered with dolmens, as many as ten in a group; the two main sites are at Carrazedo de Alvão and Lixa do Alvão, both along the N206 just west of Aguiar. You can't miss the one in Aguiar itself: it marks the middle of a roundabout.

Accommodation and food in Vila Pouca de Aguiar

Casa de Cerrado € *Agunchos, Cerva (20km west of Vila Pouca de Aguiar); tel: (059) 472 18.* Old granite farmhouse in a tiny village conceals a pleasant, bright, up-to-date interior of cushy chairs and floral motifs.

Casa da Nogueirinha € *Pontido (5km southwest of Vila Pouca de Aguiar); tel: (059) 465 77.* A classic example of the area's manorial architecture, this lodging features wide verandas facing the central stone courtyard. Rooms are understated and elegant, allowing old furniture to shine. Above is the ruined *castelo*.

Pensão Costa do Sol € *R. Imperador Teodosio 22 (Estrada do Minho); tel: (059) 423 38, fax: (059) 41 60 15.* Tidy, comfortable rooms in the town, with a dining room for travellers too weary to wander in search of dinner.

O Tijolo € *Largo Camilo Castelo Branco; tel: (059) 424 24.* Brazilian-style grilled meats in plentiful servings.

VILA REAL❖

ⓘ Tourist Information *Av. Carvalho Araújo 94; tel: (059) 32 28 19, fax: (059) 32 17 12. Open Jun–Oct daily, 0930–1900, Nov–May Mon–Sat 0930–1230, 1400–1700.*

National Park Information Office *R. Alves Torgo 22, 3rd Floor; tel: (059) 241 38, fax: (059) 738 69, open Mon–Fri 0900–1230, 1400–1700.* Has brochures on local topics and plenty of information on wildlife and the environment.

ⓗ Solar de Mateus *€€ gardens only € take R. Dr Augusto Rua from centre; tel: (059) 32 31 21, open daily 0900–1300, 1400–1800, 1900 summer, 1400–1800 spring and autumn.*

At the confluence of the Corgo and Cabril rivers, with the Serra Marão rising sharply behind, Vila Real is a city of fine old homes from the 16th–18th centuries, and a lively commercial centre. The Italian architect Nasoni spent time here, and his influence shows in the baroque façades and interiors of Vila Real's churches, especially the Capela Nova and the Igreja São Pedro, which has fine gilt carving.

Life centres on the Avenida Carvalho Araújo, lined with sidewalk cafés in front of mirror-walled pastry shops out of the 1920s. Jardim Carreira is a garden fragrant with linden trees in June and July. An esplanade through former castle grounds has good views into the river gorge. **Quinta São Domingos**❖ *(open Mon–Fri 0900–1230, 1400–1700)*, the estate lodge of a foremost Port producer, offers tours and samples.

On June 28–29 at Capela Nova, the Feira de São Pedro is a big fair especially for local potters. At Bisalhães, 5km away in the mountains, potters still produce a silvery-black pottery; nearby Agarez is known for its handwoven linen.

In the village of Flores is the Roman Piscais Bridge and remains of a Roman road. But the area's best known site is the **Solar de Mateus**❖❖ the epitome of all Portuguese Baroque architecture. The grand entrance to the manor house is encrusted with stone details – a coat of arms looms proportionate to the heroic-sized classical figures flanking it. A double staircase branches down from the front, and surrounding balustrades are graced by statuary. Part of the house is open to the public, and the viewable rooms match the outside festooned with velvet drapes and ornate carvings. Visitors can also wander through the extensive and wonderful gardens, with hedges, cyprus, and more statues creating a romantic atmosphere.

Also in Mateus, the **Santuário de Panoias**❖ *(open Wed–Sun 0900–1200, 1400–1700, Tue 0900–1200)* is among the oddest of ancient sites. Three huge boulders, well accessed by ladders, have been carved with large, precisely shaped hollows. Inscriptions show i

Restaurante Espadeiro € *Av. Almeida Lucena; tel: (059) 32 23 02.* Walking the fine line between elegant and relaxed, with an outstanding wine cave. Fine local foods, such as trout are the speciality; on Sundays they serve succulent roast kid.

Tue and Fri are market days.

Corpus Christi in Vila Real is a solemn medieval procession, with bright cloaks and silver insignias, through corridors of embroidered cloths hung as banners from upper storey windows.

Below
The solar de Mateus

to be a Roman sanctuary to Serapis, and speak of its use for animal sacrifices.

Accommodation and food in Vila Real

Hotel Mira Corgo € *Av. 1º de Maio 78; tel: (059) 32 50 01, fax: (059) 32 50 06.* Modern hotel with balconies and dizzying views, in the heart of Vila Real. Public areas are big, bright, and comfortable, and rooms are spacious and full of amenities, like direct-dial telephones and hairdriers. Saunas, big indoor pool, and a dining room whose menu extends beyond Portuguese cuisine.

Casa Agricola da Levada €–€€ *Timpeira (1.5km northeast of Vila Real); tel: (059) 32 21 90, fax: (059) 34 69 55.* Gracious and welcoming, near Solar de Mateus, landscaped stone-edged pool, hedges and gardens extend into the woods from a 1920s home designed by a prominent architect. The farm produces bread, honey, jams and traditional smoked sausage.

Casa do Mineiro € *Tras do Vale, Campeã (11km west of Vila Real); tel: (059) 97 97 20, fax: (059) 729 95.* Unassuming stone farmhouse conceals a charming interior, where guests in the two rooms have access to a 'typical' rural kitchen, with fireplace and lace tablecloths. Walking distance to swimming, fishing and restaurants, ideal for families.

Above
São Gonçalo, Amarante

◐ Pousada de Barão de Forrester €–€€
Alijó; tel: (059) 95 92 15, fax: (059) 95 93 04.
Named after the Baron James Forrester, champion of quality Port, this attractive lodging is more rustic than its stately *pousada* cousins.

Casa da Lage €–€€ S. Miguel de Paredes (10km south of Penafiel); tel: (055) 61 22 19. The outside of this 16th-century stone house may not be ornate, but rooms are big and gracious, with antique furniture, artwork, and simple details.

Suggested tour

Total distance: 152km; 219km with detours.

Time: 5 hours driving. Allow 2 days for the main route, 3 days with detours. Those with limited time should concentrate on Amarante and the Douro Valley.

Links: Vila Real and Pêso da Régua both lie on the N2, which leads to Lamego and the South of the Douro route (*see page 125*). Amarante is connected to Porto (*see page 136*) via the IP4 and to Guimarães by the N101, for the North of Porto route (*see page 155*).

Route: Leave **AMARANTE** ❶ on the N101 for the **DOURO VALLEY** ❷, following signs to **Mesão Frio**. Take the N108 and continue along the north bank of the Douro to **Pêso da Régua**, crossing to follow the south bank on the N222, and then recrossing to **Pinhão** to take the N323 north to **Sabrosa** in 15 km.

Detour: From Pinhão, the N322-3 climbs steeply through beautiful terraced hillsides of the Douro Valley to the mountain town of **Alijó**. The N322 returns, by an equally circuitous road, to rejoin the main route in **Sabrosa**.

Hotel Horus € *Av. Dr Leonardo Coimbra, Felgueiras; tel: (055) 31 24 00.* Modern hotel with many extras – gym, sauna, hairdresser, air-conditioning, lobby shops – that more rustic lodgings lack.

Leave **Sabrosa** on the N322 through **Mateus** to **VILA REAL ❸**, following the N2 north to **VILA POUCA DE AGUIAR ❹**. Take the N206 west through **Ribeira de Pena**, turning left (south) on the N312 through Cerva, dropping into the Tâmega valley at **MONDIM DE BASTO ❺**. Climb back out on the N304, following this scenic corniche road through the **PARQUE NATURAL DE SERRA DA ALVAO ❻**, detouring briefly to the **Fiscas de Ermilo** waterfall. Turn right (west) on the N15, following signs to the IP4 and Amarante.

Detour: Leave Amarante on the N15, which climbs northwards through several undistinguished towns before dropping south again, past the fine Romanesque monastery of **Travanca**, a short distance from the road, to **Penafiel**. Your goal here is the beautiful **Quinta da Aveleda***, built in 1671 and still owned by the same family. Known especially for its vinho verde, this wine estate is set in the most romantic of gardens, replete with fairy-tale follies. Tiny thatched cottages sit on islands reached by twig bridges, mossy stone fountains spurt graceful streams, and geraniums spring from gnarled tree trunks. Reached by grand avenues of towering trees, the gardens decend to more formal beds overlooking the vineyards. Visit the cellars and taste the wines while there. Return to Amarante on the IP4.

Also worth exploring

The N101, north of Amarante, leads to **Felgueiras** where, at a roundabout with an unusual fountain, brown monument signs point west (left) to several sites. At a second roundabout further along the N101, more signs point west. These signs sometimes lead you straight to your quarry, others leave you puzzled, even lost. But by perservering, you will find, within a fairly small area, the **Ponte de São Adrião** (a splendid Roman bridge and section of road), **Capela a Tocha**, and **Mosteiro Pombeiro**, a vast monastery founded in 1059, with good stonecarving and ruined cloisters under preservation. Several other sites are nearby but signage is inconsistent, creating a serendipitous treasure hunt. Look for signs reading *Calçada Romana, Ponte Romana, Cruzeiro* and *Mosteiro*.

Porto

Ratings

Art	●●●●○
Scenery	●●●●○
Architecture	●●●○○
Food and drink	●●●○○
Historical sights	●●●○○
Museums	●●●○○
Walking	●●●○○
Children	●○○○○

The Romans called the settlement near the mouth of the Douro river 'Port o Cale', giving the country its name. Porto clings to the steep north wall of the gorge where the Douro narrows, with Nova de Gaia, the home of Port wineries, facing from the opposite shore. The city rises from the river in switchbacks, some connecting by stone stairways where even the steps must carve a zigzag route. From a boat on the river or from the Gaia shore, the city appears as a solid wall of buildings, belvederes and streets set one on top of the other in layers running up the hillsides. But even in its most crowded warrens, nearly every window and largo has a view of the river, increasing the sense of intimacy between the city, the river and the nearby Atlantic Ocean.

Getting there and getting around

ⓘ **Turismo de Porto**
Praça General Humberto Delgado; tel: (02) 31 27 40, and at Praça Dom João I, south side of the square; tel: (02) 31 75 14, open Mon–Fri 0900–1900, Sat 0900–1600, Sun 1000–1300.

Walking
Everything is up- or downhill. The Ponte de Dom Luís I is a bridge with two levels, one connecting the tops of Porto and Gaia, the other their riverbanks. Walking, the only way to navigate the city, can be difficult because of the steep streets. Fortunately the area of interest to most visitors is relatively compact.

Public transport
Buses and trams are difficult to use because there are no system maps. Take buses to outlying parts of the city from Praça da Liberdade.

Parking
Chose a hotel with parking facilities and leave the car there. Streets are narrow in the old part of town and there is virtually no parking.

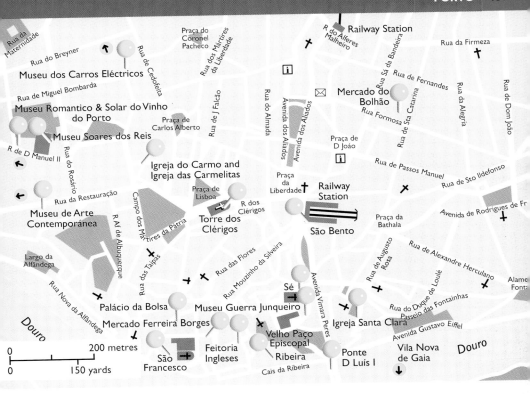

available. If you must bring a car into the city centre, you may find spaces on the west side of Avenida Dom Afonso Henriques just north of the Sé; also try near the Torre dos Clérigos on R. das Carmelitas and on R. Nova da Alfándega along the river west of the Ribeira.

By boat
Graceful *rabelos* once filled the river Douro, their long prows and sterns engaged in the mundane business of bringing wine to the Port lodges. Today only a few are left, and you can cruise the river from the deck of one. **Via D'Ouro Emprendimentos Turísticos** (€€-€€€ *Praceta D. Nuno Alvares Pereira 20; tel: (02) 938 88 16, fax: 938 85 39*) runs several cruises, from a full-day between Porto and Pêso da Régua, to a scenic cruise between the bridges (busiest between 1630 and 1830). Another company, **Douro Azul** (€€€ *Barca de Alva to Porto; tel: (02) 208 32 94, fax: (02) 208 34 07*), offers one-way boat excursions (€€€) the length of the Douro, from the Atlantic Ocean to the Spanish border, and several others. You can return to Porto on one of Iberia's most scenic train rides. Day and weekend trips on the river are offered by **Vistadouro** (€€€ *tel: (02) 938 79 49, fax: (02) 938 79 50*. The quay is at the Ribeira west of Ponte de Dom Luís I.

Sights

Estação São Bento
Praça de Almeida Garrett, near Praça da Liberdade.

Igreja do Carmo and Igreja das Carmelitas *R. do Carmo, at Praça Gomes Texeira.*

Igreja e Torre dos Clérigos € *R. dos Clérigos, from Praça da Liberdade. Tower open Thu–Tue 1030–1200, 1430–1700.*

Igreja Santa Clara *off R. Saraiva de Carvalho east of Av. Vimara Peres. Open 0930–1130, 1500–1800.*

Igreja São Francisco € *Praça Infante Dom Henrique, open Mon–Sat 0930–1230, 1400–1600.*

Estação São Bento✛
The fine old railway station, built in 1896, was embellished in 1930 by the addition of *azulejos* in the waiting room. Among the best of the 20th-century revival of *azulejos*, tile panels depict historical events and scenes of rural Portugal.

Feitoria Ingleses✛
This unpretentious house (*R. São João and R. Infante Dom Henrique*) was the hub of English merchants who operated the great 18th- and 19th-century wine houses, and the heart of the sizeable British colony. Designed by John Whithead, a British consul who did much to establish standards of quality in the port industry, it is still the home of the British Association; the interior is open only by invitation.

Igreja do Carmo and Igreja das Carmelitas✛✛
Built in 1756, the Carmo church has a huge blue and white *azulejo* panel on its outside wall depicting a solemn ecclesiastical procession and the founding of the Carmelite order of Mount Carmel. The adjoining Igreja das Carmelitas was built in 1619 and remodelled in 1756. Both churches are fine examples of the use of decorative tiles.

Igreja e Torre dos Clérigos✛✛
An elegant 75-metre clock tower that dominates the city's hilltop skyline, Torre dos Clérigos has 240 steps leading the energetic to the top and to spectacular panoramic views. The chancel of the church is punctuated with an oval dome and gilt-embellished side altars.

Igreja Santa Clara✛✛
The plain exterior of the little church of Santa Clara, built in 1416, gives little clue to the riches inside, a gold extravaganza of angels, cherubs, scrolls and leaves executed in 1730. The choir, with its painted ceiling and carved stalls, is not to be missed. Behind Santa Clara, further along R. Saraiva de Carvalho and turning right, is one of the best-preserved sections of the old town wall.

Igreja São Francisco✛✛✛
On the high altar, berobed Franciscan monks pose amongst the gilt rococo columns. Begun as a Gothic church in the 13th and 14th centuries, São Francisco's elaborate interior is 18th century. It took over 100kg of gold to encrust the heavily carved walls and ceiling as well as the baroque and rococo side altars, lit from one end by a plain glass rose window. In the midst of the mass of gold is an outstanding

**Igreja da
Misericórdia** € R.
*das Flores 15; tel: (02) 200
20 10, guided tours, open
Mon–Fri 0900–1200,
1430–1730.*

Jesse Tree of free-standing polychrome figures. A tour of the church also includes catacombs, an ossuary and a museum.

Igreja da Misericórdia*

The treasure of this 16th-century church is the Renaissance painting *Fons Vitae* depicting King Manuel I with his wife, eight children and courtiers gathering the blood of Christ at the foot of the cross. The sister of the king, Dona Leonor, was the founder of the charitable Casa da Misericórdia.

Mercado do Bolhão
*R. da Sá de Bandeira
and R. Formosa, open
Mon–Fri 0700–1700, Sat
0700–1300.*

**Museu de Arte
Contemporánea €**
*R. de Serralves; tel: (02) 618
00 57. Open Mon–Fri
1400–1800, Sat–Sun
1000–2000. 7km from
downtown, access by tram.*

**Museu Guerra
Junqueiro €** *R. Dom Hugo
32 , behind the Cathedral;
tel: (02) 31 36 44. Check at
the tourist office for opening
times.*

Museu Soares dos Reis
*€ R. Dom Manuel II. Open
Tue–Sun 1000–1230,
1400–1730.*

Museu Romântico € *R.
de Entrequintas 220; tel:
(02) 609 11 31, guided
tours Tue–Sat 1000–1200,
1400–1700, Sun
1400–1730, closed holidays.*

Mercado do Bolhão✶✶
The city's colourful, vibrant produce market, sells vegetables, fish, meat, cheese, bread and flowers, in a bright courtyard with an upper storey. Stock up for a picnic and sample the flavour of everyday life.

Mercado Ferreira Borges✶
The façade of this classic 19th-century public building is red-painted cast iron on a granite base foundation. Built in 1888 on the Praça Infante Dom Henrique, it is a rare example of iron architecture in Porto.

Museu de Arte Contemporánea✶✶
Also called the Fundação de Serralves, the museum features prominent examples of contemporary Portuguese art and architecture. All exhibits are temporary so there is always something new. Check to be sure it is not closed during a two-week re-hanging period. The museum occupies the Casa de Serralves, built in the 1930s in the art deco style with decoration by René Lalique, and outstanding gardens in an 18-hectare park.

Museu dos Carros Eléctricos✶
Dedicated to the preservation of the now-romantic conveyance, the tram museum (€ *Alameda Basílio Teles; open Tue–Sat 0900–1200, 1400–1700*) is housed in a huge old switching house. The No.18, Porto's only remaining tram, will take you there.

Museu Guerra Junqueiro✶✶
The mansion of Portuguese poet Guerra Junqueiro contains tapestries, statuary, gold and silver plate, furniture and pottery, most from the 15th and 16th centuries. The museum also has beautiful gardens.

Museu Soares dos Reis✶✶
Built by a wealthy Jewish family in 1795, the palace was headqurters to French General Soult, who abandoned it in 1809 when attacked halfway through dinner by Sir Arthur Wellesley (later Duke of Wellington). It was bought by Dom Pedro V in 1861 and houses a fine collection of 19th-century Portuguese works by António Soares dos Reis, Teixeira Lopes, Henrique Pousão, Marquês de Oliveira and Silva Porto.

Museu Romântico✶✶
When King Carlo Alberto of Sardinia lost his bid for the kingdom of Italy in 1849, after the battle of Novara, he retired here to the Quinta da Macieirinha, overlooking the city. The museum is furnished in the period with paintings (including early views of the city), portraits and English, French and Portuguese furniture. Look for the portrait of Baron Forrester, who brought order to the chaotic port wine industry of the 19th century (see also Solar do Vinho do Porto).

Palácio da Bolsa–Arab Room
€ *Praça do Infante Dom Henrique. Open Mon–Fri 0900–1300, 1400–1800, Sat–Sun 1000–1300, 1400–1900.*

Palácio da Bolsa✦✦✦

A 19th-century pinnacle of *azulejos* in renewal styles, the Great Hall of the *Bolsa* (stock exchange) is a glass-domed patio of pink stucco with neo-Moorish columns and arches. The **Arab Room**✦ celebrates the Moorish heritage of the Alhambra in a huge galleried salon executed in exquisite polychrome *azulejos* and gilt stucco work. It looks more like a Turkish harem than a centre of commerce.

Ponte de Dom Luís I✦

Two levels of bridge, 30 vertical metres apart, simultaneously connect the tops and the waterfronts of Porto and Vila Nova de Gaia. Steep curving streets and stairs lead from one level to the other. The bridge was designed in 1886 by Theophile Seyring, an assistant of Gustave Eiffel. Eiffel himself designed the Ponte Dona Maria Pia, a bit further east, in 1877.

Ribeira✦✦✦

The Ribeira is to Porto what the Alfama is to Lisbon, the oldest part of the city, clinging tenaciously to the steep hillsides. The Ribeira lies along the Douro just west of the Ponte de Dom Luís I and rises steeply up through a warren of streets and steps to the R. Infante Dom Henrique just below the Sé. Wander through this colourful neighbourhood to glimpse everyday life as it is played out in the streets. While you can reach the alleys and lanes of the Ribeira from the quay along the river, it is less tiring to explore it from the top down.

Below
Oporto's riverside Ribeira district

Sé (cloisters €)
*Largo da Sé. Open daily
0900–1200, 1430–1730.*

**Solar do Vinho do
Porto** *R. de Entrequintas
220, beneath the Museu
Romântico; tel: (02) 69 77
93, Mon–Sat 1100–2400.*

Turismo de Gaia *next to
the Sandeman lodge; tel:
(02) 30 19 02. Open
Mon–Fri 0900–1230 and
1400–1730, Sat
1400–1800.*

East of the large park
between Praça da
Liberdade and Praça
General Humberto
Delgado, R. Santa Catarina
is the most fashionable
street of the pedestrian
zone. Smart shops and
cafés abound. Like a
museum where you can
shop? Look for handicrafts
at the **Centre for
Traditional Arts and
Crafts** (*R. de Reboleira
37*), in the Ribeira. Try
also Galerias Paladium, the
city's major department
store. A morning street
market at Rua dos
Clérigos sells food.

Students let off steam
and enliven the city at
the **Queimas das Fitas**
which marks the end of
the university's academic
year, in May. Also in May is
the **Festival de
Marionetas** with puppet
theatre performances.
September sees the
Grande Noite de Fado,
a great festival of *fado*.

Above
Wine boats on the
River Douro

Sé✲✲
The Cathedral dates from the 12th and 13th centuries, with much subsequent embellishment and restoration. Its Romanesque façade has short square twin towers topped with cupolas. The chapel to the left of the fine baroque chancel has a silver altar crafted by nine silversmiths between 1632 and 1683. In 1809 it was quickly painted white to save it from theft by Napoleon's troops. On the far side of the cloister, the Capela de São Vicente has an ornate gold altar and polychrome bas-reliefs. On the upper level, above the cloisters, the chapter house has a painted ceiling and houses works of art.

Solar do Vinho do Porto✲✲
For connoisseurs of port wine this welcoming institute is a required stop, with literally hundreds of types to try. The institute is housed on the lower level of the Museu Romântico.

Vila Nova de Gaia✲✲✲
On the opposite banks of the Douro, the much smaller city of Vila Nova de Gaia was until 1987 the only place where port wine could be aged. Almost all the major port houses have their lodges on this hillside. Of the 58 port companies here, 20 offer tours, including Taylor, Ferreira, Rozes, Sandeman, Osborne, Cálem, Real Vinicola and Ramos Pinto. Tours are during normal business hours Mon–Sat. Taylor has an excellent restaurant overlooking the city from its garden and terrace. Sandeman, Real Vinicola and Osborne offer Sunday tours.

Reach Gaia from the lower level of the Ponte Dom Luís I and follow Av. Diogo Leite. Along the river is a pleasant park with some of the few remaining historic *rabelos* anchored in the river. Until the 1950s these high-prowed boats each brought 60 barrels of newly fermented wine down river for aging and finishing.

The large, stern building above the Ponte Dom Luís I is the **Mosteiro da Serra do Pilar***, built in the 16th century with an unusual round church and cloister. The church is open during Sun services but the cloister is part of an army installation and is closed. Its belvedere has good views of the city.

Accommodation and food

Hotel Infante de Sagres €€-€€€ *Praça Dona Filipa de Lencastre 62; tel: (02) 200 81 01, fax: 231 49 37*, has an old-fashioned elegance that fits the city, as well as a very good dining room, the **Dona Filipa** (€€-€€€).

Hotel Le Meridien Park Atlantic €€€ *Av. da Boavista 1466; tel: (02) 607 25 00, fax: 600 20 31.* A new grand hotel, modern and stylish in glass and marble, with luxury-level rooms and top service. **Les Terrasses** (€€€) with continental take on Portuguese cuisine is one of the city's best.

Hotel São João €-€€ *R. do Bomjardim 120; tel: (02) 200 16 62, fax: 31 61 14.* On the top floor (3rd) of a newish office building, with quite elegant rooms and public areas.

Solar São Gabriel € *R. da Alegria 98 (a block east of R. Santa Catarina); tel: (02) 200 54 99, fax: 332 39 57.* Rooms have air-conditioning, in-room phone and TV, in a fashionable in-town neighbourhood. Parking is available.

Aquario Marisqueiro €-€€ *R. Rodrigues Sampaio 179; tel: (02) 200 22 31* serves excellent seafood and other Portuguese specialities from lunch until late evening. Closed Mon.

Café Imperial €€ *Praça da Liberdade 125; tel: (02) 200 72 32.* The stained glass of this art deco café celebrates coffee, its production, transport and use.

Café Majestic €€ *R. de Santa Catarina 2a; tel: (02) 200 38 87.* Another grand old coffee house in art nouveau style on the main shopping street of the city.

Mercearia €€ *R. Cais da Ribeira 32; tel: (02) 200 43 89.* Attractive views of the port while you dine on local dishes that are well prepared and well served. Reservations are needed at busy times.

Portucale €€-€€€ *R. da Alegria 598; tel: (02) 57 07 17.* Very popular spot on the top floor of the Albergaria Miradouro with good views of the

city. There are linen tablecloths and fine china on the tables and tapestries on the walls.

Near the University and the Torre dos Clérigos are small, inexpensive **lunch restaurants**; most close in the evening. Look also on the Campo Alegre and streets around the Praça da Ribeira near the river.

Suggested tour

Begin at the blue-tiled **IGREJA DO CARMO ❶**, on Praça Gomes Texeira, walking past the large building of the old academy into the tree-lined boulevards of **Jardim de João Chagas**, a favourite haunt for lovers and black-caped students. Turn left to the impressive **Igreja e Torre dos Clerigos**, one of the tallest buildings in Portugal, then right on to a street beside it and bear left on Rua dos Caldeireiros. Follow the street as it curves downhill to Rua das Flores where you turn right. Rua das Flores bends to the left at the **Igreja da Misericordia** and leads to the **Mercado Ferreira Borges** and the garden below it. Facing the garden is **Palacio da Bolsa**, behind which is the **Igreja Saõ Francisco**.

Below the church of São Francisco, cross over Rua Infante Dom Henrique, turning left at the **Lavanderia São Nicolau** on to the charming and narrow Rua de Reboleira, past the **CENTRE FOR TRADITIONAL ARTS AND CRAFTS** ❷. Beyond, at a little *largo* with a pleasant café, begins the **CAIS DA RIBEIRA** ❸, the lively waterfront of busy market stalls and the boarding point for river cruises.

Leave the waterfront on Rua de São João and follow it to the long, straight Rua Mouzinho D Silveira, an interesting street of small shops and old buildings, to Praça de Almeida Garrett, bordered on the left by the **ESTAÇÃO SÃO BENTO** ❹, Porto's railway station.

Detour: Bear right at the upper end of Praça de Almeida Garrett on to Rua Sá da Bandeira, passing Praça Dom João, to the **Mercado do Bolhão**. Return to **PRAÇA DOM JOÃO** ❺, turning right to the grand **Praça da Liberdade**, where you rejoin the main route.

Bear left at the upper end of the square from Estacão São Bento, into Praça da Liberdade, continuing past the art deco **Café Imperial** to the street that crosses through the centre of the long plaza. Turn left, crossing the park for a good view of its **formal gardens**, and continuing straight up into a small square, past the Hotel Infante de Sagres, and eventually to **PRAÇA CARLOS ALBERTO** ❻, just behind your starting point of Igreja do Carmo.

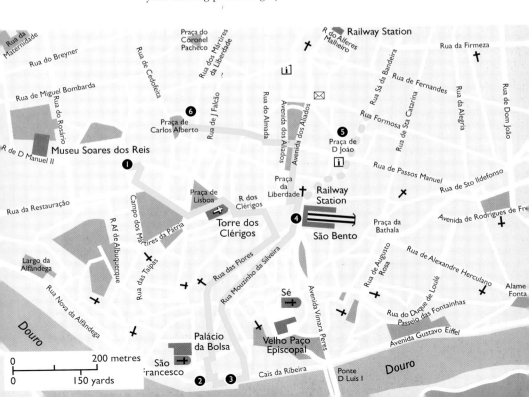

North of Porto

Ratings

Art and crafts	●●●● ○
Markets	●●●● ○
Architecture	●●● ○ ○
Historical sights	●●● ○ ○
Museums	●●● ○ ○
Castles	●● ○ ○ ○
Walking	●● ○ ○ ○
Beaches	● ○ ○ ○ ○

This route, although shorter than some, is one of great variety. Travellers can leave their cars to walk through the lonely Celtic settlement of Sanfins, and to explore the medieval streets and squares of Guimarães, one of Portugal's most appealing small cities. Two *pousadas* occupy historic buildings in Guimarães, one between two picturesque squares, the other in a spacious former monastery on a hillside high above. The battle of São Mamede, which took place in 1128 just north of the *castelo*, marked the beginning of Portugal as a nation. Here Dom Afonso Henriques was victorious over the Castilian forces, establishing Portugal's independence and his own sovereignty. The Portuguese revere Guimarães as the cradle of their country, and its castle, also thought to be their first king's birthplace, as the symbol of its birth.

BARCELOS✣

ⓘ Tourist Information, *Largo da Porta Nova (Torre de Menagem); tel: (053) 81 18 82. Open Mon–Fri 0900–1230, 1430–1800, Sat–Sun 0900–1600.*

An agricultural centre, Barcelos is best known for its weekly farmers' market where row upon row of stalls display fresh breads, honey, flowers, fruit, vegetables, pastries, cheese, olives, chickens, rabbits, and dried beans. Also in the giant shaded plaza are pottery and household wares. It is worth juggling your itinerary to be here on market day (Thur), but don't expect to find a room without advance reservations.

Adjacent to the market square is a stunning public garden, formal beds filled in riotous colours, with stone benches to enjoy it from. Above stands the unusual octagonal Igreja do Bom Jesus da Cruz, like a domed hatbox. Opposite, on the north side of the Campo da Feira (formally the Campo da República), is the Igreja de Nóssa Senhora do Terco, its walls covered in *azulejos* from the height of their artistic period in the 18th century. The painted ceiling and gilded carved pulpit are equally outstanding.

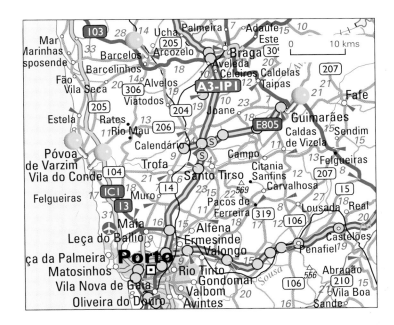

Feira de Barcelos *every Thursday. Even droves of tourists can't overwhelm a market this big; you can find examples of rural folkarts (one corner is devoted to pottery) and functional objects; the earlier you arrive, the fewer other tourists will be there with you. No weekly market in Portugal beats this one for size, colour or local atmosphere.*

Centro de Artesanato *in the tourist office (same hours) sells local handicrafts, for those who can't get to the market.*

Downhill from the garden is the tower of 15th-century defensive walls, with the tourist office and craft centre, and beyond, near the river, is the **Museu de Olaria**⁺ (€ *R. Cónego Joaquim Gaiolas, open Tue–Sun 1000–1230, 1400–1800*). This pottery museum not only explores the breadth and history of local work, but contrasts it with Portugal's other regional styles. Barcelos was the home of Rosa Romalho, whose creative ochre-coloured figures began the local art pottery movement. Labels are in Portuguese, but exhibits are self-explanatory.

The ruined Paço dos Condes (Counts' Palace) provides an open-air setting for the **Museu Arqueológico**⁺ (*open daily 0900–1730, 1830 in the summer*), a wondrous miscellany of local findings – prehistoric, Roman, medieval, and 18th century. One exhibit is the 14th-century Cruzeiro do Senhor do Galo, a crucifix reputedly commissioned by the pilgrim saved by the rooster of local ubiquity. The palace overlooks the River Cávado and a 15th-century bridge.

Accommodation and food in Barcelos

Pensão Arantes € *Av. da Liberdade 35; tel: (053) 81 13 26*. In a lovely old home, first-floor rooms open on to a marble parlour overlooking the market square and octagonal church; front-facing rooms have wrought-iron balconies. The restaurant (€) specialises in grilled chicken, and lamprey when in season.

Casa do Monte € *Lugar de Barreiro, Abade de Neiva (3km west of Barcelos); tel: (053) 81 15 19.* Pretty country house surrounded by gardens and forests has a comfortable, homey interior.

Quinta da Santa Comba € *Lugar de Crujães, Varzea (5km south of Barcelos); tel: (053) 83 21 01, fax: (053) 83 21 01.* Stone detail and stucco walls on the outside, warm country style inside, this lodging remains part of a farming estate that produces *vinho verde*.

Quinta de São João e do Espírito Santo € *Lugar do Espírito Santo, Vila Boa (1km north of Barcelos); tel: (053) 81 14 92.* Blocky Renaissance estate house of granite sits on a pond, surrounded by box hedge gardens and forest. Basic, pleasant rooms.

Solar Real €€ *Praça Pontevedra 15; tel: (053) 81 34 39.* Lovely dining room with a genteel air, starched linens and a more sophisticated menu than most, based on local ingredients.

Restaurante Tres Marias € *R. Baretta; tel: (053) 81 32 00.* No frills, but the three Marias cook up good food.

Restaurante Bagoeira €–€€ *Av. Dr Sidonio Pais 495; tel: (053) 81 12 36, fax: (053) 82 45 88.* Chequered tablecloths and a hum of activity gives this popular local restaurant a cheery atmosphere; terrace tables overlook the market square. Look for roast suckling pig or kid on the menu. Reserve upstairs *Pensão* rooms well in advance for Wed or Thur.

The Barcelos Cock

The traditional, brightly painted cockerels sold throughout Portugal came to fame when a pilgrim bound for Santiago was accused of theft in Barcelos and sentenced to die. He swore his innocence before a judge, who was eating dinner when the pilgrim came before him. The pilgrim called upon the roast cockerel on the judge's plate to stand up and crow to prove his innocence. Of course, the cockerel did, or there would be no story, and fewer market stalls.

GUIMARAES✦✦✦

ⓘ Officina de Tourismo (city)
Praça de Santiago; tel: (053) 51 87 90, open Mon–Fri 0900–1230, 1400–1730 in winter, Jun–Aug open Mon–Fri 0900–1900, Sat–Sun 1000–1300, 1500–1700.

Zona de Turismo de Guimarães (regional)
Largo Cónego José Maria Gomes; tel: (053) 51 83 94, fax: (053) 51 51 34, www.cm-guimaraes.pt

An almost perfect-sized city for walkers, Guimarães (pronounced GEEM-arahnge) spaces its attractions along charming medieval streets. In fact, you can dine, lodge and sightsee without ever leaving the few blocks of the old city. Square follows graceful square, most with sidewalk cafés and fountains. They are alive with children kicking footballs (with occasional help from passersby) or playing hide-and-seek among the arches.

Even without its history, the **Castelo✦** would be a good castle to visit, with its crenellated towers and battlements to walk. That the castle still exists is fortunate, since in 1836, when historic sites were not valued, it came within one vote of demolition to be used for street pavement. The small Romanesque **Igreja de São Miguel do Castelo✦** just under the castle walls is considered to be Afonso Henrique's baptismal church.

The imposing façade at the top of the square opposite is Santo António dos Capuchos, built in the 1600s of stones from the castle and ducal palace.

Castelo accessible from R. de Dona Teresa; tel: (053) 41 22 73, open Tue–Sun 0930–1730, 1830 in the summer.

Igreja de São Miguel do Castelo on castle grounds between castelo and the Ducal Palace; tel: (053) 41 22 73. Open daily 0930–1730, 1830 in the summer.

Paço dos Duques € R. Conde Dom Henrique; tel: (053) 41 22 73 Open daily 0930–1700, 1900 in the summer. Guided tours half-hourly. Free admission Sun mornings and for students.

Above
Largo da Oliveira, Guimarães

The already ruined **Paço dos Duques de Bragança**[*] was almost completely destroyed by such use of its stones and the building of a military barracks in its midst, when its reconstruction began in the 1930s. A storm of controversy greeted the results, but although today's palace probably bears very little resemblance to the original, it make a good setting for the antiques and tapestries on show inside.

Below the palace, past the Igreja do Carmo (which has a splendid baroque door and good woodcarving), Rua Santa Maria enters the warren of narrow streets, passing the former Convento de Santa Clara, now the town hall. With elegant balconies, ornamental stone work, and spanned by the Casa do Arco, this street was the most exclusive address in medieval Guimarães.

Rua Santa Maria leads past Praça de Santiago, its layers of balconies hung with flowers and laundry, and into one of Europe's best medieval city squares, Largo da Oliveira. Along the upper end of the square is the arcade of the old town hall and the Pousada da Oliveira. At the lower end is a 16th-century Gothic market cross. Balconies form vertical flower gardens facing the 13th-century castellated tower and fine Gothic façade of the Igreja da Senhora da Oliveira. Centuries of renovations have left little of its Romanesque beginnings, but the silver altar in the Capela do Santissimo Sacramento is beautiful.

Lace-making is the specialty of **Trofa**, 7km east of Guimarães. Local linen is hand spun from sun-bleached flax and woven in intricate patterns or plain weave as a base for embroidery. In Guimarães, **Casa dos Linhas** (*Av. da Resistencia*) is an old an well respected store. **Enxovais**, at the end of the Almeida, is another worthwhile shop.

Buy picnic supplies at the municipal market, *R. Paio Galvão at R. Gil Vicente.*

Casa de Sezim
Santo Amaro (4km southwest of Guimarães); tel: (053) 52 30 00, fax: (053) 52 31 96, has a riding school and horse trails, and a covered arena for winter.

Right
Santa Marinha da Costa, Guimarães

Museu Alberto Sampaio € R. Alfredo Guimarães facing Largo da República do Brasil; tel: (053) 41 24 65. Free admission Sun am and for students.

Igrega de São Francisco facing the Alameda; tel: (053) 51 25 07. Open Tue–Sat 0900–1200, 1500–1700.

Museu Martins Sarmento € R. de Paio Galvão; tel: (053) 41 59 69. Open Tue–Sat 0930–1200, 1400–1700, Sun 1000–1200, 1400–1700. Free for students.

Restaurante Típico Vale de Donas € R. Vale de Donas at Largo João Franco; tel: (053) 51 14 11, open 1900–0200, except Mon. A moderately elegant interior, also warm-weather tables in a stone courtyard; grilled sardines are heavenly, as is the lamprey in the spring. To get there, look on the city map for Casa dos Carvalhos.

Restaurante Solar do Arco €€ R. de Santa Maria; tel: (053) 51 30 72, open 1200–2400. Directly behind the pousada, linen napery sets off grey stone walls. A sophisticated approach to traditional dishes; the daily tourist menu brings midday prices down (€).

The church's L-shaped medieval cloister is now part of the **Museu Alberto Sampaio**✷, entered round the corner. This excellent museum shows gold treasuries and art works from several churches, including a splendid Spanish tryptic, booty from the battle of Aljubarrota. In fact the church was built in gratitude for the victory at Aljubarrota in 1385. The medieval sculpture is outstanding and a not-so-meditative noughts and crosses is carved into the stone rail of the cloister.

The street leaves the old city and reaches the broad leafy Almeida, passing one of the several small chapels representing the Stations of the Cross, which are tucked away in corners all over Guimarães. Below a sloping formal garden, is the remarkable façade of the Igreja dos Santos Passos. This is the best view of it; the inside is not nearly as interesting.

On the lower side of the Almeida is the **Igrega de São Francisco**✷, its entrance and chancel walls lined in azulejos. Spiral columns flank its ornate gold altar and the side altars have good polychromes. A façade beside the church is also covered in azulejos.

At its far end, the Almeida becomes the Largo do Toural, and beyond is the **Museu Martins Sarmento**✷, one of Portugal's two major archaeology museums, containing most of the carved stonework found at the nearby Celtic hillforts of Briteiros and Sabrosa, together with other prehistoric artifacts. Collections spill into the cloister of the adjacent Convento de São Domingos, where you will find the Pedra Formosa, one of the most interesting – and puzzling – pieces of early stone carving.

High on the side of Penha, a mountain overlooking the city, is the former Convento da Costa, once a very wealthy monastery, now a pousada. Visitors are welcome to stroll its gardens, whose formal boxwood hedges filled with massed flowers are behind the convento, reached via an azulejo-lined granite staircase. At the far end of the upper floor, a beautiful stone porch with a fountain overlooks the gardens and mountain.

The adjoining church, Santa Marinha da Costa, is interesting mainly for its figural organ loft and its sacristy, to the right of the altar. The best time to go is late afternoon, when the carved fountains and balustrades of the terrace are silhouetted against an orange sunset.

Further up, Monte da Penha has a sanctuary and trails to chapels, grottoes, springs and several interesting rock formations. A popular spot for weekend excursions, its cafés and restaurant may be very crowded in good weather. On the second Sunday of September each year thousand of pilgrims take part in a Romaria to the sanctuary from the Igreja dos Santos Passos in the town.

The Gualterianas, a festival which dates back to 1452, takes place on the first weekend of August, to celebrate Guimarães' annual free market with a colourful parade, agricultural shows and fireworks. In Santo Tirso, 20km southwest of Guimarães, the Feiras Artesanato (craft fair) is on the second weekend in August.

Grelhados do Mar €€
Largo Condessa do Juncal 27; tel: (053) 51 84 27. Try the excellent fish soup or seafood salad for starters, then proceed to *espadarte* of shrimp (brochette) or the daily catch, which you can watch grill behind a glass window.

🌙 **Parque de Campismo da Penha €** *Monte de Penha; tel: (053) 51 74 51, fax: (053) 51 65 69. Open May–Oct,* this campsite has a small pool.

Pensão das Trinas € *R. das Trinas 29; tel: (053) 51 73 58, fax: (053) 51 73 62.* Pleasant, unassuming little *residencial* on a quiet back street, within walking distance of everything.

Accommodation and food in Guimarães

Pousada da Nossa Senhora da Oliveira €€ *R. de Santa Maria; tel: (053) 51 41 57, fax: (053) 51 42 04.* Spacious rooms decorated with antiques, in the best location in town, if early morning church bells don't bother you. The dining room looks directly on to Largo de Oliveira.

Pousada de Santa Marinha €€ *Penha National Park (1km northwest of Guimarães); tel: (053) 51 44 53, fax: (053) 51 44 59.* Splendid setting with sweeping sunset views from a restored monastery setting. Rooms are far from cell-like, richly furnished in antiques. The bar overlooks the cloister.

Casa de Sezim €€ *R. de Sezim, Santo Amaro (4km southwest of Guimarães); tel: (053) 52 30 00, fax: (053) 52 31 96, e–mail: sezimmail@telepac.pt* Pink and white 18th-century façade encloses a 14th–17th-century manor house, decorated with rare French panoramic wallpapers. The vineyards (known for white wines) and the overgrown gardens overlooked by an atmospheric veranda, are a romantic's dream.

Hotel Toural €€ *Largo A. L. Carvalho; tel: (053) 51 71 84, fax: 51 71 49.* Rather modern hotel inside an older building, with more amenities than usual.

VILA DO CONDE AND PÓVOA DE VARZIM*

ℹ️ **Tourist Information Vila do Conde** *R. 25 de Abril 103; tel: (052) 64 27 00, fax: (052) 64 18 76, open Jun–Sep daily 0900–1230, 1400–1730, rest of the year open weekdays only.*

Tourist Information, Póvoa de Varzim *Av. Mouzinho de Albuquerque 166; tel: (052) 61 46 09, fax: (052) 61 78 72.*

🛒 **Market day** *R. 25 de Abril, Vila do Conde (near TIC) every Friday.* Sells both crafts and agricultural products, good place to look for local lace and other handiwork from the makers' hands.

Not bristling with sights, but interesting nonetheless, these towns sit on the coast, a scant 3km apart. Póvoa is a highly developed seaside resort with all the accompanying razzmatazz; Vila do Conde is a working town, and has been since the days when Prince Henry the Navigator had his ships built there. While the men built ships, women made lace, a needle art still very much alive. Not surprisingly, most of the places to see are in Vila do Conde.

The **Mosteiro de Santa Clara*** (*open daily 0900–1200, 1400–1530*) is the focal point of Vila do Conde, its huge walls rising above the town. The church has a 16th-century founder's chapel with good stone vaulting, sculpted stone tombs, and a lovely rose window. Its unfinished cloister features a carved fountain fed by an aqueduct.

The front portal of the Igreja Matriz, usually described as Manueline (and in that period), shows more Spanish Plateresque, and was in fact created by a Spanish artist. Built at the turn of the 16th century, the rest of the church is more Manueline and has polychrome relief carvings and a fine gilded wood pulpit. The church's **Museu da Arte Sacra*** (*€ R. da Igreja, open 1000–1200, 1400–1600*) shows ecclesiastic pieces from this and other churches. The *pelourinho* in front, brandishing a sword, represents justice, oddly.

Centro de Artesanato, R. 5 de Outubro, Vila do Conde, open Fri–Tue 1000–1300, 1500–1900, except closed Sun am. Local lace, not cheap, but genuine.

Corpus Christi June, about every four years, Vila do Conde. Streets are decorated with carpets of flower petals in beautiful designs. The four-year cycle may be changed for special events; last held in 1997.

Feira de Artesanato Vila do Conde, last week of Jul–first week in Aug features regional crafts.

Feira Grande de Augosto, Romaria de Senhora das Neves first Fri and Sun Aug. A fair and a procession, called the 'Sweethearts Fair' because wedding rings are bought there.

The 16th-century Misericórdia, on Av. Bento de Freitas, has *azulejo* panels and, unlike many churches, few side altars to interrupt them.

Still quite active, the **Escola de Rendas*** (School of Lacemaking R. de São Bento, visits arranged through the tourist office) is a rarity, founded in 1918 to pass on the local lacemaking tradition to young girls. The local lace is called *bilros* (bone lace), and is made with 30–50 bobbins of gossamer-fine thread worked on a round cushion with lightning speed. There is a small display of show-stopping pieces, as well as demonstrations; the Centro de Artesanato (*see sidebar*) also has occasional demonstrations.

Ever year, to celebrate the Festa de São João on June 23, there is a candlelit procession of lacemakers from the village to the beach. The nicely arranged **Museu de Póvoa de Varzim*** (€ *open Tue–Sun 1000–1230, 1430–1800*), covers local folk life, focusing primarily on the sea and fishing, although the towns's tiny fishing port, to the south, is largely crowded out by its holiday beach development. Póvoa's has more facilities, but the beach south of Vila do Conde is nicer, quieter and less crowded.

Accommodation and food in Vila do Conde and Póvoa de Varzim

Costa Verde € *Av. Vasco da Gama 56, Póvoa de Varzim; tel: (052) 61 55 31, fax: (052) 61 59 31.* Nice clean lodgings, right in town.

Quinta São Miguel de Arcos € *R. de Igreja 209, Arcos (10km east of Vila do Conde and Póvoa de Varzim); tel: (052) 65 20 94, fax: (052) 65 20 94.* Lovely farm setting for this country estate house, featuring stone-walled bedrooms.

Le Villageois €€ *Praça da República 94, Vila do Conde; tel: (052) 63 11 19. Closed Mondays.* Terrace for outdoor eating; serves dinner, and in high-season lunch, of nicely prepared local specialities. They also have modest lodgings (€).

Estrela do Mar € *R. Caetano de Oliveira 144, Póvoa do Varzim; tel: (052) 68 49 75.* Locals-mostly restaurant with seafood menu.

Suggested tour

Total distance: 164km; 210km with detours.

Time: 3 hours driving. Allow 3 days, with or without detours. Those with limited time should concentrate on Guimarães.

Opposite
Santa Oliveira, Guimarães

Previous Page
Praca de Santiago, Guimarães

Links: From Guimarães, the N101 leads north to Braga and on to the Gerês Mountains (*see page 170*). Viana do Castelo, gateway to the

Right
The village of São Lourenço

Minho Valley (*see page 165*) is connected to Barcelos by the N103. To the south, Amarante (*see page 126*) is attached to Guimarães via the winding N101.

Route: Leave **PORTO** ❶ on the A3-IP1, heading north; take the exit east on to the A7-IC5 to **GUIMARAES** ❷.

Detour: Leave Porto on the N105 through Emesinde to Agua Longa, turning right on the N207 to Paços de Ferreira, then north on the N209 through Meixomil. In about 5km, turn left following signs to the village of **Sanfins**. Continue, bearing left and uphill, past the small museum, to the top of the hill and **Citânia de Sanfins***. This Celtic hillfort covers the entire hilltop, its streets and round house foundations intact. Most travellers who find their way here prefer it to Briteiros (*see page 179*). Return to the N209, joining the N106 north through the spa town of Vizela to Guimarães.

Leave Guimarães heading west on the N206, paralleling the motorway to **Vila Nova de Famalição**, taking the N204 north to **BARCELOS** ❸. Follow the N103-1 west to the seaside town of **Esposende**, turning south along the shore on the N13 to **POVOA DE VARZIM** ❹ and **VILA DO CONDE** ❺, returning to Porto on the IC1.

Detour: Just north of Vila do Condo, the N205 leads east 7km to **Rio Mau**, stopping at the Romanesque **Igreja São Cristóvão** which has carved granite capitals, rough mid-12th-century ones on the three portals; more complex, later ones inside. Two km further on, a left turning leads to **Rates**, where the **Igreja de São Pedro**, from the same period, has a five-arched front portal decorated with animals and a carved tympanum. Inside are more fine carved capitals and a rose window.

Follow the N306 south to the N104, turning left (east) to Trofa, known for its handspun linen, and returning to Porto on the N14.

Also worth exploring

From Monte da Penha, near Guimarães, you can see to the north twin towers of **Irmandade de São Torcato**, still under construction as a sanctuary for the incorrupt relics of the saint. Visitors can watch artists working at the school of stonemasonry, and the **Museu Etnográfico** has folk art and exhibits on hand linen production. Above, via a narrow stone street, a former monastery of Visigothic origin has some finely carved friezes at the rear. On the way, seek out the tiny waterside mill village of **São Lourenço**, its colourful and picturesque houses beside a **Roman bridge**.

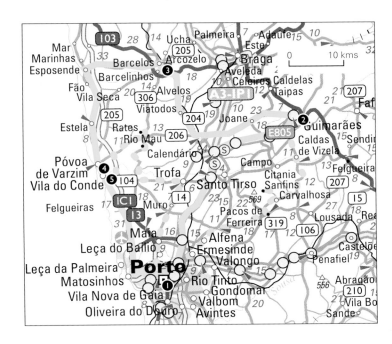

The Minho

Ratings

Beaches	●●●●○
Scenery	●●●●○
Architecture	●●●○○
Villages	●●●○○
Crafts	●●○○○
Children	●●○○○
Historical sights	●●○○○
Museums	●●○○○

Surrounded on two sides by Spain and on one side by ocean, this northernmost part of Portugal offers a fully fortified border town, several graceful small cities, two lovely river valleys, a national park and mountains. Altogether, it is one of Portugal's most charming areas, with few block-buster sights, but a fine selection of experiences, all neatly spaced. Travel around its river and ocean perimeters is mostly free of narrow, steep roads; even the trip back through its centre is not a hair-raising one, so those who shun mountainous roads will find it comfortable. Attractions in the traditional sense – museums, monuments, major churches or palaces – are few, but in few other places will you find such a succession of likeable, picturesque towns.

CAMINHA✦

ⓘ Tourist Information R. Ricardo Joachim de Sousa, Caminha; tel: (058) 92 19 52. Open Mon–Sat 0930–1230, 1430–1800.

Largo do Municipio, Vila Nova de Cerveira; tel: (051) 79 57 87.

Caminha clusters in its original shape, as though thick medieval walls still held it together. The 15th-century Igreja Matriz is fortified, although it is hard to take seriously a building whose gargoyles spit rainwater on to pedestrians. The carved side portal includes skulls and griffins, and inside is an excellent carved Mudéjar ceiling.

Rua Direita leads through the 14th-century arch of Torre do Relogio into a broad medieval plaza surrounding a splendid fountain. The **Misericórdia**, beyond an arcaded façade, has gold baroque altars and painted chancel ceiling. Local archaeological finds are exhibited at the **Museu Municipal**, in the library.

South of Caminha, **Anta Barrosa✦✦** is a well-preserved dolmen near Vila Praia da Ancora (east 0.2km to roundabout; turn left). The dolmen, which is behind a stone wall on the left, supports its huge capstone on seven flat uprights with an eighth at the end. Vila Praia stretches behind the beach from a diminutive fortress guarding bright fishing

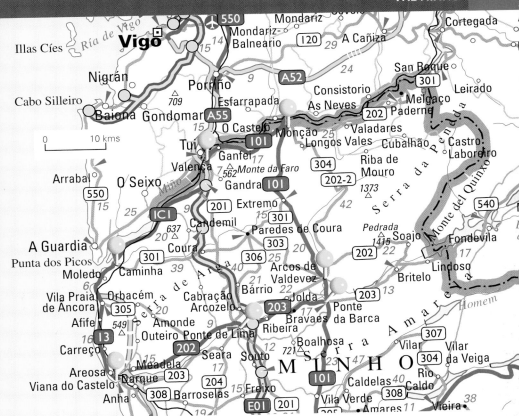

boats to a promenade-lined **swimming beach**◆◆, rarely crowded. Another beach backed by dunes is reached by a boardwalk from a park with a good children's playground.

To the north, Vilar de Mouros, 3km from the N13, has shaded stone picnic tables beside a Roman bridge. Further north still, facing Spain across the wide Rio Minho, Vila Nova de Cerveira spreads around its fortress; a Misericórdia and a *pousada* hide within the walls.

Clube Celtas do Minho◆ (*Vila Nova de Cerveira, tel: (0933) 325 11 66), open Tue, Thur, Sat 0930–1730*) sponsors easy-to-moderate 8–10km monthly walks and hikes, focusing on history, ecology, culture or simply the beautiful Minho scenery. The tourist office has schedules.

Accommodation and food in Caminha

Hotel Porta do Sol €-€€ *N13 (Av. Marginal); tel: (058) 72 23 40*. Facing the water and conveniently located on the main highway, within easy walk of the old town.

Afluente *Lugar de Sentinela, Lanhelas (Caminha); tel: (058) 72 70 17,www.angelfire.com/biz/afluente* offer a 3-hour **Canoe Safari** (*€€€*) on the Minho. *Daily departures 1000 and 1500.* They also have kayaks.

Museu Municipal € *Biblioteca, off R. Direita; tel: (058) 71 03 10, open mid-Sep–Jun Tue–Fri 1000–1230, 1400–1730, Sat–Sun to 1830, Jul–mid-Sep Tue–Fri 1000–1230, 1500–1830, Sat–Sun to 1930.*

Articobre *Seixas do Minho (3km north of Caminha); tel: (058) 72 21 26,* specialises in metalware, especially copper.

Weekly markets are Wednesday in Caminha and Saturday in Vila Nova de Cerveira.

Casa de Anta €–€€ *Lanhelas (5km north of Caminha); tel: (058) 72 15 95; fax: (058) 72 12 14, e-mail: pnvm.anta@cartaopostal.com http://www.cartaopostal.com/pnvmouros* Stone building houses an expanding country lodging popular with coach tours. Folkloric entertainment livens Saturday dinner and Sunday lunch. Advance booking suggested.

Pousada Dom Dinis €€ *Vila Nova de Cerveira; tel: (051) 79 56 01, fax: (051) 79 56 04.* Inside the fortress, rooms have terraces bounded by old city walls, and views over the estuary.

Restaurante Duque de Caminha €€ *R. Ricardo Joaquim de Sousa, Caminha; tel: (058) 72 20 46.* Elegant dining room with stone and dark wood décor; impeccable service. Closed Mondays.

Restaurante O Barão €€ *R. Barão de San Roque, Caminha, tel: (058) 72 11 30.* Historic old home turned upscale dining room, in town centre.

A Petisqueira Costa e Machados € *R. Direita 32, Caminha; tel: (058) 72 14 78.* Wonderful family-run place with stone walls and immaculately polished woodwork hidden a few steps below street level.

Restaurante Coral €€ *Av. Campo do Castelo, Vila Praia de Ancora; tel: (058) 91 10 98.* First-floor dining room overlooks fishing port and little fort; fish is so fresh you can meet it before it goes to the kitchen.

MONCAO

Tourist Information *Praça da República and Praça Deula Deu; tel: (051) 65 27 57, open 0930–1230, 1400–1800, with later hours in the summer.*

Taberna Ponte de Lima € *Praça da República 72; tel: (051) 65 22 23.* A darkly atmospheric tavern with the local wine on tap and local specialities abounding. Also has some guest-rooms upstairs.

Wander the narrow old streets in Monção's centre, stopping to see the fine painted ceiling and two primitive altar statues in the Misericórdia. The Igreja Matriz, near the river, has a fine Romanesque door and a strange St Christopher in a glass case. A belvedere has good views of the Minho. Three km south, a long wall beside the N101 ends abruptly a the gates of the Palácio da Brejoeira, well known for its *vinho verde* and said to be the last great house built in Portugal. Although it is not open to the public, the façade is visible through the gates.

East of town in **Ponte de Mouro**, now bypassed by the N202, is a narrow arched bridge where King João met John of Gaunt in 1386 to arrange his marriage to John of Gaunt's daughter, Philippa of Lancaster, later mother of Prince Henry the Navigator.

Accommodation and food in Monção

Solar de Serrade € *Mazedo (1.4km southeast); tel: (051) 65 40 08, fax: (051) 65 40 41.* Seventeenth-century manor house with simple, stately interior – canopy beds, tasteful carpets, and understated detailing.

Right
Bravães, the Igreja Matriz

PONTE DA BARCA AND ARCOS DE VALDEVEZ✤✤

ⓘ Tourist Information, *Largo da Misericórdia 10, Ponte da Barca; tel: (058) 428 99, open Mon–Fri 0900–1230, 1430–1800, Sat 0900–1230 (and 1430–1800 summer).*

🍴 Restaurante "Bom Grelhado" € *Ponte da Barca; tel: (058) 444 92.* Local eating spot with regional specialities.

A graceful 15th-century bridge spans the Lima River at Ponte da Barca, an attractive but uneventful town, except on alternate Wednesdays, when it fairly hums with market life. It is the gateway to the western segment of the **Parque Nacional da Peneda-Gerês.**

Four km north, Arcos de Valdevez sits on a riverbend in a deep valley, a *pelourinho* at the centre of its cluster of old houses. A deep-arched bridge, somewhat reminiscent of the one in Amarante (*see page 126*), spans the River Vez. Stop to see the oval Igreja de Nossa Senhora da Lapa, very baroque, and more interesting outside than in.

West of Ponte da Barca, in Bravães, the Igreja Matriz has one of the most beautifully carved Romanesque portals in this country of fine Romanesque churches. Carved into five layers of arches and four sets of pillars, sculpted figures stand upon the heads of others, animals cling to columns and intricate sculpted knot patterns can only have been inspired by the Celts. Inside, flanking its stone-carved arch, are some early frescoes.

PONTE DE LIMA✦✦

ⓘ **Tourist Information** *Praça da República; tel: (058) 94 23 35, open Mon–Sat 0930–1230, 1400–1800, Sun 0930–1230.*

🏛 **Solares de Portugal (Turismo de Habitação)** *Praça da República (above TIC), tel: (058) 74 28 29,* headquarters has information on private residences and estates that welcome guests, but bookings can also be made through tourist offices.

◐ **Casa de Cortinhas** € *N101, Paço; tel: (058) 52 21 90, fax: (058) 651 88.* Granite house is a pleasant blend of traditional (in its interior tilework) and modern amenities (most notably their large swimming pool).

● The large, very lively market is on alternate Mondays

Long before it was an important waystop on the route to Santiago, Ponte de Lima was a Roman settlement, where the main road north to Astoria bridged the River Lima. Five original Roman arches remain. The river is not always low and serene; look at the wall opposite the bridge for a record of high water marks.

The town is filled with fine buildings from Romanesque to neo-classical periods. Near the end of the bridge, the 14th-century tower, now a craft centre, has needlework demonstrations. Behind, the Igreja Matriz has a good Romanesque doorway and a vaulted chapel with a deeply carved altar – ungilded for a change. Along the river, the **Museu dos Terceiros**✦ (€ *open Wed–Mon 0900–1200, 1430–1700*) shows sacred and folk art in the convent of a baroque church with excellent carving, this time gilded.

But the best part of Ponte de Lima is simply wandering through its streets. Another of its attractions is the opportunity to stay in one of the inordinate number of fine manor houses and *solares* that fill the region. These are not open to view, so staying in them is the only way to look inside. Most regal of all is the Paço de Calheiros (*see Accommodation*) which once hosted a king.

The Feiras Novas, in the third weekend of September, is a local harvest festival and a good opportunity to see a religious procession of children in angel costumes and a market devoted to trading farm tools.

Accommodation and food in Ponte de Lima

Paço de Calheiros €€ *Calheiros (7km north); tel: (058) 94 71 64, fax: (058) 94 72 94.* Grand manor-house in stucco and stone is still operated by the noble family that built it. Tastefully decorated, comfortable and with a gracious atmosphere, thanks to the solicitous host. The view from the terrace swimming pool is glorious.

Azenha de Estorãos €–€€ *Estorãos (7km west of Ponte de Lima); tel: (058) 94 15 46, fax: (058) 94 15 46.* On the banks of a brook, adjoining a 14th-century bridge, this old watermill has been renovated for guests, but retains relics, including an old baking oven.

Torre de Refoios €–€€ *Refoios (6km east of Ponte de Lima); tel: (058) 75 10 30; fax: (058) 75 10 30.* Medieval crenellated tower offers views of the glorious rural surroundings and interior; more comfortable than it was for the monks who first lived there, though care has been taken to preserve the dark wood and plaster interior.

Casa de Sabadão €–€€ *Arcozelo (2km east of Ponte de Lima); tel: (058) 94 19 63.* Manor-house is entered through an elaborate gate to the courtyard, all dating from the 17th century. Updated interior is respectful of its history, with unusual ceiling treatments tempering old stone windowseats.

Casa de Pomarchão € *Arcozelo (2km northeast of Ponte de Lima); tel: (058) 74 17 42, fax: (058) 74 27 42.* Grand Baroque home built in 1775, complete with its own chapel. Simple, spacious rooms lead to verandas where guests have a view of the valley below.

Quinta de Pomarchão € *Arcozelo (2km northeast of Ponte de Lima); tel: (058) 74 17 42.* A stone house with red tile roof conceals four lovely apartments on an operating farm estate. Rooms fuse modern tastes for balconies and bay windows with the traditional rural styles, such as beautifully painted furniture.

Quinta de Vermil €€ *Ardegão (16 km southwest of Ponte de Lima); tel: (058) 76 15 95, fax: (058) 76 18 01.* Mansion sits amidst lush, multi-level gardens of hedges, fountains, and wild profusion; vineyards extend into the surrounding countryside. Rooms are well-appointed and bright.

Restaurante Casa Gaio € *R. Agostinho José Taveira; (058) 94 12 51.* Good spot to try the local cuisine, especially *rojões de sarrabulho*, a dish of minced pork.

Restaurante Churrasqueira O Garfo €–€€ *Castro-Ribeira; tel: (058) 94 14 60.* Accessible restaurant featuring grilled meats and several varieties of *bacalhau* (salt cod).

Below
Ponte de Lima: azulejo panel

Valença do Minho❖❖

ⓘ **Tourist Information** *off Av. Espanha; tel: (051) 233 74, open Mon–Sat 0900–1200, 1400–1800, Sun 0900–1200.*

Ⓟ Park below the walls of the fortress and walk through the arched passageway.

A most unusual arrangement of two separate fortified towns, Valença overhangs the River Minho facing Tuy, in Spain. Connected by a bridge over a deep-walled ditch, their bastioned walls follow a French Vauban design, great six-pointed stars dating from the 16th century. Busy in the daytime, overrun at weekends, the narrow passages and fountain-filled squares become quiet and cosy in the evening, as the low sun mellows the colours of the tiled façades and stone walls.

From the far end there are fine views over the river and into Spain, and each turn brings a fresh vignette of low white buildings, tiny statues and flower-decked doorsteps. Churches are interesting mostly for their provincial folk art, especially the Capela São Sebastião, just inside the gate, which has some good polychrome statuary. A Roman milestone is near the Renaissance façade of Igreja de São Estevão.

The new town is uninteresting except for the small **Museu Ferroviario**❖ (Railway Museum) in the train station (€ *tel: (051) 82 41*

Right
The fortified town of
Valença do Minho

55). Colourful pottery, *azulejos*, copper ware and needlework line the main street and are scattered throughout the town. Many goods displayed are ordinary household linens aimed at Spanish shoppers. Market stalls often spread out below the fortress, becoming a fully fledged fair on the second and last Sundays of each month. Bread, cheese, local olives, cured ham and sausages for picnics are available at the municipal market (*N13–N202 intersection*).

It is almost irresistible to make a foray across the Eiffel bridge into Tuy, Spain. The town rises from a band of restaurants and cafés along the river to its cathedral, a cast-iron bandstand and a warren of old streets. Lunch at the parador, enjoying the view back on to Valença.

Accommodation and food in Ponte de Lima

Pousada de São Teotonio €€ *Fortaleza da Valença; tel: (051) 82 40 20, fax: (051) 82 43 97.* Modern building on a garden-painted terrace inside the fortress.

Restaurante Fortaleza €–€€ *Centro Histórico.* Open-air eating, where diners can admire the softly lit gates and grass-topped walls while enjoying their speciality fish dish – *Pescada a Romana* – or the braised kid.

VIANA DO CASTELO❖❖

ⓘ Tourist Information *Praça da Erva (R. Hospital Velha); tel: (058) 82 26 20. Open Mon–Sat 0930–1230, 1430–1800, Sun 0930–1230.*

ⓟ *A large parking area is located along the river, in the town centre.*

ⓢ Funicular to Santa Luzia (€) *Av. 25 de Abril, hourly 0900–1300, half-hourly 1330–1900.*

ⓜ Misericórdia *open 0930–1230, 1400–1730, except Sun during mass 1100–1230.*

Museu Municipal € *R. Manuel Esprigueira, open Tue–Sun 0930–1230, 1400–1700.*

Another thoroughly likeable small city, this one with a penchant for colourful embroidery that brightens its shopfronts, Viana is a place of broad streets and elegant buildings. Its fortune in maritime trade was translated into fine Renaissance, Manueline and Baroque architecture. Unlike many cities, Viana's wide streets make its buildings easy to admire.

All roads ultimately lead to the Praça da República, and to Viana's best-known building, the Renaissance **Misericórdia**❖, its balcony supported by a row of magnificent caryatids. Beside it is the entrance to a chapel, which has *azulejos* and a provincial painted ceiling. At the centre of the Praça stands a 16th-century fountain, behind which is the crenellated old town hall with an arcaded front.

The wide street beside the Misericórdia is bordered by the elegant late-baroque façade of the new town hall, formerly a ducal palace. Off the head of the square is the Igreja de Santa Maria Maior, or Sé, with a carved Gothic portal and a *tromp-l'oeil* ceiling painted in monochrome. The narrow Rua São Pedro, beyond, is lined with fine old buildings, including one exceptional Manueline window.

The collections of *azulejos*, Portuguese ceramics and ivory-inlaid Goan-Portuguese furniture in the **Museu Municipal**❖ are excellent, as are the ceilings in the palace that houses it. Some archaeological relics from the Celtic Citânia de Santa Luzia are here, as well.

The **Basílica de Santa Luzia***, poised on its mountain and more attractive from afar, is reached by funicular or road. Rose windows and frescoes highlight its neo-Byzantine interior. The view from its Miradouro reaching to the rivermouth, beaches and valley farmlands, is even better from the dome, but be aware that the last part of the climb is claustrophobic. Behind the basilica there are shaded tables for picnics (drinks are available from kiosks in front).

More interesting to the historically minded are the remains of the 4th-century **Citânia de Santa Luzia***, behind the elegant *pousada* above. Although its location lacks the romance of the remote *citânias*, it is well interpreted and accessible by boardwalks.

Basilica Santa Luzia, *Monte de Santa Luzia (follow R. 25 de Abril to Estrada S. Luzia, near the hospital), open **0930–1230, 1400–1730** (€ for entrance to dome and lift).

Citânia de Santa Luzia, *open Tue–Sun 1000–1200, 1400–1700 Oct–Mar, 0900–1200, 1400–1800 Apr–Sep.*

An excellent beach is on the opposite side of the river, at **Praia de Cabedelo**. Others are north, along the N13.

The main market building is on R. Martim Velho. Every Friday there is a market next to the Castelo de São Tiago da Barra, strong on jumble, clothes, antiques, and some crafts

Right
The Renaissance-style Misericórdia in Viana do Castelo

The Romaria de Nossa Senhora da Agonia, usually the third Friday of August, and continuing through the weekend, is the biggest of many regional festivals. It starts as a sombre religious occasion on the Friday, drinks itself into merriment by Saturday, and bottoms out in a bleary stupor by Sunday night. Parades, folk costumes, papier mâché figures, and children fill the streets, which are bedecked in elaborately arranged coloured sawdust designs. The city is jam-packed this week, so book far in advance.

Accommodation and food in Viana do Castelo

Pousada do Monte Santa Luzia €€ *Monte Santa Luzia; tel: (058) 82 88 89, fax: (058) 82 88 92*. Newly renovated in chic art deco, this well-run hotel has sweeping views from most rooms, marble baths in all. If you have not yet tried *bacalhau* (salt cod), do it here; it is heavenly in cream, mushrooms and shredded carrot.

Casa de Santa Maria € *Lugar do Xisto, Santa Maria de Geraz do Lima (11km west of Viana do Castelo); tel: (058) 73 23 96, fax: (058) 73 23 96*. Granite country home with exterior staircase leading into tranquil gardens. Natural stone walls, red tiled floors, dark wooden furnishings, and rugs make a cosy, rustic atmosphere.

Casa dos Costa Barros €€ *R. de São Pedro; tel: (058) 82 37 05, fax: (058) 82 81 37*. In the historic city centre, the building is famed for its elaborate Manueline window and exterior details. Inside, rooms are ornate and decorated with fine local arts – paintings, ceramics, and French-style furniture.

Casa Grande da Bandeira €€ *Largo das Carmelitas 488; tel: (058) 82 31 69*. Pretty in-town lodgings facing onto a quiet street, with comfortable rooms and a small garden of old camellias and black bamboo.

Os Tres Potes €–€€€ *B. dos Fornos 7; tel: (058) 82 99 28*. Central location and Saturday folkloric shows make this a hit with tourists, but the food is quite good. Quieter at lunchtime; in season sample the local lamprey.

Restaurante Bar Minho € *R. Gago Coutinho 103; tel: (058) 82 32 61*. Family-run place, family-style eating, local specialities in portions big enough to last right through the next day.

Suggested tour

Total distance: 158km; 220km with detours.

Time: 4 hours driving. Allow 2–3 days for the main route, with or without detours. Those with limited time should concentrate on Viana do Castelo and Valença.

**ⓘ Tourist
Information** *R. da
Loja Nova, Melgaço; tel:
(051) 424 40.*

**Ⓐ Adega Quintas de
Melgaço** *Lugar de
Ferreiro, Alvaredo; tel: (051)
446 37, cellars where you
can sample Melgaço's
wines.*

Ⓡ Adega Real €
*Terreiro, Vila Nova de
Cerveira, is a good place for
lunch and small snacks
with local wine*

Right
The Roman bridge
in Amonde

Links: Viana do Castelo is connected to Barcelos and the North of
Porto route (*see page 146*) along the IC1 and N103. From Ponte da
Barca, the N101 connects to Braga, 33km to the south, for the
beginning of the Gerês Mountains route (*see page 180*).

Route: Head north on the N13 from **VIANA DO CASTELO ❶**, along
the dunes to **Vila Praia de Ancora**. Keep hugging the coast to
CAMINHA ❷, at the mouth of the Minho, and along the river to **Vila
Nova de Cerveira**.

Continue north to **VALENÇA DO MINHO ❸**, at the Spanish frontier,
turning east on to the N202, passing the enormous crowned gate of
Quinta do Crasto, now stranded below road level. The attractive town
of **Lapella** clusters on the riverbank around a 12th-century tower.
Follow its tiny narrow streets to the tower to see an excellent group of
Minho granaries. Continue to **MONÇÃO ❹**.

Detour: Drive east along the narrowing Minho, through the **Ponte de
Mouro** to **Melgaço** (Friday is market day). Either backtrack to Monção or,
if feeling adventurous, follow a series of unnumbered, but paved roads
southwest along the foothills of the Serra da Peneda, through **Roussas,
Ceivães, Tangil** and **Merufe**, there taking the N202-2 south to **Azere** and
ARCOS DE VALDEVEZ ❺, where you will rejoin the main route.

Head south on the N101 from Monção, over hilly countryside, with
good views eastward over the **Serra da Peneda** from just south of
Barrocas. The entire road is scenic, as it drops almost straight south to

ARCOS DE VALDEVEZ. Crossing the River Lima at **PONTE DA BARCA 6**, head west on the N203, through **Bravães**, recrossing to the north side of the river at **PONTE DE LIMA 7**. Follow the N202 west to **VIANA DO CASTELO**.

Detour: Just west of **Lanheses**, follow the N305 north for about 10km. As you leave **Amonde**, look out on the right for a particularly fine **Roman bridge**** with sharp humpback, huge paving stones and a granite cross at its centre. The perfect ensemble of the bridge and adjacent stone farmhouse with a porch, in a setting of green fields and mountains, invites an artist.

Also worth exploring

Castro Laboreiro, south of Melgaço, and **Lindoso**, east of Arcos de Valdevez, are each remote mountain towns deep in the Parque Nacional. For adventurous drivers, the trip between the two, over the mountains on precipitous (but paved) roads, is a fascinating day's travel. Castro Laboreiro is surrounded by megalithic sites and each town has a castle.

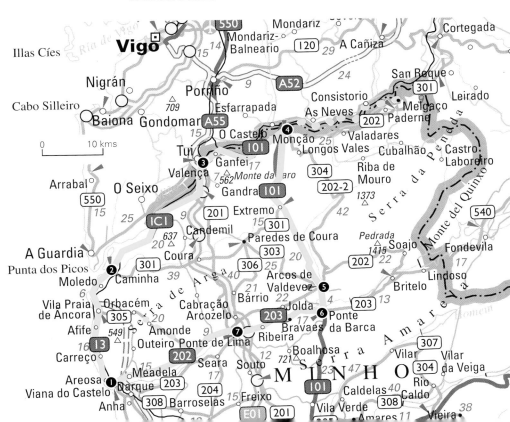

Braga and the Gerês Mountains

Ratings

Mountains	●●●●●
Architecture	●●●●
Nature	●●●●
Scenery	●●●●
Villages	●●●●
History	●●●
Outdoor activities	●●●
Walking	●●

The contrast between prim ecclesiastical Braga and the wild, untamed landscapes of the Parque Nacional da Peneda-Gerês, less than 30km away, make this route particularly interesting. The architecture ranges from the rough stones of ancient dolmens and one of Portugal's finest Celtic hillforts, through a rare Visigothic chapel, Roman bridges and medieval churches to the refined lines of early baroque churches and manor houses and the flamboyance of later baroque. Roads leading north from the N103, the principal east–west route, converge near Caniçadas to cross the Cávado River, impounded and widened to lake proportions by a long string of dams. You will follow the shores – often from considerable height – of these huge reservoirs wherever you travel here. High in the mountains, stone villages seem to grow from the rocky land, many looking much as they would have in the Middle Ages.

BRAGA❖❖

ℹ **Turismo** *Av. Liberdade 1 (Praça da República); tel: (053) 26 25 50, open daily 0900–1900.*

🅿 Public parking is at Praça de Conde Agrolongo, a block from the Sé.

🛈 **Sé** € *open 0830–1230, 1330–1830, until 1730 Sep–May. The church itself is free; tours last one hour, it's better to wander on your own.*

A city of flowers and fountains, Braga is known for its churches, which seem to outnumber restaurants. Even the **Sé❖** is not content to be just one church, but includes several separate chapels off the cloister. In the nave, rows of very plain stone scoured columns end at a wildly ornamented baroque altar. Side chapels flank it, one with *azulejos*, the other has a fine polychrome wood altar. Overhead, two highly decorated organs are encrusted with cherubs.

The cloister chapels include the Capela da Glória, in sombre-toned Arabian Nights frescoes, and São Geraldo, lined with *azulejos*. The Capelo dos Reis contains tombs of the parents of Portugal's first king, and the mummified body of a 14th-century archbishop. The Capela de Santa Catarina is usually filled with votive offerings. The Tesoro (Treasury), on two floors in the chapter house, is a mixed lot, with some very good pieces (gem-encrusted silver and goldwork, vestments, a 10th-century ivory chest) poorly displayed and ill-cared-

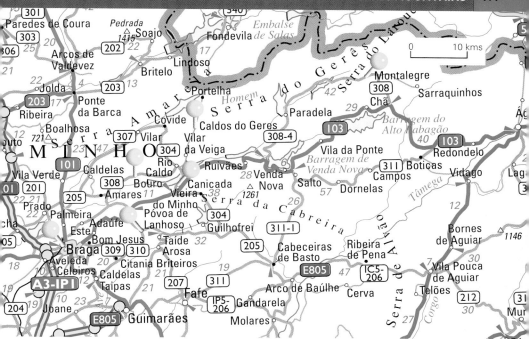

Palácio dos Biscainhos € *R. dos Biscainhos, 30-minute tours begin Tue–Sun 1000–1145, 1400–1700. Free Sun am.*

Bom Jesus *funicular (€) operates 0800–2000, half-hourly.*

Capela de São Frutuoso € *north on N201, signposted to the right in São Jeronimo Real, open Wed–Sun 1000–1230, 1400–1730.*

for. But it gives access to the *coro alto* (choir loft) and its richly carved and gilded stalls.

Next door, the Paço Episcopal, now a library, dates from the 14th to 18th centuries. The reading room ceiling is magnificent. Beyond is the brilliant Jardim de Santa Bárbara, filled with colourful flowers almost all year round. Many of Braga's churches are thick with gilded baroque carving; the chancel of the Misericórdia, behind the cathedral, is completely covered in gold.

To see how the not-so-holy lived in this opulent era, visit the **Palácio dos Biscainhos***, a noble mansion, now a museum, set in formal gardens with pools, fountains and statuary. The *palácio* is decorated with baroque stucco work, panelled walls and *azulejos*, and is furnished with antiques. The Igreja Santa Cruz, at the opposite end of R. do Anjo, has a startlingly baroque exterior, with better proportions inside.

The pilgrimage sanctuary of **Bom Jesus***, 6km east, is known not so much for the church as the setting. The flight after flight of baroque stairs leading to its entrance, climbed by penitents on their knees, is lined with chapels, terracotta statues and fountains. A funicular gets the unrepentant there faster, or you can drive to the top.

Just north of Braga, the **Capela de São Frutuoso*** is a tiny Visigothic church thought to date from the 7th century. Built in the shape of a cross, São Frutuoso extends its equilateral arms in vaulted chapels,

ⓘ **São Martinho de Tibães** € *Mira do Tibães, open Tue–Sun 0900–1230, 1400–1730.*

🜂 Market day is Tue, at Largo da Feira, south of the city centre.

🜂 **Semana Santa** *the week before Easter*, sees Braga's streets lined with wayside chapels and, on Thu night, with black-hooded penitents swinging long-handled lanterns.

São João *Jun 23–24*, processions, dancing and celebrations.

supported on plain columns with acanthus leaf capitals. The feeling is solid, sturdy and very old. Outside, narrow bands of delicately carved marble decorate the frieze and pediment. Enter through the newer Igreja de São Francisco, whose ornate high altar and well-restored painted ceiling are best appreciated from the *coro alto* (choir), entered from outside. Lift the choir seats to see the ornately carved misericords on the Renaissance stalls. A little museum in the sacristy corridor explains São Frutuoso's archaeology.

After the monasteries were dissolved in 1834, the great Benedictine **Mosteiro de São Martinho de Tibães*** spent more than a century in private hands, finally falling to a family who systematically sold everything they could pull or hammer loose, allowing roofs to collapse and the property to crumble into decay. Now the government has begun the long task of stabilising and restoring the enormous monastic buildings and the remarkable gardens, whose current overgrown and neglected state has its own romantic charm.

The attached church, which remained in ecclesiastical hands, was well cared for. Its high altar is among the finest examples of gilded baroque woodcarving in Portugal, and its choir stalls are separated by caryatids.

But it is the gardens that enchant. Their decay has simply made them more romantic, and the long Rua das Fontes is all the more charming for the moss and herbs that overgrow its stones and *azulejos*. This long series of terraces joined by double staircases, with fountains set at each level and trees overhead, is one of the loveliest pieces of garden architecture in Europe. Elsewhere are mossy stone fountains, an aqueduct, a pond ringed by camellias and giant conifers and boxwood hedges grown to trees.

Accommodation and food in Braga

Castelo Bom-Jesus €€ *Bom Jesus (5.5km east of Braga); tel: (053) 67 65 66, fax: (053) 67 76 91.* Glorious park setting of old trees and lush gardens with fountains and pools, overlooking Braga. Inside is as opulent, with finest rooms featuring domed carved ceilings, and gilt detailing.

Albergaria Senhora-a-Branca € *Largo da Senhora-a-Branca 58; tel: (053) 299 38, fax: (053) 299 37.* Covered carpark and convenient main street location, easily accessible to major highway routes.

Restaurante Cruz Sobral € *Campo das Hortas 7–8; tel: (053) 61 66 48, closed Mon and late May.* On restaurant row, with few surprises on menu of well-prepared regional dishes.

The best view of Braga may be from one of the atmospheric old cafés, either the art deco **Astoria**, *Praça da República*, or **Lusitania**, overlooking Jardim de Santa Bárbara.

Opposite
The gardens of the Mosteiro de São Martinho de Tibães

CANICADA AND BOURO✢

Although towns on the two sides of the dam look close together, the N304 climbs steeply to meet the N103, not a comfortable road to travel at night.

Rent paddleboats, canoes and kayaks on the N308-1, north of Canicada bridge. Park by Café Beira Rio, overlooking the lake, and rent watercraft on the beach below.

This area, near the intersection of main roads, is a good central base, with two *pousadas* and water-side communities providing lodgings close to the bridge.

A decade ago the vast Santa Maria al Bouro monastery lay, like Tibães, in desolate ruin, its walls rising roofless. That's hard to remember now, in the cool stone corridors surrounding the cloister of this sparkling new *pousada*. The monastery's vast kitchen is today's dining room, with a huge stone table as its centrepiece and the inside of the mammoth chimney forming the ceiling. Non-guests are welcome to visit the monastery, stroll in its gardens and dine in its cavernous kitchen.

Albufeira de Canicada, the impounded reservoir, stretches northwards in two arms, providing swimming and other water sports based at the southern end near the bridge.

Accommodation and food in Canicada and Bouro

Pousada de Santa Maria do Bouro €€ *Mosteiro de Santa Maria do Bouro, Amares (northeast of Braga); tel: (053) 37 19 71, fax: (053) 37 19 76.* In contrast to the massive granite walls, guest rooms are sleekly contemporary with cleverly disguised mini-bars. The dining room (€€–€€€) serves regional dishes, perhaps lamprey or kid, to strains of *ars antigua* and monastic choirs. The delicious starter of *bacalhau* (salt-codfish) with eggs and potatoes (€) is enough for a main course.

Pousada de São Bento € *Vieira do Minho (between the N103 and the Canicada Bridge); tel: (053) 64 71 90, fax: (053) 64 78 67.* Suspended high above the Cávado river, this rustic *pousada's* rooms are decorated in sturdy pine furniture, wrought-iron and woven rugs. A good chef offers updated regional specialities.

Casa de São Paio € *São Paio de Eira Velha (1.5km north of Vieira do Minho); tel: (053) 64 74 31.* Near the N103 and the main intersection at Canicada bridge, this stone house contains two apartments and one suite, perfect for families. Exposed stonework is offset with dark wood accents for a cosy atmosphere.

Restaurante Morais € *Bouro, opposite the pousada,* serves standard fare in a pleasant setting.

Opposite
Canicada's reservoir

CALDOS DO GERES❖❖

ℹ **Turismo de Gerês**
*Termas Colunat; tel:
(053) 39 11 33, open
Mon–Sat 0900–1200,
1400–1800, Sun
0900–1200.* For walking
and activities within the
Parque Nacional, the
turismo is more helpful
than park office, just north.

Park maps available at TIC
or park offices are not
accurate enough for hiking
and footpaths, although
plentiful, are not
waymarked.

🅿 On summer
weekends, parking in
Gerês is virtually
impossible. Everyone parks
along the main road.

There's no mistaking this town for anything but an old-time spa resort. Strung out in a narrow valley above a river are the tell-tale candy-coloured once-grand hotels – one of which has almost completely fallen in behind its blue façade, another is undergoing a facelift. Uphill, a crescent-shaped colonnade with the spring and some baths is also being refurbished.

Gerês welcomes casual visitors to its baths (€), saunas (€€) and massages (€€€). Apart from soaking, shopping and sitting in cafés, there's not much to do in town, which is just as its devotees like it. More active pleasures lie all around.

The road climbs steeply from Gerês, poised above a ravine so sheer you can see the road lying in coils directly below. Forested slopes with picnic parks, crowded at weekends, open to sweeping mountain views.

At the deserted Spanish border station, and along the road from Portela do Homem to Campo do Gerês, stands Iberia's largest collection of Roman milestones, placed along the Via Nova between AD79 and 350. Wild ponies, *garranos*, are unique to these mountains, as are more than a dozen plant species.

Another road leaves Rio Caldo on the west side of the Canicada reservoir, climbing over a rock-strewn mountain to Vilarinho das Furnas and its long reservoir at tiny Campo do Gerês. At a crossroads

Empresa das Aguas do Gerês (Spa)
€–€€€ Av. Manuel F Costa; tel: (052) 39 11 13, open Mon–Sat 0800–1200, 1500–1800 May–Oct.

Small shops sell earthenware, straw and wicker, embroidery, rag rugs, copper, honey and teas from local herbs. At the southern end a tiny shop sells easy-to-carry fretwork woodenware.

Hire horses from **Equi Campo €€-€€€** *Campo do Gerês; tel: (053) 35 70 22.*

is a Roman column and cross with well-preserved inscriptions. The poignant Museu Etnográfico de Vilarinho das Furnas tells the story of the little town drowned by the dam. Run on a communal basis, with shared work and property, Furnas's way of life disappeared with the rising waters in 1972. When water levels drop in the middle of the summer, you can sometimes see the upper ramparts of the old town walls rising out of the waters beyond.

A tree-shaded hike along the Vilarhino das Furnas Reservoir takes about 3 hours of easy, level walking. Park at the gate alongside the reservoir and walk north on the unpaved road, or along the shore past remnants of the flooded village. After about 1km, a miniature waterfall drops through mossy rocks, then the roadside is littered with huge moss-covered boulders. A little further on the Ribeiro do Pedredo cascades past a group of inscribed Roman milestones, and traces of the Roman road are discernible. At 3km a footpath leads left downhill where waterfalls drop over sculptured rocks and potholes. Return to the road and continue walking until you find another cluster of milestones shortly beyond. The road crosses the cascades of the Rio Maceira (4.2km), a good turning point before the ascent to the Gerês road, 400m further on.

Above
Roman Milestones along the Furnas Reservoir path

Opposite
Pitões das Júnias

Accommodation and food in Caldas do Gerês

Most lodgings close Nov–Apr and are booked solid June–Aug. Reserve ahead, especially summer for weekends.

Hotel Universal €–€€ *Av. Manuel Francisco da Costa; tel: (053) 39 11 70, fax: (053) 39 11 02.* Forest-green cast-iron filigree columns and arcades wrap around the beautiful mosaic atrium-lobby dripping with plants. Rooms are pleasant and modern with tasteful use of *azulejos*.

Pensão Casa da Ponte € *N308-1; tel: (053) 39 11 25.* Hard to miss, just as you enter the village, it is clean and hospitable, with few frills.

Estalagem de São Bento € *Seara, Rio Caldo; tel: (053) 39 11 06.* Opposite the shrine, this well-appointed hotel has been converted from the buildings of a former convent.

Pousada da Juventude de Vilarinho das Furnas € *Campo do Gerês; tel: (053) 35 13 39.* More than just a youth hostel, it is a centre for park activities and the best source of maps and trail information. Dorms, doubles and quad rooms just right for families.

Restaurante Nova Sol € *tel: (053) 39 11 08*, regional dishes, including *receita do cozido*, bean stew with pork, kale and local smoke-cured meats.

Restaurante Pensão Adelaide € *tel: (053) 39 00 20*, serves regional dishes, including local trout.

MONTALEGRE✤

Turismo *Praça do Município; tel: (076) 527 65.*

O Pote Barrosão €-€€ *R. do Outeiro 8; tel: (076) 51 11 52.* Rusticated restaurant of local cuisine, specialising in meat pies.

Buy really good ham and cured sausage for picnics at **Fumeiro de Barroso**, paired with bread and other titbits from **Cruz and Cruz, Ltda Supermercados**, *R. Direita 9.*

A restored late-medieval castle looks down on the red rooftops of Montalegre. Its huge window arches in three-metre-thick walls narrow to tiny slits, allowing bowmen to take aim inside with plenty of elbow room.

The Misericórdia, below, has a good altar and columns whose spirals continue into the arches. Casa Cerrada, opposite the town hall, is a manor house with the armourial crest of a noble family, once tax collectors for the king.

From the Corujeira vantage point there are fine views of the castle and the town, to the green and amber farms and the mountains beyond.

Northwest of Montalegre an unnumbered road leads over moors reminiscent of Yorkshire, dividing right to Tourem, where it continues into Spain, and left Pitões das Júnias, where it ends altogether. Both towns have dolmen and Pitões has daunting mountain views and a tiny ruined Cistercian monastery hidden in a vale.

At São Vicente da Cha, 5km south on the M509, is an Iron Age hillfort, and in Gralhos, also south and off the N308, is a well-preserved section of Roman road and a Roman bridge.

Several organizations in or near Montalegre offer a variety of sporting activities in the national park. The **Club Nautical de Alto Rabagão** (*Penedones; tel/fax: (076) 55 50 32*) rents sailing and other boats and organises group sailing trips. **Trote Gerês** (*tel/fax: (053) 65*

98 60) runs kayak tours of the Paradela and Salamonde reservoirs, while guided horse-riding tours are arranged by **Clube do Cavalo** *(Padornelos; tel: (076) 521 14)*.

There are dozens of small festivals in this area such as the Festa do Senhor da Piedade and the Fastas do Concelho at the beginning of August, or the Feira do Fumeiro de Barroso (meat-smokers' fair), during the second weekend of January.

Povoa de Lanhoso❖❖

🏛 **Citânia Briteiros €**
Briteiros, open daily 0900–1800, 0900–1700 in winter.

🌀 **Romaria de Nossa Senhora do Porto de Ave** *Sep 5–8,* with processions filling the great granite stairs and terraces.

🍴 **Tasquina do Guarda €** *Largo Principal, Cabril,* Café serving light meals and hardier fare, along with local wines.

Restaurante Sol Rio € *N308, Paradela; tel: (076) 561 67.* Serves good, simple mountain dishes.

The main square of this busy town is surrounded by buildings faced with coloured tiles. Although no signs point the way, Castelo de Póvoa de Lanhoso is easy to find, visible above the town; simply head uphill towards it, until you see signs. Watch for the round foundations of buildings from an Iron Age *castro*, in the woods beside the road.

The 12th-century castle, whose entrance is hidden around to the left, commands a 360-degree view from its parapets. At the top a map shows locations of the many nearby *castro* sites, as well as the route of the Roman road and other Roman, medieval and prehistoric sites.

About 7km southeast of Póvoa, the N207-4 passes through the centre of the sanctuary of Nossa Senhora do Porto de Ave in Taide, an attractive town rising steeply from the valley. Rising with it are the stairways leading to the sanctuary, an imposing white-and-granite baroque church on a terrace above the river. Wide granite staircases connect a series of terraces, one with a mossy garden and fountain, another overlooked by balconies. Narrower stairs ascend a wooded hillside past small chapels.

Ten km south of Póvoa is Portugal's best known and largest Iron-Age hillfort, **Citânia Briteiros❖❖❖**. Its stone-paved streets climb past the earliest round rough-stone foundations to those built of slabs set on end, and finally to square-cornered Roman foundations. Parts of three defensive walls remain, some restored. Also restored are two round houses, but nearly all the carved stonework has been removed to the Museu Martins Sarmento in Guimarães *(see page 151)*. Briteiros is thought to be one of the last strongholds of the Celts in Portugal, finally falling to the Romans.

Accommodation and food in Póvoa do Lanhoso

Quinta de São Vicente €-€€ *Lugar de Portas, Gerês do Minho (6km north of Póvoa do Lanhoso); tel: (053) 63 24 66, fax: (053) 63 24 66.* Rural estate house nestled amid gardens with 17th-century chapel.

Opposite
The iron-age hillfort at Citânia Briteiros

Restaurante Castelo € *Monte Pilar; tel: (053) 61 12 21, closed Mon.* Carved wooden ox-yokes form bench-backs at the tables of this classy little restaurant below the castle. Panoramic views compete for attention with fork-tender *lombo assado* (roast pork) and the crisp, slightly sparkling house wine.

Suggested tour

Total distance: 216km; 219km with detours.

Time: 5 hours driving. Allow 2 days, plus a day for Braga. Those with limited time should concentrate on Braga and Citânia Briteiros.

Links: At the eastern end of the route, the N103 continues to Chaves and Route 13 (*see page 184*). Braga is close to Guimarães via the N101 (*see page 148*) and Ponte de Lima on the N201 (*see page 162*).

Route: Leave BRAGA on the N103 then the N309, following signs to Chaves and the sanctuary of **Bom Jesus**. Continue right and follow signs towards Guimarães, then to **Citânia Briteiros**. Follow the N310 north to **POVOA DE LANHOSO** ❶, just beyond which is the N103. Turn right (east) bypassing a left turn to **CANICADA** ❷ and **Rio Caldo**, unless stopping there for the night.

The N103 continues east, high above the southern shore of the widened Cavado river through **Venda Nova**, then **Pisões** and along the low, relatively level northern shore of the reservoir. Turn left (north) on the N308 to **MONTALEGRE** ❸. Stay on the N308 through **Paredes do Rio**, stopping to see the church, mills and *canastros* (corncribs) and detouring north in **Outeiro** to **Parada**, another picturesque stone village. From **Outeiro** take the N308 south past beautiful views of the Serra do Gerês to **Paradela**. Turn right (west) on the 103-8, across the dam and through **Sirvozelo**'s stone houses and stone corncribs built amid giant boulders. In **Cabril** stop to see the community olive press.

Right
Montalegre

Follow an unnumbered road west to the N308-1 in **Veiga**. Turn right (north) to **GERÊS** ❹ and continue north, climbing through beautiful forested mountains, crossing a bridge with a waterfall upstream just before the Spanish border at **Portela do Homem**. Milestones have been assembled from the old Roman road, which you can see south of the bridge. Return on the same road through Gerês to Rio Caldo. The upper stretch of this road through the **Mata de Albergaria**, a forest of rare virgin oak and chestnut, may be subject to timed travel. You will be given a ticket to show at the other end within 15 minutes, proving that you have not stopped *en route*.

Detour: From **Portela do Homem**, backtrack 2.4km to a right turn on to an unpaved but quite passable road (except after prolonged rains). Drive through wooded glades past several groups of Roman milestones and moss-covered boulders, to the shore of the **Vilarinho das Furnas** reservoir. If the water is low, the submerged walls and foundations of the flooded town will be visible. Continue to **Campo do Gerês**, past a Roman column, to **Covide**, then on through **São Bento da Porta Aberta** until you meet the N304 in **Rio Caldo**. If this route is closed, you can access the lower end, as far as the **Vilarinho das Furnas** reservoir, from Rio Caldo and explore this scenic, level route on foot.

Follow the N308 west to **BOURO** ❺ and **Amares**, then take the N205-4 and the N101 to Braga.

The Northern Mountains

Ratings

Mountains	●●●●
Scenery	●●●●
Villages	●●●●
Historical sights	●●●
Nature	●●●
Walking	●●●
Castles	●●
Museums	●●

Trás-os-Montes lies in long folds of mountain ranges, or *serras*. Nowhere are they out of sight, and rarely is the ground level. This makes driving interesting, but most main roads are well-surfaced, with rails separating them from the valley below. Unpaved roads and tracks between remote villages in the Serra de Montesinho make splendid walking routes through mountain-ringed moorlands of heather and broom. Wildlife, including boar and deer, flourishes in the park's lowlands, and overhead you may see rare golden eagles or black storks. Chaves, since ancient times the 'key' to this region, is a small lively city with just enough attractions to make it interesting, plenty of restaurants and a relaxed air. Evidence of the region's distant past is all around, in Iron-Age *castros*, Roman bridges, and castles that once defended Portugal's northern outpost.

BOTICAS❖

ℹ **Turismo** *R. 5 de Outubro; tel: (076) 422 03.*

⚲ **Mesinha de São Sebastião** *Vila Grande (Dornelas), Jan 20.* A linen-covered table, 400 metres long, stretches through town, serving pilgrims and visitors a midday meal of bread, rice and pork stew. This colourful, if cold, occasion is accompanied by the saint's image, to which donations are expected. BYO cutlery and drink.

Boticas is a pleasant, but not memorable town in a fertile valley. Several nearby attractions are worth a stop for unhurried travellers with time to enjoy the views and to admire the golden-brown cattle with curved horns and soft eyes, that munch placidly by the roadsides.

Carvalhelhos, 6km west of Boticas, has a bosky spa park with springs used since Roman times. An Iron-Age fortified village is about 1km away, with some restored houses curiously outside its protective walls. South of Carvalhelhos, on the N519, a footpath leads from the village of Campos to Castro Lesenho, a Roman settlement where four warrior statues were found, now in museums elsewhere. Between Boticas and Carvalhelhos, north beside the N311, is Ponte da Pedrinha, a medieval bridge with a watermill.

Sapiãos, a stone town 4km east, is also medieval. A downhill turn at the Café Bem Estar leads, bearing left, to a stone slab bridge surrounded by stone houses with exterior stairs, and a granite cross.

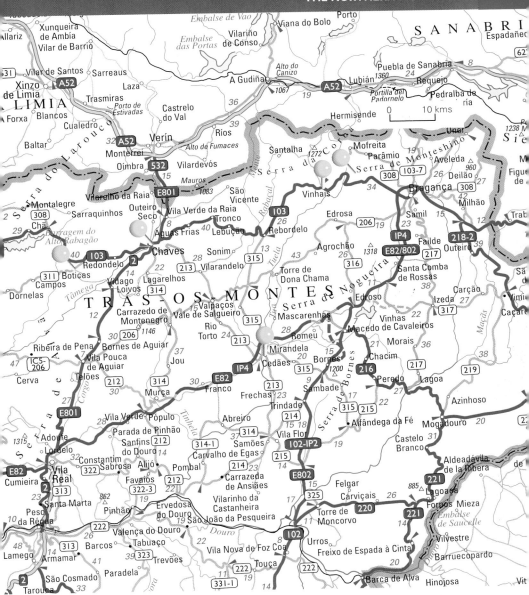

Roman gold mines at Poço das Freitas, near Ardãos, are reached by a northbound road from the N103, west of Sapiãos. Approached on foot or by jeep across a Roman bridge, the mines have hidden sink-holes and should not be visited without a guide recommended by the tourist office in Boticas or Chaves.

CHAVES✥✥

On the Tâmega River, the town of Chaves is only 10km from Spain, at a crossroads important since ancient times. The 16-arch Roman bridge, still in regular use, has columns with Roman inscriptions and was built by the Emperor Trajan. It is best viewed from the gardens which stretch along the river to the **Caldas de Chaves✥** (Parque Termal; tel: (076) 33 24 45), hotsprings which provided a further attraction to the bath-loving Romans.

Narrow streets wind up from the river, passing parks and flower-filled gardens. Most of the city's attractions are on a terrace above the river, where the early settlement clustered around the Torre de Menagem, sole remnant of the castle built to protect 14th-century Chaves. In the keep, the **Museu Militar✥** has exhibits relating to ancient, colonial and modern wars. A long climb brings roof-top views of the city, farmlands and gardens below. These gardens of brilliant annuals are interspersed with samples of the wealth of Roman and prehistoric stones housed, along with other exhibits, in the adjacent **Museu da Região Flaviense✥**, a former palace of the Dukes of Bragança. A highlight is a 4000-year-old megalith in human form.

The extraordinary Misericórdia church, next to the palace, is completely walled in *azulejo* scenes from the New Testament, which rise to a painted ceiling and end at a gold baroque high altar. At the bottom of the square is the Igreja Matriz, modernised during the Renaissance, but with a very old stone statue of the Virgin Mary in a niche of the apse.

Praça Camões and the adjacent square facing the castle gardens are lined by houses with wooden balconies, some carved, others brightly painted, quite different from other northern towns.

Forte São Francisco caps a second hill, guarded by Vauban fortifications, and with more stunning flower gardens below. The fort conceals a convent, newly restored and converted into a *pousada*-like hotel. Guests can access its bright baroque chapel and see the antiques and Arraiolos carpets that decorate the inn. A vaulted brick cistern is the hotel's wine cellar, among Portugal's finest.

North along the river towards Outeiro Seco, is the 13th-century Romanesque Nossa Senhora da Azinheira, with wonderful animal-face corbels outside and possibly Portugal's oldest frescoes inside (which you may have to view through the large keyhole if no one is nearby to find the key).

About 12km east of Chaves along the N103, **Castelo Montforte✥** (Aguas Frias, open Wed–Sun 0930–1230, 1400–1730, Mon–Tues 1400–1530) stands on a hilltop, a well-preserved fortress, whose outer walls can easily be scaled up a path to the left of the entrance, should the gate be closed. Rather grand picnic pavilions sit below. Just beyond is the Pedra Bolideira, a large split glacial erratic, which no longer rocks with a nudge, as popularly reported.

Adega Faustino €
*Travessa do Olival; tel:
(076) 32 21 42, closed Sun.*
Cavernous tavern with
uncomfortable wooden
stools, but good food,
served as *petiscos*, so you
get exactly the amount you
want, with big glasses of
youthful wine.

Restaurant Sergio €
*Travessa do Olival; tel: (076)
32 11 70.* Nothing fancy,
but fresh trout and cutlets
with mushrooms are well
prepared.

Confeitaria Aurora €
*off R. de Santo António, next
to the post office.* Admire
the gardens opposite, as
you sip coffee and munch
pastry and good croissants.

Passeios a Cavalo,
*Quinta dos Borralhos,
Pastoria (Curalha); tel: (076)
32 83 67.* Historical and
cultural horse-riding tours
with a professor well-
versed in the local area.

Feira de Santos *Oct
26–Nov 1.* The major
event, climaxing last two
days.

Feira Dia de Cicade *Jul
8.* Parades and fireworks
mark this secular festival.

Festa do Folar, *Apr 3,*
fills the Praça de Camões
with food stalls and music.

**Romaria de São
Caetano** *second Sun in
Aug.* A major point in the
religious calendar, the
devoted make a 15km
pilgrimage to the rural
sanctuary.

Right
Chaves

Accommodation and food in Chaves

Forte de Sãu Francisco €–€€ *R. do Tabolado 35, Forte de S. Francisco; tel: (076) 33 37 00, fax: (076) 33 37 01.* Top-of-the-line, with warmth often lacking in such well-polished hotels. Guests can loll among antiques and explore the crannies of this former convent, although guestrooms are almost too lovely to leave. The restaurant (€€) does nice things with local game, such as *feijoada* with wild boar.

Pensão Casa das Termas € *R. do Tabolado 7; tel: (076) 33 32 80.* Plain but pleasant *residencial*, with flowers tucked into ironwork outside every window; new without being glaringly 'modern'. The best restaurants are in sight.

Quinta de Santa Isabel € *Santo Estevão (7km east of Chaves); tel: (076) 35 18 18, fax: (076) 35 18 18.* Rustic exterior gives no hint of its brief moment of fame: the Sainted Queen Isabel stayed the night here before she wed King Dinis. The interior is graceful, with dark wood and plaster walls softened by floral drapes and lacy bedspreads, very romantic.

Below
Mirandela

MIRANDELA

Tourist Information *Praça do Mercado; tel: (078) 257 68. Open 0930–1230, 1400–1700,* relatively useless.

Museu Municipal Armindo Teixeira Lopes € *town centre; tel: (078) 26 57 68. Open 0930–1230, 1400–1800.*

Without any 'must-see' sights, Mirandela is a very pleasant town to be in. The best view is from across the impressive medieval bridge as the late afternoon sun hits the old town, which rises in layers above the river. The bridge's 17 graceful arches, built on Roman foundations, draw your eye to the façade of the Palácio dos Távoras, grandly dominating the hill. Now the Town Hall, its ornate granite pediments with spiral-carved tips and window casements highlight its 18th-century exterior. Beside it is one of the city's many gardens, small flower-beds filled with brilliant colour.

Mirandela has an inordinate amount of recent public sculpture: below the palace, a beneficent Pope John Paul II reflects the city's gentility in his face; an allegorical female poises above the river; a mother reads to her children; St Francis stands before a crumbling balconied house.

The small **Museu Municipal Armindo Teixeira Lopes**✦ focuses on 20th-century Portuguese art including views of the surrounding area by the local artist after whom the museum was named.

🏛 **Museu das Curiosidades €**
Romeu (about 10km east of Mirandela); tel: (078) 931 34.

🍴 The well-designed Mercado Municipal has shops on two levels around a central atrium for seasonal stalls. *Artesanatos* sell local baskets and food shops have fresh breads, local honey, cheeses and a wide choice of smoked meats. In front is a nice playground, a vintage olive oil press and a wooden oxcart.

Although it is 10km east in Romeu, who could resist a museum called the **Museu das Curiosidades**⁺? The curiosities were collected by a local benefactor and include all kinds of mechanical doodahs, unusual musical boxes and vintage cars.

From Mirandela, a scenic narrow-gauge train follows the Tua River to its confluence with the Douro in Tua, two hours away. Of five daily trains, only two return trips run during daylight. They allow for one or two hours for strolling round Tua. Check with the tourist office for times.

Accommodation and food in Mirandela

Grand Hotel Dom Dinis €–€€ *Av. Nossa Senhora do Amparo; tel: (078) 26 01 00, fax (078) 26 01 01*. New hotel taking advantage of the best views in town; balconies overlook the river and medieval bridge, five-minute stroll from centre. Modern rooms, very accommodating staff and good restaurant (€€).

Parque de Campismo € *Quinta da Maravilha; tel: (078) 26 31 77*, has a restaurant at the campsite and is open all year.

Restaurante O Recanto € *Traversa de Santa Luzia; tel: (078) 26 25 24*. Giant portions of local dishes; beware the *alheiras de Mirandela*, an over-rich sausage.

Restaurante O Arco € *R. Santo António 10; tel (078) 26 51 45, open daily 0800–2400*. Good selection of fish and the usual meats in a casual atmosphere near the town hall.

Restaurante Luso Brasileiro € *R. Santa Luzia 18; tel: (078) 26 12 22*. Standard dishes with daily bargain tourist menu.

VINHAIS AND THE SERRA DE MONTESHINO⁺⁺

ℹ️ **Parque Natural de Montesinho**
Delagação de Vinhais; tel: (073) 724 16.

➡️ Use the park's own map, inside the park brochure, as it's much more reliable than highway maps, some of which show non-existent connecting roads.

Vinhais is a long, narrow corniche town far more interesting than it first appears from the N103, its main street. West of the centre, the mountainside is so steep that you look almost straight into two belltowers. An impressive staircase leads down to a long façade encompassing two churches of the former Mosteiro de São Francisco. The monastery buildings are now a school, where someone will open the church to show the polychrome and gold altar, an unusual multi-windowed reliquary, and ornate carved vestment chests.

From a square at the east end of town, a street winds up through the gate of a crumbling castle to a tiny village once enclosed by its walls. Only a few of the higgledy-piggledy buildings have been restored; most retain their medieval air, heightened by chickens and rabbits in the street and a nice old *pelhourinho*.

Romaria de Nossa Senhora da Assunção, *Aug 15*, and **Romaria de Santo António**, *first Sat in Sept, in Vinhais.*

Don't be put off by the thought of venturing into the Serra de Montesinho, which fills the land between the N103 and the Spanish border. These are kinder, gentler mountains than neighbouring ranges, and roads to their tiny rock-built villages are blessedly free of cliff-hanging hairpin bends. Watch for traditional white oval dovecotes with flat roofs.

Streets were almost an afterthought in Travança, a gathering of medieval stone farmhouses north of Vinhais. Hay and straw spills out on to the narrow cobbled streets from ground-floor barns, homes above them are reached by exterior stone staircases. Shepherds watch flocks of grazing sheep nearby and donkey carts are common on the roads.

At Moimenta, almost on the Spanish frontier, a Roman bridge crosses the River Tuela, known for its trout fishing (and its trout, which you will find on menus throughout the area).

Pinheiro Novo and Sernande are end-of-the-road towns reached through Tuizelo and Seixas. The mountain views are spectacular, especially between Salgueiros (where there are more dovecotes) and Moimenta, where the road crosses the Serra da Coroa.

Vinhais and the mountain villages to the north are known for their wooden ware. However, it is not always easy to find, so look out for *trabalhos em madeira* signs.

Food in Vinhais and the Serra de Monteshino

Restaurante Encontro € *R. de Corujeira 4, Vinhais; tel: (073) 715 05.* No menu, but hearty *feijoadas* and platter-sized steaks at minuscule prices, a few steps from the main street.

Suggested tour

Total distance: 263km; 336km with detours.

Time: 5–6 hours driving. Allow 3 days for the main route, 4 days with detours. Those with limited time should concentrate on Chaves.

Links: From Boticas, head west on the N103 to join the Gerês Mountains route (*see page 180*). The IP4 leads from Murça to Vila Real and the North of the Douro (*see page 132*), while Bragança begins the route exploring the Northeastern Borderlands (*see page 198*).

Route: Head east from **CHAVES ❶** on the N103, passing **Castelo de Montforte** and **Pedra Bolideira** on the newly improved road along a ridge surrounded by green agricultural valleys dotted with red-roofed villages rising to layers of mountains. Just before reaching **Rebordelo**, the road drops down a rocky hillside to skirt the end of a deep ravine. After climbing the other side, it continues to **VINHAIS ❷**.

ⓘ Citânia Curalha R. do Castro, Curalha, turn south, left at 0.3km, park at football pitch and follow footpath 2 minutes.

🍴 Cafetaria Restaurante Royal € Fonte Fernandes, Rebordelo; tel: (076 3 61 76), a lunch stop en route.

🌙 Vidago Palace Hotel €€ Parque de Vidago; tel: (076) 97 37 37, fax (076)90 73 59. A full-service resort hotel replete with belle époque grandeur.

Detour: A left turn from Vinhais leads to the **Serra da Coroa** and the greener western part of **PARQUE NATURAL DE MONTESINHO ❸**. A good circuit, with spur roads leading to more remote villages, leads north to **Moimenta**, west to **Seixas** and south through **Tuizelo** and **Peleias.**

From Vinhais patches of rocky mountainside intersperse with terraced sheep pastures, gardens, and vineyards borrowed from the plunging earth. Chestnut trees line the roads. Outside **Bragança** (see page 192) turn south onto the IP4 to **MIRANDELA ❹**.

Detour: Those not weary of mountain roads can leave Bragança on the N206; the road across the **Serra da Noueira** is often tortuous but the scenery is splendid. In the village of **Bouca**, which has a nice little Romanesque church, turn south onto the 206-1, along a valley to **Mirandela.**

From **MIRANDELA** follow the IP4 to **Murça**, a trimly modern town with a prehistoric pig prominently displayed in its main square. Above is another square with an excellent pelourinho and balconied houses. Murça also has a Roman bridge, still in use.

Turn north on the N212, over an other-worldly landscape of giant stone outcrops along a gently rolling highland, to the N2 in **Vila Pouca de Aguiar** (see page 131). Continue north through the spa towns of **Pedras Salgadas** and **Vidago**. Each has an extensive verdant spa park, the former with fountained gardens, the latter centring around the showy pink Palace Hotel. Just north, turn left (west) on the N311 to **BOTICAS ❺**.

From Boticos drive east 4km to **Sapiãos**, turning right onto the N103. At **Curalha**, stop at **Citânia Curalha**, a particularly good Iron Age hillfort crowned by a single cyprus. Its outer line of walls encloses the entire hilltop, and the square-cornered houses built into the walls suggest it was occupied later than others. Shortly beyond, just before the old Tâmega rail station, is a **slab bridge**, then **CHAVES**.

Hot springs of the Alto Tâmega

Caldas de Chaves is one in a chain of thermal springs caused by a fault line roughly paralleling the River Tâmega. In Chaves, the 70°C soda springs are incorporated into a modern treatment centre for rheumatic complaints and hypertension. Further south along the fault, bicarbonated waters of Vidago and Pedras Salgadas are surrounded by the belle époque elegance of spa parks.

Also worth exploring

The central area enclosed by this route is crossed by several scenic roads, one of which, the N213, shortens the route back to Chaves, returning directly from Mirandela. It crosses over a ridge and winds along a valley rim through **Valpaços**, known for its large rock outcrop with a hole in it, called **Pedra Furada**. Several roads lead off the N213 into the **Serra da Padrela**.

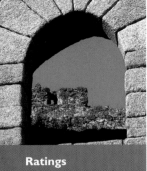

The Northeastern Borderlands

Ratings

Castles	●●●●
Crafts	●●●
Geology	●●●
Historical sights	●●●
Mountains	●●●
Nature	●●●
Scenery	●●●
Villages	●●

Now connected to the rest of Portugal by a motorway, this region whose history has been one of isolation is beginning to see more tourists. But changes are slow, and Bragança still feels like a country town. Landscapes are not as dramatically vertical towards this eastern border, a welcome break for drivers just arriving from the central or northern mountains. The road from Miranda do Douro to Mogadouro is almost level, although the landscape is far from monotonous. This is one area where a loop route is not practical, since the region is not laced with roads and most attractions are spread along a single route. The Northeastern Borderlands route makes a good connecting link between the mountains of the north and the castellated towns to the south. But that does not mean that the traveller should rush through it.

BRAGANÇA✦✦✦

ⓘ Tourist Information Av. Cidade de Zamora; tel: (073) 38 12 73, open Mon–Sat 0900–1230, 1400–1900, Sun 0900–1230.

Castelo and Museu Militar € Cidadela; tel: (073) 223 78, open Fri–Wed 0900–1200, 1400–1700, free Sun am.

Centro Artesanato, a local craft co-operative, is inside the citadel.

Bragança rises from a wide plain hemmed in by mountains, giving glorious scenery in all directions. The well-preserved **Cidadela✦** stands out over a base of uneven tile rooftops that cling to the hill it crowns. In the morning when castle walls loom dark and foreboding over sun-drenched roofs, or the afternoon when the scene is softened with the rosiness of a low sun, the castle is a splendid centrepiece.

Maintained long after its military service was over, the castle never really fell into ruin. This makes it particularly attractive to children (or those of us who are prone to relapse), for around every corner are ramparts to walk, crenellations to peer between, and arrow slits to safely spy from. Instead of hordes of Spanish archers, the view is of rolling green and gold farmlands and forest, or of red roofs and winding streets.

These tiny surrounding houses, part of the old castle town and often built on to its walls, with their backyard gardens, laundry lines, chickens, and flowerpots crammed on to impossibly small doorsteps are a charming study in the use of space.

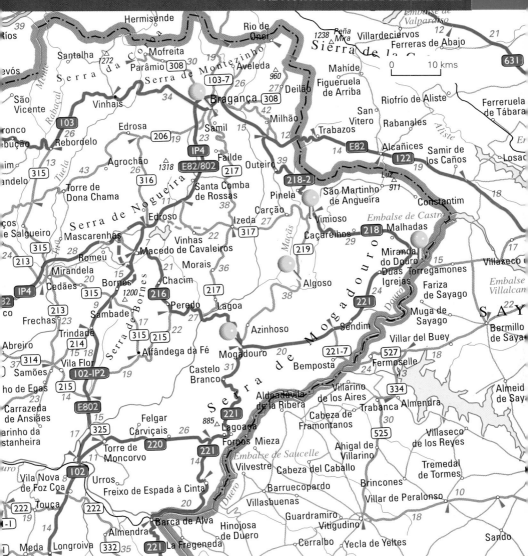

By the castle gate is a prominent example of a regional archaeological mystery – a stone *berrão*, or sow. This one has the shaft of a particularly interesting *pelourinho* through it, and a dented snout.

The baroque Igreja Santa Maria, within the citadel walls, has a remarkable *trompe-l'oeil* of the Assumption, one of the city's many fine painted church ceilings. The polychrome statues are also very good. Opposite stands an exceedingly rare example of a large Romanesque

Museu do Abade de Baçal € R. Abilio Bessa; tel: (073) 33 15 95, open Tue–Fri 1000–1700; Sat–Sun 1000–1800, admission free on Sun and holidays until 1400.

Market day is the 3rd, 12th, and 21st of each month, unless it is a weekend, when the market is the following Monday. For everyday fresh produce, the **Municipal Market**, behind the cathedral, is open in the mornings.

Romaria de Santa Cruz May 3, combines pilgrimage with a song festival; **Romaria de Nossa Senhora das Graças** Aug 12–22 and **Romaria de Nossa Senhora da Serra** Sep 8.

Berrões

Carved stone pigs found throughout the Trás-os-Montes region are of ancient but uncertain origin. These towns were Celtic settlements, and pigs are perhaps connected with the Scottish use of boars to denote kingship. Interestingly, they are always called by the Portuguese word for 'sow' – even those whose maleness is quite evident. Look for others in Murça, Castro de Avelas and as far south as Castelo Mendo (see page 201).

council chamber, this one roofed, and with five unequal walls and carved stone faces of humans and animals supporting its ceiling. This Domus Municipalis, like the tiny ones surviving elsewhere, is over a cistern. To see the interior of this or Igreja Santa Maria ask at any house.

The ceiling of Igreja de São Bento, just outside the walls, is a breath of stylistic fresh air, the Italianate columns and figures on a barrel-arched ceiling contrasting sharply with the baroque of most churches. The much older choir-loft ceiling is reached via stairs in the rear.

Yet another splendid ceiling, in the Igreja São Vicente, has the four evangelists carved into its corners. Long-running rumour holds that it was here that future King Pedro and Inês de Castro were secretly wed, although of course there was no written record because the marriage was forbidden by Pedro's father, King Afonso IV.

Just off the same *largo*, the **Museu do Abade de Baçal*** is an outstanding museum, named after the abbot who wrote an 11-volume historical and archaeological study of the region. Nicely displayed exhibits (labelled in Portuguese) begin with the prehistoric: stone-age tools, early pottery and more pigs. Reminders of the long Roman occupation include funerary artifacts and milestones, all displayed in the former episcopal palace, with art and polychrome statues from its chapels.

Beyond is the Misericórdia, one of the earliest, with a fine Renaissance high altar and good polychromes. To the right is the Igreja de Santa Clara, with another good ceiling. The Sé, which ascended late to the rank of cathedral and was not built for such an august position, is relatively plain, with *azulejos*, and fan tracery in the Gothic roof. Two large polychrome statues stand under a naively exuberant painted ceiling in the sacristy, off a graceful cloister.

South of the N103, about 7km west of Bragança, is Castro de Avelas and its near-ruined 12th-century monastery. Brick walls, very rare in Portugal, and closed Mozarabic arcades make you wonder if you have strayed across the border into Spain.

Accommodation and food in Bragança

Pousada de São Bartolomeu €€ Estrada do Turismo; tel: (073) 33 14 93, fax: (073) 234 53. The modern-style *pousada* offers a fabulous view (from many rooms) of the castle and city. Fellow guests will most likely be Spanish and Portuguese.

Pensão Classis € Av. João da Cruz 102; tel: (073) 33 16 31, fax: (073) 234 58. No-frills, un-folksy, but good, inexpensive lodgings right in town, with breakfast.

Parque de Campismo do Sabor € N103-7 (to Portelo); tel: (073) 33 15 35, fax: (073) 272 52. Pleasant and well-equipped campsite; recent

Above
Bragança

planting has provided more shade. Café, restaurant and small market all used by locals.

O Bolha €–€€ *corner R. da República and R. da Praça ; tel: (073) 232 40.* Excellent pork dishes, like bean and pork stew and marinated pork casserole, prepared with a trained hand.

Principe Negro € *Av. João da Cruz 8; tel: (073) 234 57.* Traditional and regional foods in an ordinary atmosphere.

Restaurante Esplanada € *Av. das Cantarias 82; tel: (073) 31 27 72.* Local specialities, patronised by tourists and locals alike.

Miranda do Douro*

ⓘ Tourist Information *Largo do Menino Jesus da Cartolinha; tel: (073) 411 32, open Mon–Fri 0900–1230, 1400–1730.*

Sé *R. de Dom Turibio Lopes. Open Tue–Sun, closed to visitors during services.* Public conveniences are in the garden behind the cathedral.

Museu Regional da Terra de Miranda € *Praça Dom João III; tel: (073) 411 64, open Tue–Sun 1000–1245, 1430–1745.*

Festa de Santa Bárbara *first Sun after Aug 15.*

Wellington had a better view of the yawning chasm that separates Miranda from its Spanish neighbours (he was slung across it in a basket to reconnoitre during the Peninsular Wars) but the view from the brink is still impressive.

Little remains of the castle, which was destroyed two centuries ago when the powder store exploded inside. The Renaissance **Sé***, which lost its cathedral status less than a decade after the castle blew into oblivion, did not lose its name (at least not locally) nor its grandeur. Inside is an elaborate altarpiece of the Assumption, an impressive carved and gilded organ, and the statue of Menino Jesus da Cartolinha. This Boy Jesus wears a top hat, and devoted local women sew his wardrobe of suits to wear in processions on Dia dos Reis.

To learn more about Miranda's festivals, visit the **Museu Regional da Terra de Miranda***, which has especially interesting collections of rural household and farm tools; a bit like poking about in someone else's grandmother's attic.

Ruins of the bishop's palace behind the cathedral are now a public garden overlooking the Douro gorge and accented by cloister arches. Houses in this old neighbourhood are from the 16th century, some with amusing stonework and gargoyles.

Miranda is a centre for crafts, especially woven woollens, hand-crocheted lace bedspreads and wrought iron work. Several shops sell handwork including the Centro do Artesanato (*off Praça Dom João III*).

Accommodation and food in Miranda do Douro

Pousada de Santa Caterina €–€€ *tel: (073) 410 05, fax: (073) 410 65.* Highlighted by the view of the Douro, deep in the gorge below, the *pousada* has a good dining room and bright spacious rooms.

Pensão Morgadinha € *R. do Mercado 57; tel: (073) 43 80 50, fax: (073) 43 80 51.* Modern, tidy in-town hotel, all rooms with balconies.

Albergaria Restaurante O Mirandes €–€€ *Largo da Moagem (by the municipal swimming pool); tel: (073) 43 28 23.* Dining room with a view, serving traditional and regional specialities. Look for fresh local fish.

Mogadouro*

The keep of a Knights Templars castle built on solid rock is a reminder that most of these border towns began as guard stations. A 15th-century convent church of São Francisco dominates the attractive square, and the later Igreja Matriz has good carved and gilded work. The Miradouro do Santuario de São Cristovão is a scenic spot for a picnic.

ⓘ Turismo *Largo de Santo Cristo; tel: (079) 323 10.*

🍴 Adega Típica do Alves € *Av. Nossa Senhora do Caminho 56; tel: (079) 34 10 12,* serves home-style local food, specialising in fish fillets and *bacalhau* (salt cod).

⚘ Feira dos Gorazes, *Oct 15–16,* is a religious procession and village fair.

Azinhoso, 6km north of Mogadouro, has a 12th-century church, but continue 3km further to Penas Roias, where another tower remains of a ruined medieval castle. The little town clusters around it, with farm buildings built into its walls.

Local crafts include hand-crocheted lace, other needle arts, and leather work.

Right
Mogadouro castle

Accommodation and food in Mogadouro

A Lareira € *Av. Nossa Senhora do Caminho 58; tel: (079) 34 23 63.* French restaurant, an oddity in rural Portugal, but quite good. They also have ten guest-rooms.

VIMIOSO AND ALGOSO✣

🍴 Restaurante Gabriela € *Largo da Praça 28, Sendim.* A rather famous chef presides here, serving up hearthy wood-grilled lunches and dinners, cooked over olive wood in the winter and grape vines in the summer.

Vimioso has more left of its Roman occupation than most towns in the region, with Roman bridges crossing three nearby rivers. Its church, which dominates the sloping main square, is one of the few where the early painting has not been scoured off the chancel stonework; perhaps the two excellent polychrome angels have guarded it.

The Igreja Matriz in Algoso, 15km south, is a treasury of ecclesiastical folk art, with polychrome angels, cherubs and a large bas relief of Christ saving souls from Hell. This primitive masterpiece is complete with leering black demons, and a monk busily pulling grateful little souls from the flames.

Romaria de Nossa Senhora das Graças, *Sendim, Sun before Aug 15*, is a religious procession with accompanying festivities.

Festas São Lourenço *Aug 10, Vimioso*. The local saint's day, with processions and fair tables selling local products and allsorts.

Restaurante Charneca € *R. do Hospital, Largo de São Sebastião, Vimioso; tel: (073) 521 92.* Small restaurant in a *pensão*, a good lunch stop.

In front of stone houses you may see women working on squares, which they assemble into beautiful bedspreads. Although referred to as crochet, they are actually knitted, in pattern stitches using two metal crochet hooks in place of knitting needles. Also look for hand-crocheted lace bedspreads as well as basketwork, copper, and weaving. Perched on a pinnacle south of town, the stone tower of Algoso's **Castelo**✶✶ commands a 360-degree view over the surrounding countryside of almond and olive groves. A track winds down into a deep vale, crossing a tiny Roman bridge almost directly below. On clear days the castle of Azinhoso is visible to the south.

Suggested tour

Total distance: 250km; 304km with detours.

Time: 6 hours driving. Allow 3 days with or without detours. Those with limited time should head directly south from Bragança on the IP4 and IP2 to the fortified towns or follow the more scenic route south through Vimioso and Mogadouro.

Links: Bragança, the starting point for this route, connects with the Northern Mountains (*see page 182*). At the southern end, Mogadouro is 68km north of Torre de Moncorvo, on the route through the fortified towns (*see page 206*).

Route: Leave **BRAGANÇA** ❶ heading east on the N218, toward the Spanish border, branching right (south) on the N218 near **Rio Frio**.

Detour: At **Gimonde** turn left on the N308 into the **Parque Natural de Montesinho**, continuing along the park border past **Babe**, **Caravela** and **Palácios** – each of which has a small rural museum – to **São Julião**. Turn left to **Guadramil**, a village deep in the interior of the park, with traditional stone houses. Return to São Julião and continue south to **Quintanilha**, on the Spanish border, turning right on the N218-1 to rejoin the main route on the N218 in Rio Frio.

Continue south to **Carção**, turning left (east) on to the N317 to **VIMIOSO** ❷.

Detour: Turn right (south) on the N219 to **ALGOSO** ❸ to visit the castle, backtracking to Vimioso.

The N218 continues east to **MIRANDA DO DOURO** ❹, where you head south on the N221, passing through **Sendim** to **MOGADOURO** ❺.

In Mogadouro, the N219 leads north 9km to the castle at **Penas Roias**. From Mogadouro, either continue south on the N221 to join the Fortified Towns route (*see page 206*), or return west via the N216, IP2 and IP4 to Bragança.

Also worth exploring

As you head south from **Mogadouro** on the N221, you pass the N221-6, left, to **Picote** and the **Barragem de Picote**, another of the series of dams that impound the Douro, at the bottom of its dizzyingly deep gorge. All along the N221, you can follow these small roads towards the Douro and its *barragens*, or dams. This area along the river gorge is a wonderland for birders, who may spot or hear as many as 63 species, including nightingales, larks and cuckoos.

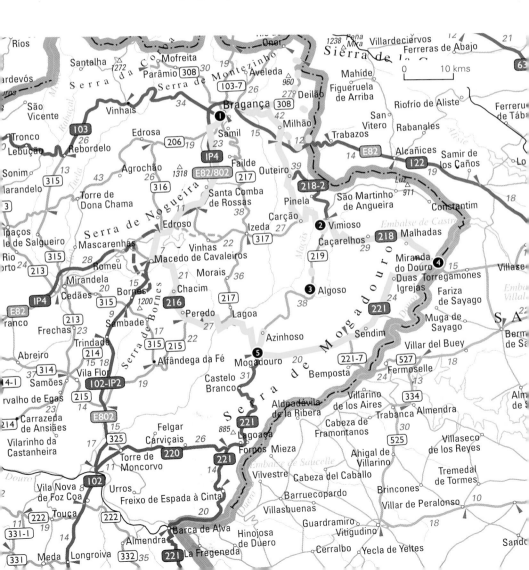

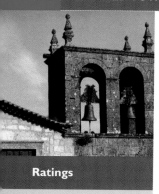

Fortified towns

Ratings

Castles	●●●●●
Historical sights	●●●●
Villages	●●●●
Architecture	●●●
Children	●●●
Mountains	●●●
Scenery	●●●
Geology	●●

The landscape along the border is often a barren rock-strewn one, broken by oases of forest and olive and almond groves in the watered valleys. High points were fortified, many by King Dinis, as watchtowers and military garrisons, at a time when Portugal was trying to assert independence from Castile. Few of the towns that grew around these castles have 'sights' in the traditional sense, although their castles are reason enough for visiting them. They vary enormously, from active and bustling towns inside their walls to abandoned hilltop ghost towns. Although at the end of a day's explorations, you may not remember them all by name, each will stand out in memory as quite different from the others. The town of Guarda, with good restaurants and lodging, makes a convenient base for both the fortified towns and the Serra da Estrela (*see pages 208–19*).

ALMEIDA*

ⓘ Look just outside the town gates for less pricy restaurants.

The only hint of sleepy Almeida's stormy history is in its shape: its six-pointed fortifications are said to have been supervised by Vauban himself. Entered through its sally-port or impressive arched gateways above the wide defensive ditch, the town is compact and tidy. Although it was built to withstand attacks from its Iberian neighbours, it was in fact captured more often by the French; nowadays, however, the only invaders are Spanish tourists. Much of village life takes place in the streets of Almeida which are wider and straighter than in other castellated towns and are lined by a blend of fine and modest homes, some sheathed in tiles.

Accommodation and food in Almeida

Pousada Senhora das Neves €€ *Almeida; tel: (071) 542 83, fax: (071) 543 20.* Its modern construction jars, but its well-appointed rooms command good views. The dining room (€€) offers braised kid and delicious breakfast breads.

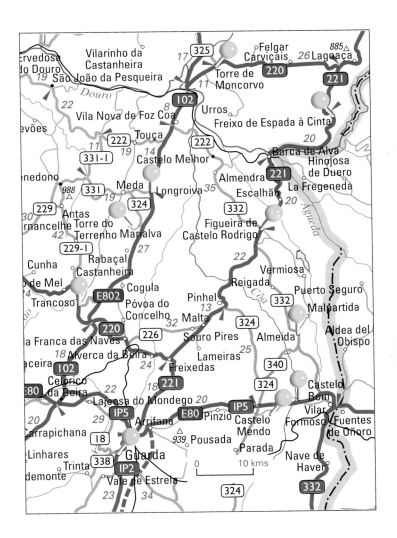

CASTELO BOM AND CASTELO MENDO*

Be sure to take the N16, not the limited access IP5, which has no interchanges near.

Of Castelo Bom's *castelo*, only a fragment of tower and a stretch of wall with an arched gate remain. But the atmosphere of this appealing castellated village makes up for its lack of ramparts. Atop a rocky mound, its old enclosure is still lived in and each house seems to vie for the brightest patio garden.

Castelo Mendo is larger, above a deep rockstrewn ravine. Enter through a gate flanked by truncated towers and a pair of stone pigs.

Homes inside have graceful stone staircases and pillared porches, both usually lined with pots of bright flowers. The *pelourinho* – extraordinarily tall with a stone cage on top – and several good Renaissance buildings border winding stone streets.

Although the town rises sharply from the landscape, its low *castelo* walls encircle a flat top. Wide steps carved into bedrock reach a ruined chapel; inside, the stone font, altar and pulpit stairs are still intact.

CASTELO RODRIGO*

Pensão Figueirense
€ Av. 25 de Abril; tel: (071) 325 17, is not fancy, but comfortable and with a restaurant.

The old town towers over younger Figueira de Castelo Rodrigo, whose 18th-century Igreja Matriz has gold baroque altars and an arch made entirely of interlocked S-shaped stones. The road ascends past a fountain and through a gate in the walls. Inside, stone streets of stone houses cluster around the stone walls and tower of the *castelo*. The best views of the gate and bastions are from the bell tower, which has iron steps clinging to its back.

The abandoned Convento de Santa Maria de Aguiar crumbles beside the road towards Redonda. The cloister is now a farmyard, but owners will show you the once-magnificent church, sadly stripped of its decoration by the accursed Ancient Monuments' Commission. A Manueline door and stone tombs remain, along with a fine vaulted chapter house ceiling.

Above
Castelo Mendo

About 6km further on, after a left turn signposted 'Almofala' is the large and curious Casarão da Torre. Its base is Roman – evidently it was a temple of impressive size – with a somewhat later structure on top.

FREIXO DE ESPADA✧

Romaria da Senhora dos Montes Ermos, Aug 15, is a colourful, low-key religious procession.

Unexpectedly in such a small remote town, the Igreja Matriz resembles a pint-sized Mosteiro dos Jerónimos (*see page 50*), with vaulting, columns and floor-plan similar to the Belém monastery. More impressive still are the painted panels of the altarpiece, thought to be by Grão Vasco. The Torre de Galo, a seven-sided tower, is a relic from the medieval defensive walls. Several stone houses in the village have Manueline embellishments and the *pelourinho* is topped by a stone human head.

The Miradouro Penedo Durão has sweeping valley views, especially beautiful when blooming almond trees paint it white in early spring. Silk goods and crocheted lace bedspreads are local specialities. This is also the place to buy almond-based sweets.

GUARDA✧

Posto Turismo *Praça de Luís Camões;* tel: (071) 22 22 51 open daily 1000–1900. Very helpful staff; ask about walking trail book (€), free restaurant map and illustrated *Roteiro* map of the fortified towns, a good souvenir.

Arriving from any direction, head uphill to Praça Luís de Camões and the Sé.

Not a beautiful city by any account, and often cold and windy, but Guarda does have some fine noble homes overlooking its older hilltop streets. Travellers who wander its atmospheric stone lanes will be rewarded by some very good restaurants, and local hospitality is as warm as the wind is cold.

The massive **Sé**✧, or cathedral (*open daily 0900–1200, 1400–1700*), stands on the uphill side of the arcaded Praça de Luís Camões, making its dark granite magnitude look even taller. It does not, as many guides suggest, look like Batalha (they shared an architect), any more than it looks like Notre Dame just because it has flying buttresses and gargoyles. Although high overhead, these are worth inspection, lightening the cathedral's sobriety, as do grimacing misericords under the choir seats inside. Soaring on clustered and twisted columns, the interior is best known for its four-layer Renaissance altarpiece of carved stone figures. For a gargoyle's-eye view of the city, climb to the roof (ask for access) on stairs to the right of the nave.

The white baroque façade of the Misericórdia faces a narrow *largo*; uphill, the Torre dos Ferreiros is a relic of the old town walls. The **Museu Regional**✧ (€ *open Tue–Sun 1000–1230, 1400–1730, free Sun am*), in the former episcopal palace, has a Renaissance cloister with local folk artifacts and archaeological findings; interesting but not outstanding.

Arte Portuguese *Largo D Manuel Alascão (above the Sé),* has antiques and decorative crafts, including ceramics and Arraiolas rugs. Across the square, opposite the Sé's towers, **Artesanato Junta de Sé** has folk crafts, including baskets. On R. 31 de Janeiro, off Praça de Luís Camões, is another antique shop. On first and third Wednesdays a big market is held below, near the railway station.

Guarda's big fairs are Jun 24 and Oct 4.

The old town merits a wander, especially along the narrow streets below Praça Luís Camões. Only a few inscriptions remain of the old Jewish neighbourhood behind Igreja São Vicente, which has elaborate *azulejo*-lined walls.

In nearby Pêra do Moço, off the N221 to the north, is a dolmen whose thin stones give it an almost fragile air.

Accommodation and food in Guarda

Hotel Turismo €€ *Praça do Municipio; tel: (071) 22 33 66, fax: (071) 22 33 99.* Full-service hotel with a solid reputation, located near the old city centre.

Solar de Alcarção €–€€ *Largo D Manuel Alascão (above the Sé); tel: (071) 21 43 92.* In-town manor house, with its own chapel and a garden; the location is perfect, behind the cathedral, with parking. Owner speaks no English, but radiates hospitality. Ask to see the grand salon's panelled ceiling and the exceptionally fine Arraiolos carpets used as wall hangings.

O Ferrinho € *R Francisco de Passos 21; tel: (071) 21 19 90.* Well-spaced tables are upstairs, where discreet waiters do not hover as you read the menu, which is more interesting than most. Duck is excellent and a steaming bowl of their *caldo verde* will warm you to the toes.

O Montneve € *Praça Luís de Camões 24; tel: (071) 21 27 99, closed Mon.* Another above-average dining room, in a former noble home. Daily specials include kid on Sundays and rich, tasty *feijoada* of beans and meats on Friday. Salmon with river clams is outstanding. The attached *pastelaria* is a good breakfast stop.

A Floresta € *R Francisco de Passos 40; tel: (071) 21 23 62, closed Mon.* More modest but good, serving traditional regional dishes, with very inexpensive daily 'student plate'.

Frigata € *R 31 de Janeiro,* filled with local families. Grilled trout and roast suckling pig are on the menu, available in English.

MARIALVA AND LONGROIVA✦✦✦

To reach **Marialva's castle**, drive to the far end of town and head upward, bearing left.

.

The medieval equivalent of a Celtic hillfort, Marialva is deserted, romantic in ruin, a place to commune with ghosts of ages past. At the top of a granite town, an entire stone village enclosed by 12th-century castle walls lies roofless and empty. Once-fine homes are carpeted with grass, birds fly through arched doors and windows. In the centre a stone fountain still runs, used by black-shawled women preparing for Holy Week processions. These begin at the only remaining buildings

➔ **Longroiva's castle** is clearly visible and easy to aim for. Park behind the church.

🍴 **O Marquês €** *below the castle, Marialva*, is a cheery café with outdoor tables and light lunch dishes.

with roofs, the chapels at the upper end of the village. The Rua Direita, stone-paved in a pattern, leads from the open gate to the keep, a square tower guarding the highest corner. A 15th-century *pelourinho* and Manueline doorway on the church seem modern.

Longroiva, which has only a single square keep in its castle walls, is built on rocks that drop straight down into the valley. Beside it is a sleepy, white-washed stone village whose inhabitants tend narrow terraced gardens on the steep slope below.

TORRE DE MONCORVO❖

ⓘ **Tourist Information**, R *Manuel Seixas; tel: (079) 25 22 89; fax: (079) 25 27 28.*

A hill town surrounded by orchards on the northern slope of the Serra do Reboredo, Moncorvo has two good Renaissance churches: the Misericórdia with a 16th-century carved choir, and the Igreja Matriz, begun in 1544, with a carved and polychromed Gothic triptych. The narrow streets wind past several early houses with escutcheons above their doors. On Aug 15 there is a procession and local celebration of the Romaria de Nossa Senhora da Assunção.

TRANCOSO❖❖

King Dinis, the 13th-century monarch responsible for building so many of Portugal's border castles, chose Trancoso for his wedding to Isabel of Aragon. She was enchanted when townspeople covered the streets in rose petals for her. Still gracious and welcoming, the old town is wrapped in original walls with picket-fence merlons; the battlements have 15 turrets and four gates, which you can inspect from a street

Above
Longroiva

ⓘ Turismo de Trancoso Largo Santa Maria de Guimarães; tel: (071) 81 11 47. Parking is outside the castle gate.

ⓘ Restaurante O Museu € Largo Santa Maria de Guimarães; tel: (071) 81 18 10. Tidy and somewhat up-market for the area, with a good menu specialising in seafood.

Restaurante São Marcos € Largo Luís Albuquerque; tel: (071) 81 13 26. Plain, local cooking in low-key setting.

ⓒ Pensão Brasilia € N220, Torre de Moncorvo, Torre de Moncorvo; tel: (079) 224 94. Pleasant lodgings in a modern building, easy to find.

around their perimeter. Inside the **castle*** (open 0930–1230, 1400–1730; if closed, the key is at the Posta da Guarda Nacional) is a ruined chapel, its stones yellow with lichens.

Of the large Judiaria, there remains Casa do Gato Preto, near the Misericórdia, in front of which stands a Manueline pelourinho. Casa dos Arcos, a 16th-century arcaded building, marks another side of the square and the Palácio Ducal faces a garden at the far end. Just outside the walls, at Portas do Prado, medieval sepulchres are carved into bedrock in startlingly human shapes.

Suggested tour

Total distance: 290km; 339km with detours.

Time: 6 hours driving. Allow 3 days for the main route, 4 days with detours. Those with limited time should concentrate on Marialva and Trancoso.

Links: Guarda is 75km from Viseu via the IP5; a closer link to the South of the Douro route (see page 122) is between Trancoso and Aguiar de Beira. The Northeastern Borderlands route (see page 198) is near the intersection of the N220 and N221, east of Torre de Moncorvo. The Serra da Estrela Route (see page 216) also begins in Guarda.

Route: From **GUARDA** ❶ take the IP5 east to **Vilar Formosa**, backtracking on the N16 to

CASTELO MENDO ❷ and **CASTELO BOM** ❸. Head north on the N332 to **ALMEIDA** ❹.

Detour: For a challenging scenic drive, follow the N340 west from Almeida, turning right (north) on the N324 to **Pinhel**. From here, the N221 heads north over what is locally called the 'excommunicated' or 'cursed' road through the narrow **Coa Valley** and over **Serra Marofa**, which rises to over 3 000 feet before descending to the green landscape of **CASTELO RODRIGO** ❺.

From **ALMEIDA** go north on the N332 to Castelo Rodrigo, then on the N221 to **FREIXO DE ESPADA A CINTA** ❻. The N221 continues north to a junction with views of Douro near **Fornos**; turn left (west) onto the N220 towards **TORRE DE MONCORVO** ❼.

Turn left (south) again when the N220 meets the N102, shortly beyond, passing **Vila Nova Pascoa**. Detour right, 17km south, to **LONGROIVA** ❽ and, 8km further south, to **MARIALVA** ❾. Later, the N226 turns west to **TRANCOSO** ❿.

Detour: From **Longroiva**, continue west through **Meda** and **Ranhados** to **Penedono**, where the lovely small triangular **castle**** has sweeping views of the Serra da Estrella. Follow the N229-1 south to Trancoso.

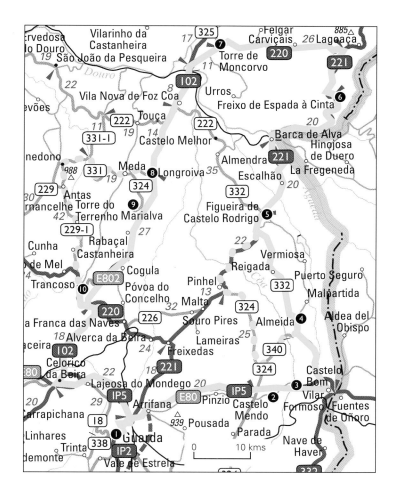

Parque Arqueológico do Vale do Coa €–€€
Castelo Melhor; tel: (079) 733 44, fax: (079) 76 52 57.

The N102 carries on south into **Celorica de Beira**, from which the IP5 returns to Guarda.

Also worth exploring

The Coa Valley made headlines in 1996 when the discovery of outstanding Palaeolithic drawings stopped construction of a major hydroelectric dam. The easiest approach to this remote site is through **Castelo Melhor**, south on the N332 from Vila Nova de Foz Coa. Access is controlled, and in high season you must reserve two months in advance. Jeep trips to **Penascosa** take under two hours, leaving from the reserve headquarters.

The Serra da Estrela

Ratings

Mountains	●●●●●
Scenery	●●●●○
Castles	●●●●○
Geology	●●●●○
Outdoor activities	●●●●○
Historical sights	●●●○○
Nature	●●●○○
Walking	●●●○○

The mountain range, including its towns, is inside the boundaries of the Parque Natural Serra da Estrela. In its centre, Torre, the highest mountain in Portugal, rises over a landscape sculpted by glaciers and scattered with boulders dropped from their melting ice. Its higher slopes are alpine in environment, the lower slopes terraced for farming. The park's well-marked system of trails is rare in Portugal, but few hikers use them, so even in high season they will be uncrowded. But do not expect solitude on the roads, especially not across Torre on weekends. And, of course, expect tortuous roads clinging to the steep mountainsides, climbing in long series of switch-back loops. In reward, however, you can look forward to some of Portugal's finest wines, since this is the home of the velvety and aromatic Dão.

BELMONTE❖❖

ℹ️ **Turismo** *Praça da República; tel: (075) 91 14 18.*

🖐️ An English-speaking teacher organises horse-riding tours at **Parque Equestre**, *Quinta de Santo António do Rio, Terlamente; tel: (075) 92 18 94.*

🛍️ Several *artesanatos* face Praça da República.

The keep and walls of **Castelo de Belmonte**❖ (*open daily 1000–1230, 1400–1700*) are of gold-coloured stone, with an early Manueline window. The parents of explorer Pedro Alvares Cabral, who was born here, are buried in the adjoining **Capela de Saõ Tiago**❖ (*open daily 1000–1230, 1400–1700*), of Romanesque origin with a free-standing bell tower. Inside are stone carvings and a fine polychrome granite pietà from the 13th century.

Just north, Centum Cellas is a striking three-storey stone Roman building. Recently excavated lower storeys are well preserved, but the third, which was not buried, shows signs of later use; upper courses of stone are missing and window openings are coarsely filled with stone. Carved cornices show some sophistication. From the unexcavated west wall you can see how the lower part filled in over the years, leaving only upper walls exposed.

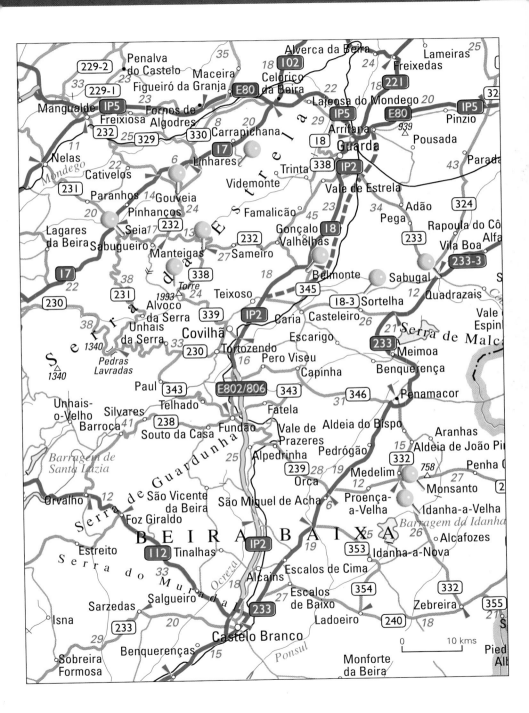

Penalva do Castelo
229-2
Maceira
Celorico da Beira
102
Alverca da Beira
Lameiras
Freixedas
229-1
Figueiró da Granja
E80
221
Fornos de
Mangualde
IP5
Algodres
Carrapichana
Lajeosa do Mondego
IP5
E80
IP5
Freixiosa
Arriana
Pinzio
232
329
330
17
Linhares
18
Guarda
Pousada
Nelas
Cativelos
Trinta
338
IP2
Parada
231
Paranhos
Gouveia
Videmonte
Vale de Estrela
Pinhanços
232
Famalicão
Adão
324
Lagares da Beira
Seia
232
Gonçalo
18
Pega
Rapoula do Cô
233
Sabugueiro
232
Valhelhas
Vila Boa
Alfa
Manteigas
Sameiro
233-3
17
338
Belmonte
Sabugal
230
231
Torre
Teixoso
345
Quadrazais
Alvoco da Serra
339
18-3
Sortelha
Vale Espin
Unhais da Serra
IP2
Caria
Casteleiro
Serra de Malc
Covilhã
Escarigo
233
Pedras Lavradas
Tortozendo
Pero Viseu
Meimoa
Capinha
Benquerença
Paul
343
E802/806
343
346
Penamacor
Unhais-o-Velho
Silvares
Telhado
Fatela
Barroca
238
Fundão
Vale de Prazeres
Aldeia do Bispo
Aranhas
Souto da Casa
Pedrógão
Aldeia de João Pi
Barragem de Santa Luzia
Alpedrinha
332
Penha
239
Medelim
Monsanto
Orca
Proença-a-Velha
Orvalho
São Vicente da Beira
São Miguel de Acha
Idanha-a-Velha
Foz Giraldo
Barragem da Idanha
BEIRA BAIXA
Alcafozes
Estreito
112
Tinalhas
IP2
353
Idanha-a-Nova
Serra do Mura
Escalos de Cima
Salgueiro
Alcains
354
332
Sarzedas
Escalos de Baixo
Zebreira
355
Isna
233
Ladoeiro
240
Castelo Branco
Sobreira Formosa
Benquerenças
Monforte da Beira
Pied

0   10 kms

Accommodation and food in Belmonte

Hotel-Restaurant Belsol € *N18, Quinta do Rio; tel: (075) 91 22 06; fax: (075) 91 23 15, e-mail; hotelbelsol@mail.telepac.pt.* Modern with full facilities, including pool, children's pool, playground and restaurant.

Quinta de Santo António do Rio € *Terlamente; tel: (075) 92 18 94*, has tent pitches and a rustic guest house accessible along a 600-metre footpath. Meals are served at the farmhouse.

GOUVEIA*

ⓘ Turismo *Jardim Lopes da Costa; tel: (038) 421 85.*

🍷 Adega Co-operativa de São Paio *São Paio; tel: (038) 421 01* takes reservations for tours and wine tastings.

⬤ Market day is Thursday, although the municipal market, *Av. Bombeiros*, is open daily. **Supermercato**, *R. da República*, has a good selection of dried fruits and foods for hikers and campers.

A town with a sense of humour, Gouveia goes to great pains to please children. Next to its town hall is a charming children's garden with hedges trimmed in animal-shaped topiaries. A cat's arched back forms a boxwood gate, a green elephant supervises the roundabouts and oversized leafy lizards laze along hedges. Benches abound and picnic tables fill shady corners.

A more adult garden is just opposite, a cool, atmospheric outdoor museum of millstones, capitals and architectural stonework rescued from demolished churches. Birds bathe in a water-filled tomb and a mossy Romanesque pulpit stands on a pillar in a stairway, blue myrtle blooming behind it. Flowerbeds are shaded by giant cedars and alive with songbirds.

Part of the **Museu de Arte Sacra e Etnológico*** (*open Thur–Tue 0930–1230, 1400–1730*), which fills the surrounding stone buildings with an interesting miscellany, the garden is always open. Inside the adjacent former Jesuit College, now the Town Hall, are excellent modern bas-relief stone panels, including a scene of sheep with a Serra da Estrela dog.

Up the hill, the **Museu de Abel Manta*** (*Praça São Pedro, open daily 1000–1800*), in a fine old home, has a gallery of this Portuguese artist's paintings as well as changing exhibits. Below, the only level place in town is Praça de São Pedro, filled with café tables and bordered by the blue and white tiled façades of two churches.

Across the N17, 4km away in Rio Torto, a vine-draped Roman bridge and a section of Roman road are still in use. Also in Rio Torto, a lane leaves the N17 to Ante do Pedro da Orca, a large dolmen with four support stones on each side and an almost square capstone.

Accommodation and food in Gouveia

Casa Grande € *Paços da Serra (7.5km northwest of Gouveia off N232); tel: (038) 49 63 41.* Behind a stately façade are two rooms and three apartments, humbly appealing. Exposed stone walls, local pottery, and rustic detailing.

Right
The children's garden
in Gouveia

Hotel de Gouveia € *Av. 1º de Maio; tel: (038) 94 10 10, fax: (038) 413 70.* Functional modern hotel, with a few more comforts than smaller lodgings, if less charm. Convenient in-town location.

Parque Campismo Curral do Negro € *3km east of town on the way to Folgosinho; tel: (038) 49 10 08.* Campsite with pool, restaurant and free showers.

Pensão Estrela € *R. da República 36; tel: (038) 421 71.* Pleasant restaurant serving just what you'd expect – roasted meats, local wines.

LINHARES✧✧✧

Café Linharense €
R. da Igreja, below castle, offers *petiscos* for lunch

Behind the church near the castle is an *artesanato*.

Unlike most castle towns, the approach to the **castelo**✧ (*open daily 0930–1200, 1400–1730*) in Linhares is not a vertical climb. Wooden walkways over the mounds of bedrock inside the walls lead to a lower terrace and ramparts with fine views. This is a rare castle with safety railings, reassuring to those with children.

Linhares is not undiscovered, but not self-conscious; women wash laundry in the icy waters of the town fountain, while bedding airs from medieval balconies. The castle is the goal of most visitors, who ignore the beauties of the little 12th-century town and its narrow stone streets.

The ruined Ducal Palace faces the Misericórdia, its massive chimney overlooking roofless moss-grown walls, stairs rising grandly from its grass-filled foyer to a landing empty but for wild flowers growing between its stones. You can wander in to explore. On Rua Direita a tiny open Romanesque council chamber has a well underneath.

MANTEIGAS*

ⓘ Tourist Information R. Dr Esteves de Carvalho; tel: (075) 98 11 29, open Tue–Sat 0930–1200, 1400–1800, to 2000 on Sat. Not very helpful.

Parque Natural Serra da Estrela R. 1 de Maio; tel: (075) 98 23 82, fax: (075) 98 23 84, is much more helpful.

The most central base for hiking and exploring, Manteigas sprawls beneath mountains. Caldas de Manteigas has two springs, one warm (42ºC) and one cold, rich in sulphur and sodium. A spa hotel completes the settlement. To its south the Vale Glaciario do Zêzere, the largest glacial valley in Europe, is equally scenic with mountains rising like sides of a bowl.

Poço do Inferno, 6km from Caldas along a rough lane, is a wooded gorge with a waterfall, at the geological junction of two rock types, schist on one side, granite on the other. The name translates to 'Hell's Well' and you may agree, as you wade through weekend picnic debris.

Hiking is the main attraction, with several day-hike options, including the walk (8 hours return) to Nave de Santo António, up the Zêzere River through the glacial valley. The friendly park office sells maps and can suggest routes.

Between hikes, visit farmhouse cheesemakers, a kennel breeding Serra da Estrela dogs, or a **trout farm*** (open 0900–1100, 1400–1700) near the bridge over the Zêzere at Caldas, where you will see thatched stone cottages.

Accommodation and food in Manteigas

Pousada de São Lourenço €€ Parque Natural Serra da Estrela, 13km north of Manteigas; tel: (075) 98 24 50, fax: (075) 98 24 53. Well situated for walkers, mountain goats and travellers who like waking to glorious views, the pousada is atop one of Portugal's most tortuous roads. Don't even think about driving here after dark.

Albegaria Berne € Quinta de Santo António; tel: (075) 98 13 51, fax: (075) 98 21 14. Large and modern, but blends well with the setting. Basic amenities, including a pleasant restaurant.

Casa de São Roque € R. de Santo António 67; tel: (075) 98 11 25. Lovely house with graceful interior, bright colours, all immaculately maintained. Rooms with and without baths fit everyone's budgets. Breakfast in an elegant dining room.

O Abrigo € B Alardo tel: (075) 98 12 71. Hearty regional red wines and preserved meats are specialities.

MONSANTO AND IDANHA-A-VELHA✢✢

🛈 **Turismo de Monsanto** *open Tue–Fri 1000–1300, 1400–1800, Sat–Sun 1000–1800.*

🅿 Park along the road below the stone walls; there is hardly any parking inside and you may find yourself backing out of narrow streets.

🌙 **Pousada de Monsanto €–€€** *Medelim, tel: (077) 344 71, fax: (077) 344 81.* Not grand, in a simple stone building and overlooking a stone church, it's the only act in town.

Monsanto comes into view as a stark ragged granite crag protruding out of a flat, olive-leaf-coloured landscape. Reactions vary widely, depending on whether the traveller arrives on an off-season weekday, when the streets are deserted, or an April weekend when the approach road is clogged and residents pose winsomely on stone doorsteps practising their quaint folkways.

Try for the former, when Monsanto, despite a bit of tarting up, looks medieval and you can climb its steep stone streets in peace. Built into the almost vertical side of the rocky mount, its houses are wedged between, under and on top of giant boulders. Igloo-shaped stone pigpens and metre-square gardens are tucked into the scant space remaining. Above, a ruined castelo has wild flowers rooted between its stones, a glorious site for a picnic. On May 3 each year, the Festa de Cruzes colourfully recalls a medieval siege with flowers thrown from the castle.

Built in the final years of the Roman Republic, Idanha-a-Velha was designed as an administrative and economic centre for the region, an important, prosperous and highly cultured city, with two temples, wineries and educated citizens.

The tower was built by the Knights Templar on a Roman base. Inside the 16th-century church, excavated stones represent Roman and later periods; near the door are tombs carved into rock. One section of the town wall is equipped with walkways and near the tower a Roman road leads through an original arch. Amid these antiquities is a somewhat newer village, the balconies of its manor house carved like woven stone.

Right
Monsanto

SABUGAL AND SORTELHA✧✧

Turismo *Castelo;*
open Mon, Thu, Fri
0930–1300, 1400–1730,
Sat–Sun 0930–1300,
1400–1700.

Castelo de Sabugal,
open Mon, Thu, Fri
0930–1300, 1400–1730,
Sat–Sun 0930–1300,
1400–1700. See photos of
castle rehabilitation in the
office and ask for free
history of castle in English.

If possible, drive
through Sortelha's
impressive gate and head
uphill, parking at the top
outside the other gate. To
leave, drive down the
steep lane straight ahead.

Sortelha's annual fair
on Aug 15, fills the
town with singing and
dancing; in some years
bulls run through the
cobbled streets, Pamplona
style, but more
picturesque (and best seen
from an upper-storey
perch).

Castelo de Sabugal✧ is well-restored and popular with children because of the balcony in the main tower, which has holes in its stone floor for pouring boiling oil on entering attackers. The view from the top of this 30-metre pentagonal tower of granite and schist is over a panorama of fields and mountains. Below, Ponte de Sequeiros, a medieval stone bridge, crosses the River Coa.

Sortelha is a more dramatic walled town, its well-preserved walls hanging over steep slopes. The castle stands a bit aloof on a separate crag from the rest, as though posing for pictures. The square keep towers over encircling walls.

Climb to the top of town, near the bell tower to look down on the tidy houses with tiny back gardens, dotted by olive trees. A fine *pelourinho* stands in the lower square. Despite its air of prosperity, Sortelha retains its medieval atmosphere, especially in the evening, when people return from fields below, and the smoke of cooking fires drifts among its stones.

Antique and *artesanato* shops in Sortelha include O Ferrolho, outside the town walls, and Arcas Velhas, in the old town. Local crafts to look for are woollen tapestry rugs and woven baskets. Just east of Sortelha, Quinta da Corredoura sells delicious Queijo da Ovelha, a tangy white cheese, and will invite you into the kitchen, past their big Serra da Estrela dog, to see it made.

Right
Sortelha

Accommodation and food in Sabugal and Sortelha

Casa do Pateo €–€€ *Sortelha; tel: (071) 681 13, fax: (071) 685 00*. Little granite house in the village comes furnished with ornate wooden chairs, an imposing old hearth and a stone stoop to sit on. Perfect for families, it sleeps 4.

Casas do Campanario € *R. Mesquita, Sortelha; tel: (071) 38 81 98*. Granite blocks form the centuries-old walls which are hung with local pottery.

Café Santiago € *Largo Santiago (off Praça da República), Sabugal, closed Sun*, is a good lunch stop, just outside the gate.

O Alburoque, *R. Mesquita, Sortelha; tel: (071) 681 29, closed Mon*, wild boar in an atmospheric setting in the old town.

Bar do Campanario, *R. Mequita, Sortelha; tel: (071) 38 81 98*, on a terrace under the bell tower, with best view in town, and good sandwiches of local ham.

SEIA AND TORRES✦✦✦

Turismo *R. do Mercado; tel: (038) 222 72.*

As well as normal-sized wine barrels, local coopers make miniatures, along with sturdy little stave tubs.

Senorha de Desterro, *29 June, 15 Sept* pilgrimages; **Nossa Senhora da Estrela**, procession *second Sun Aug*.

Set into a landscape of sculptured green terraces rising up the mountainsides like stairs, everything in Seia is on a slant.

Outside neighbouring São Romão, Senhora do Desterro is a cluster of little white chapels around a river, where you can picnic in the shade. A path leads from the sanctuary to Cabeça da Velha, a huge stone eroded into the profile of an old woman.

Two routes leave Seia to cross the Serra's highest point, just under the summit of Torre. Either one is uphill all the way. Snowbanks at the top may be higher than your car in April, and at weekends in spring families drive here to build snowmen that line the road by late afternoon. Three ski-lifts have made the area a winter sports centre. In 1817, King João VI ordered a 7-metre tower built on the 1993-metre Torre summit, so Portugal would have a 2 000-metre elevation.

Mountain weather can change abruptly, making driving hazardous, so avoid the Torres road unless the weather is good; when hiking, be prepared for rain and sudden drops in temperature. You can also expect traffic jams near the top of the pass at Torres. They are good natured slow-downs, but can delay you an hour or two on a sunny Sunday afternoon, even in April.

East of the summit, the land drops sharply through craggy rock pillars; into one has been carved the modern bas-relief image of Nossa Senhora da Estrela. Penhas da Saude, a former health resort below, now has holidays chalets sprouting incongruously from its rocky slopes.

Accommodation and food in Seia and Torres

Quinta do Crestelo €–€€ *tel: (038) 252 00, fax: (038) 31 11 11.* A new resort with fresh, modern rooms and rustic décor. Sports facilities and, in a land of meat, a restaurant that actually grills vegetables. The menu ranges from local grilled trout to beef with mushrooms.

Casa das Tilias €–€€ *São Romão (2km south of Seia); tel: (038) 39 00 55, fax: (038) 39 01 23.* Near the Senhora de Desterro shrine, and surrounded by the fresh mountain air, this 19th-century manor house nestles into a lush green setting, with a large pool.

Suggested tour

Turismo *Alameda da Liberdade, Castelo Branco; tel: (072) 210 02, fax: (072) 33 03 24, open Mon–Fri 0900–1230, 1400–1730.*

Total distance: 430km; 472km with detours.

Time: 8–9 hours driving. Allow 4 days for the main route, 5 days with detours. Those with limited time should concentrate on Linhares, Sabugal and Sortelha, and the Seia–Torres road.

Links: IP2 continues south from Castelo Branco, connecting to the N18 and the Lower Alentejo route (*see page 244*). Guarda is also the base for the Fortified Towns route (*see page 206*).

Route: Leave **GUARDA** ❶ on the IP5 west to exit N17 signposted Gouveia and turn right. About 100 metres further on, go left, then right (both poorly signposted). The road is straight, through farmlands. After some 9km, turn left to **LINHARES** ❷. Surprisingly, a layby is conveniently placed for photographing the twin towers of the castle, ahead. Continue on the same unnumbered road, turning left back onto the N17 at Carrapichana. Make a 5km diversion left to **GOUVEIA** ❸.

Detour: From Gouveia, head up the mountains on the N232 to **MANTEIGAS** ❹ over a twisty road, past **Cabeça do Velho**, a rock profile of a toothless old man. This route is known as the most hair-raising in Portugal, especially as it drops almost straight into Manteigas, covering 4km of linear distance on 17km of twisting road with vertical drops on one side.

Head west on the N17, past the **Solar da Familia Sacadura Botte**, on the left, a manor house with a chapel and a boxwood garden with flowerbeds surrounded by a stone pergola and shaded by camellia trees. Almost immediately after is the left turn to **SEIA** ❺.

From Praça Misericórdia in Seia follow signs to *Coimbra via São Romão*, and from the centre of **São Romão** follow signs left to **Senhora de Desterro**, crossing the bridge and bearing left along the river. The road begins to climb in earnest after the shrine, winding through

Vouga 323 · 2 · 229 · Troncoso · Povoa do Concelho · 13 · 39
220 · 32 · Malta · 324 · 332
Penalva · do Castelo · 35 · Alverca da Beira · Lameiras · 25
229-2 · Maceira · 18 · 102 · 24 · Freixedas · 340
33 · 229-1 · Figueiró da Granja · Celorico · 22 · 18 · 221
23 · Fornos de · da Beira · E80 · Lajeosa do Mondego · 20 · 324 · 16
Mangualde · IP5 · Algodres · IP5 · E80 · IP5
Freixiosa · 8 · 20 · 29 · Arrifana · 939 · Pinzio
232 · 25 · 329 · 330 · Carrapichana · △ · Pousada
Nelas · Mondego · 6 · Linhares · 2 · Trinta · 338 · 1 · IP2 · 43 · Parada
11 · 22 · 17
Cativelos · Videmonte · Vale de Estrela
231 · Paranhos · 14 · Gouveia · Famalicão · 45 · 23 · 34 · Adão · 324
20 · Pinhanços · 24 · Pega
Lagares · Seia · 17 · 232 · 13 · Gonçalo · 18 · Rapoula do Côa
da Beira · Sabugueiro · 232 · Valhelhas · 233 · Vila Boa · Alfaiates
Manteigas · 4 · 27 · Sameiro · 233-3
17 · 6 · 338 · 18 · 7 · Belmonte · Sabugal · 10 · Souto
22 · Torre · Teixoso · 345 · 11 · 12 · Quadrazais
230 · 231 · 1993 · 24 · 18-3 · Sortelha · Vale de
38 · Alvoco · da Serra · 339 · IP2 · Caria · Casteleiro · 26 · 21 · Espinho
Unhais · Covilhã · Escarigo · Serra de Malcata
da Serra · 33 · 230 · Tortozendo · 233 · Meimoa
S · 1340 · Pedras · 16 · Pero Viseu · Benquerença
△ · Lavradas · Capinha
1340
Paul · 343 · E802/806 · 343 · 346 · 31 · Penamacor
Unhais- · Silvares · Telhado · Fatela
o-Velho · Barroca · 41 · 238 · Fundão · Vale de · Aldeia do Bispo · Aranhas
Souto da Casa · Prazeres · Pedrógão · 15 · Aldeia de João Pires
Barragem de · 25 · Alpedrinha · 332 · Penha Garcia
Santa Luzia · de Guardunha · 239 · 28 · 19 · Medelim · 758 · 27
Orca · 12 · △ · 239
Urvalho · 12 · São Vicente · São Miguel de Acha · 6 · Proença- · 8 · Monsanto
da Beira · 9 · a-Velha · 9 · Idanha-a-Velha
Foz Giraldo · Barragem da Idanha
B E I R A · B A I X A · 26 · Alcafozes
Estreito · 112 · Tinalhas · 19 · 353 · Idanha-a-Nova · 240
Serra · do · 33 · Escalos de Cima · 29
Muradal · 18 · Alcains · Escalos · 354 · 332 · Zebreira · 355
Sarzedas · Salgueiro · 27 · de Baixo · 21
Isna · 233 · 233 · Ladoeiro · 240 · 18 · Segura
29 · Castelo Branco · 0 · 10 kms · Piedras
Sobreira · Benquerenças · 15 · Ponsul · Monforte · Albas

Adruse *Largo do Mercado, Gouveia; tel: (038) 49 11 23, fax ; (038) 402 50,* dedicated to preserving the mountain villages' way of life, acts as clearing house for village lodgings, as well as promoting crafts and organising hiking trips.

Praça Velha €€ *Largo Luís de Camões 17; tel: (072) 32 86 40.* Fine quality cooking well worth the price. Rusticated interior, locally inspired menu.

Three traditional farms offer tent pitches, lodging and meals near Paul: **Quinta dos Penesinhos**; *tel: (075) 96 21 38,* **Quinta da Cava**, *tel: (075) 96 13 43* and **Quinta das Boochas**, *Taliscos; tel: (075) 96 14 11.*

increasingly rocky terrain until it meets the N339, where you turn right. Continue climbing past the dam and **Lago Comprida**, through precipitous boulder fields to a windswept shoulder just below the summit of **TORRE ❻**.

After the road begins to drop through jagged rocks, turn left on the N358 and continue descending to the River Zêzere, enjoying 10km of almost straight, level road through a valley whose rounded sides clearly show its glacial origins, to **Caldas de Manteigas** and **MANTEIGAS**.

Follow the N232 to **BELMONTE ❼**, turning right (south) on the N18/IP2 to **Fundão**. Stay on the N18 south over a scenic, but winding route, and turn left (east) on the N239 in Vale de Prazeres.

Detour: Continue past Fundão, taking the IP5 to **Castelo Branco**, whose outstanding attraction is the garden of the **Antigo Paço Episcopal✦** (€ *R. Frei Bartolomeu da Costa; tel: (072) 210 02, open daily 0900–1900, opens 0800 at weekends*). Terraces of sculptured boxwood frame statues of allegorical, religious and historical figures, including a stairway of Portuguese kings. Pools, fountains, tiled walls and patterned flowerbeds make this unlike any other garden. The palace itself houses the **Museu Francisco Tavares Proença✦** (€ *R. Frei Bartolomeu da Costa; tel: (072) 242 77, open Tues–Sun 1000–1200, 1430–1700*) whose collections progress from archaeological relics and ecclesiastical art through local embroidery and modern painting. Call first, as the museum has been under renovation. Opposite, the **Misericórdia** has its own museum of sacred art (**Museu de Arte Sacra✦** *tel: (072) 244 54, ext 57, open Mon–Fri 0900–1200, 1400–1800*).

Head north from **Castelo Branco** on the N233 to the N239, turning right (east) at **São Miguel de Acha** and rejoining the main route.

Right
Castelo Branco:
the Bishop's Garden

Right
Monsanto

For information

Parque Natural Serra da Estrela, Praça da República, Seia; tel: (038) 255 06, fax: (038) 256 06 and Av. Bombeiros, Gouveia; tel: (038) 424 11, open Mon–Fri 0900–1230, 1400–1700.

Region de Turismo Av. Frei Heitor Pinto, Apt 438, Covilhã; tel: (075) 31 95 60, fax: (075) 31 95 69, e-mail: turismo.estrela@mail.tele pac.port

Emergencies tel: (0931) 451 75 87 or (075) 31 54 76.

Continue east through São Miguel de Acha, **Provença-a-Velha**, where people sit in front of their houses with their feet in the narrow roadway, and **Medelim** to **MONSANTO** ❽. Return to Medelim and turn left (south) on the N332 to **IDANHA-A-VELHA** ❾.

Head north on the N332, through **Penamacor**, where the remnants of a castle stand on a steep ledge over terraced gardens. Just outside the castle gate is a *pelourinho* and the **Misericórdia**✳ (*open Mon–Sat 0900–1700*), with a Manueline door and good gilt carving.

In **Meimoa**, where the road widens into the village square, there is a 9-arch **Roman bridge** to the left. Donkey carts are a common sight on the roads here. The N233 heads north to **SABUGAL** ❿, west of which is **SORTELHA** ⓫. Further north still, the N233 continues to Guarda.

Also worth exploring

South of Seia, the N231 winds up and down over the mountains and through Loriga to the southern border of the park. The N230 then heads east, and south of it is Paul, with a renovated watermill and a folklife museum. A cultural festival is held here during the second week in August.

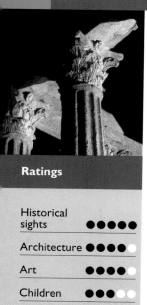

Evora

Ratings

Historical sights	●●●●●
Architecture	●●●●○
Art	●●●●○
Children	●●●○○
Museums	●●●○○
Food and drink	●●○○○
Walking	●●○○○
Outdoor activities	●○○○○

E vora is a rarity, a city still essentially contained within its historic walls. Celts inhabited the spot before the Romans came in 59 BC. The Romans lost it to the Moors in 715, who in turn lost it to Christians in 1165. Compact, and without steep hills, it is an easy city to explore on foot, which is handy, since driving inside its walls is nearly impossible. The treasures of the city cover nearly two millennia, and the nearby megaliths reach back even farther, into the mists of prehistory. Like the smaller Alentejo towns around it, Evora is largely whitewashed, giving a Moorish flavour to some of its streets. But its architecture has more substantive remains of its other inhabitants, including one of Iberia's best-preserved Roman temples and an outstanding early Renaissance church façade.

Getting there and getting around

Turismo *Praça do Giraldo 73; tel: (066) 226 71. Open Mon–Fri 0900–1900 and Sat–Sun 1230–1730.* Ask for the excellent Historical Itineraries packet. They have a city map too but better ones are available at bookstores, also on the Giraldo.

By car
To drive from one quarter of the city to another you must go back out to the ring road outside the walls and enter by another gate. When reserving a room, be sure to ask your hotel which gate to use.

By bus
The **bus station**, *tel: (066) 221 21 and (066) 242 54* is on R. da República near the Igreja São Francisco. Express buses from Lisbon take about 2 ¾ hours.

By train
The **railway station** *tel: (066) 221 25* is about a mile south of Giraldo, outside the walls. Travel straight up R. da República and go left on R. Miguel Bombarda.

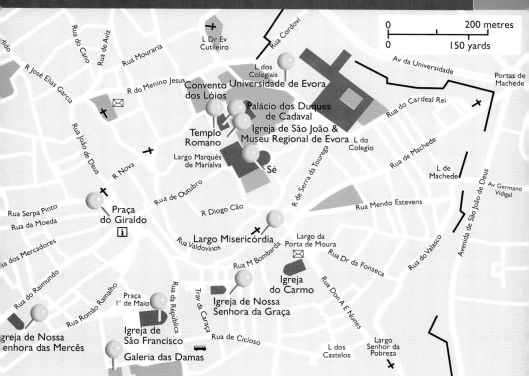

Parking
Hotel signs lead you to their parking places, usually in a nearby square. Once your car is parked, leave it there.

Walking
Praça do Giraldo is the main plaza, big and reserved for pedestrians, as are the streets between it and the cathedral, two blocks up Rua 5 de Outubro.

Sights

Galeria das Damas and Jardim Público
immediately south of Igreja São Francisco at the south end of the Praça 1° de Maio.

Galeria das Damas**
In the 15th and 16th centuries Evora was the capital and home of the royal family. No longer fearing attacks by Moors, the Palace of São Francisco was built outside the walls in 1506, combining late Gothic and Renaissance features with Moorish influences. With the Moors gone and most of their original architecture destroyed, Mudéjar style had become fashionable. Now all that remains of the palace is the Galeria das Damas, the Ladies Gallery, built into the old orange

Igreja de Nossa Senhora das Mercês/ Museu das Artes Decorativas € R. de Raimundo; tel: (066) 2 26 04, open Tue–Sun 1000–1230 and 1400–1700.

Below
Igreja de Nossa Senhora da Graça

orchard and once housing the ballroom. In the former palace grounds, the Jardim Público is good for strolling, and a pleasant vantage point for the Galeria das Damas. At its lower level, outside the walls, is a children's playground and a Museu do Brinquedo (Toy Museum).

Igreja de Nossa Senhora da Graça**

Built in the 16th-century, this church is believed to be the first example of Italian Renaissance style in Portugal. On the corners of its columned portico perch two monumental statues of the Children of Grace, their feet swinging over the edge like kids on a pier. The church (*in a narrow alley off R. da República*) is not open for visiting, but the façade and portico are the attraction.

Igreja de Nossa Senhora das Mercês*

This former church, now **Museu das Artes Decorativas***, is a part of the Museu Regional de Evora, housing religious art, including

altarpieces, vestments and statuary. The building itself has polychrome *azulejos* and baroque-rococo wood carvings. The carved and gilt arches in the transept are especially handsome.

Igreja de São Francisco**

Built in 1510 in Gothic style the unusually wide church's side chapels range from classical to baroque and rococo. In one of these, magnificent *azulejos* remain, and in the chapter houses, with spiral columns, a superb series of *azulejos* depicts the Stations of the Cross. The chapter house is reached through a small door beside the main Manueline portal, which is decorated with a pelican and a horseshoe-arched portico.

Beyond is the **Capela dos Ossos***, the church's best-known, somewhat macabre attraction. 16th-century Franciscan monks, determined to emphasise the impermanence of life, built the chapel walls from the bones of 5,000 human skeletons, sorting the bones by size and shape and creating designs with them. The vaulted ceiling has fine fresco painting, in the centre about the living and on the sides about the dead. A desiccated body hangs from one wall. In case you don't get the message, a sign over the entrance announces that these bones await your own.

Igreja de São João*

The 15th-century Convento dos Lóios, now a *pousada*, and the Igreja de São João form one side of the square facing the Roman Temple. The chapel, built in 1485, has a Gothic doorway and the nave is covered in early 18th-century *azulejos* by the noted tile-maker António Oliviera Bernardes. Grills in the floor reveal an ancient cistern and an ossuary. The convent is not open to the general public unless one can act the part of a *pousada* guest. The highlight is the Gothic cloister topped with a Renaissance gallery.

Misericórdia**

This small gem of a baroque church just south of the cathedral has extensive *azulejo* panels illustrating acts of charity, created by master tile-artist António de Oliveira Bernardes in 1716. On the ceiling above are fine 18th-century paintings framed in gilded carving.

Museu Regional de Evora**

In the old Bishop's Palace next to the Sé, exhibits trace the history of the area, beginning outside with a Roman bas-relief of a Vestal Virgin, a 14th-century Annunciation and 16th-century Holy Trinity. Roman, medieval, Manueline and Luso-Moorish sculpture is on the ground floor, while upstairs is an outstanding 13-panel altarpiece from the 16th century, as well as a 6-panel altarpiece from the Flemish school and a number of 15th- and 16th-century religious paintings. A fine cenotaph by Nicolas Chanterène honours Bishop Dom Afonso.

🛈 **Palácio dos Duques de Cadaval** € *Largo do Conde de Vila Flor, immediately north of the Roman Temple. Museum open 1000–1200 and 1400–1700, but hours can be irregular.*

Sé *Largo Marquês de Marialva, behind the Roman Temple, open Tue–Sun 0900–1200 and 1400–1700 (€ museum and cloister).*

Universidade de Evora *Rua do Colégio; follow R. Conde da Serra from the Sé to just outside the walls.*

Palácio dos Duques de Cadaval

A gift from the king to the noble Melo family in 1390, the palace is still occupied, in part, by the same family. One of two square crenellated towers was once part of the medieval town walls. A small museum in the courtyard has early paintings and two Flemish bronzes.

Praça do Giraldo*

This square has long been the centre of community life: an 18th-century fountain replaced a Roman Arch. Around the *praça* shops and cafés are busy all day and into the night.

Sé**

Only 21 years after the Moors were expelled, Sancho I ordered the construction of the cathedral, or Igreja Santa Maria. Transitional between the Romanesque and Gothic, it has square twin towers and a portal surrounded by 13th-century statues of the apostles. Inside, rose windows light the beautifully domed transept. The Renaissance organ is considered the oldest in Europe, and the choir stalls are beautifully carved with scenes of peasant life. An early cloister adjoins along with a treasury of religious art, including bejewelled reliquaries.

Templo Romano***

Fourteen columns and most of the base of this 2nd- or 3rd-century Roman temple stand just north of the cathedral. The symbol of the city, it is one of the most striking remnants of Roman civilisation in Iberia. It is particularly beautiful when lit up at night.

Universidade de Evora*

The old university, founded in 1559 by the Jesuits, was closed in the 1700s when the order was expelled from Portugal, only reopening in the 1970s. The Igreja do Espírito Santo is a fine example of the austere Jesuit Renaissance style. The sacristy ceiling is arched with frescoes and off the two-storey cloister are rooms decorated with *azulejo* panels depicting the elements, and other themes relating to the subjects studied there.

Accommodation and food

Pousada dos Lóios €€€ *Largo do Conde de Vila Flor; tel: (066) 2 40 51 and 52, fax: 2 72 48, e-mail: enatur@mail.telepac.pt* Opposite the Roman Temple in the former convent, whose graceful cloister it has appropriated. Full service and all amenities, long on luxury, short on warmth.

Hotel Dom Fernando €€ *Av. Dr Barahona 2; tel: (066) 74 17 17, fax: 74 17 16*. A modern full-service hotel, west on the ring road. It has all amenities, including restaurant (€–€€) and pool and is within walking distance of the inner city.

Pensão Monfalim €€ *Largo da Misericórdia 1; tel: (066) 2 20 31, fax: 74 23 67*. Fine location near the Misericórdia, Sé and Roman Temple, it is newly renovated and has a wonderful breakfast room and first-floor patio. Parking and individually controlled room temperature.

Pensão Riviera Residential €-€€ *R. de Octubro 49; tel: (066) 2 33 04, fax: 2 04 67*. A pleasant hotel in the centre of the old city. A nice breakfast room and very helpful staff. Reserved parking by the cathedral.

Quinta do Pintor € *Estrada dos Canaviais; tel: (066) 269 15 and 75 19 53*. On a farm outside town, rooms are attractive and have country painted furniture. On the road to Canaviais off the N18 from the Portas de Avis gate, north of the ring road.

O Antao €-€€ *R. João de Deus 5; tel: (066) 70 64 59, 1930–2300, closed Wed*. Winner of several prizes for Alentejo specialities, look for tuna with black eyed beans, partridge for two, and rabbit. Friendly and attentive service.

Adega do Neto € *R. dos Mercadores*. A limited menu of inexpensive *petiscos* and fried chicken.

Lampeão € *R. dos Mercadores 72*, Another inexpensive option for typical Portuguese meat dishes.

A Cave €-€€ *R. da República 26; tel: (066) 239 11*. Elegant more formal dining in a rustic atmosphere.

Pane & Vino €-€€ *Pateo do Salema; tel: (066) 74 69 60*. At the end of R. Diogo Cao, it is a pleasant small Italian restaurant for pasta, pizza, meat and fish dishes, closed Mon.

A Muralha € *R. 5 de Outubro; tel: (066) 22 28 4*. Popular for well-prepared meals in a pleasant setting.

Fialho €-€€ *Travessa de Mascarenhas 14; tel: (066) 2 30 79*. Serves traditional Portuguese dishes in a rustic setting.

Suggested tour

Begin at the **LARGO DO CONDE DE VILA FLOR** ❶, where you can see many of the city's attractions: the **Roman Temple**, **Convento dos Lóios**, **Igreja de São João** and the **Palácio dos Duques de Cadaval**. Go around the north end of the palace and take the street behind it through the town walls, past Largo Sextante to R. do Colégio and the **Universidade de Evora** and **IGREJA DO ESPIRITO SANTO** ❷.

At the south end of the University buildings cross the street and follow R. Conde da Serra de Tourega to the **LARGO DA PORTA DE MOURO** ❸, past the 1556 **Renaissance fountain**. On the east side of the Largo take R. da Misericórdia past the **Misericórdia** church.

Continue east to R. Miguel Bombarda and cross it, taking the first street on the right. At the next intersection look to the right for the **IGREJA DE NOSSA SENHORA DA GRACA** ❹ . From the church go east to R. da República, cross it and go south a short distance, then turn right, toward Praça 28 de Maio and the **Igreja de São Francisco**.

South of the church is the **Jardim Público** and the **Galeria das Damas**. Return to the Praça 28 de Maio and take the street west a short way to the lane north (the R. do Lagar dos Dizimos, although not signed) that leads to R. do Raimundo. Follow R. Raimundo west to the **IGREJA DE NOSSA SENHORA DAS MERCES** ❺ and the **Museu das Artes Decorativas**. Leaving the museum, take R. Raimundo east to the **PRACA DO GIRALDO** ❻ , then R. de 5 de Outubro to the **SE (IGREJA SANTA MARIA)** ❼ and the **Museu Regional de Evora**, where the tour began.

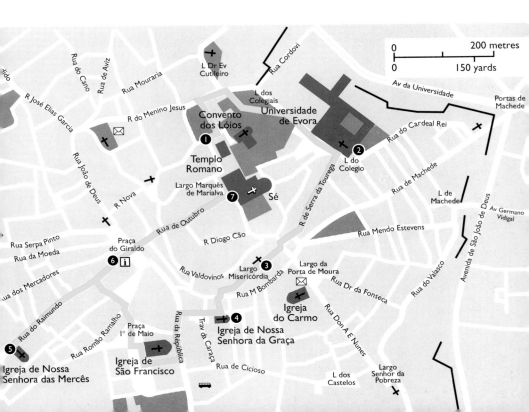

Upper Alentejo

Ratings

Castles	●●●●
Nature	●●●●
Nature	●●●○○
Villages	●●●○○
Architecture	●●○○○
Food and drink	●●○○○
Museums	●●○○○
Walking	●●○○○

Some of Portugal's prettiest villages and two former royal residences, at Estremoz and Vila Viçosa, highlight this route through the northern Alentejo. These are the country's wide open spaces, farmlands with rich, rolling plains, low hills and only a few mountains. Cork trees, chestnuts and olive trees grow in open groves, and wild flowers carpet the meadows in the spring. Summers here are hot, often brutally, a good time for travellers to avoid these sun-drenched plains. Drivers will find roads here less challenging; straight and gently rolling routes replace the snake-like mountain roads of the north. Distances grow between towns, but travel is faster, too. Prehistoric sites scatter the region, as do remnants of the long Roman occupation. At the heart of the Alentejo is the lovely city of Evora (*see pages 220–27*).

CAMPO MAIOR

ⓘ **Turismo** R. Major Talaya and Praça da República; tel: (068) 68 89 36, fax: (068) 68 89 37.

ⓘ **Museu de Arte Sacra** and **Capela dos Ossos**, R. 1° de Maio, tel: (068) 68 61 68, open Sun 1000–1200, 1400–1700 or call for Fri–Sat admission, same hours. At other times, ring the high doorbell on the door marked '6' and if the priest is there, he will show you into the chapel.

A pleasant, if slightly run-down, whitewashed town, Campo Maior sees few tourists on its streets. Homes built into the walls circling the hilltop castelo have arched dooryards, white and Moorish-looking. The castle entrance is on the lower side, from Praça Velha, but the reason for going to Campo Maior is in the town below, beside the **Museu de Arte Sacra**. The **Capela dos Ossos*** there is small and more touching than macabre. Unlike the others built from bones of monks, this is a memorial to the 1500 people who died suddenly when lightning struck the castle's gunpowder magazine in 1732. As the survivors rebuilt their town, they gathered the bones, arranging them to line this chapel.

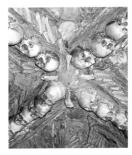

Maxieira
244-3 244
24 16
Envendos
23
3 Mação
E806 18
3
Mouriscas
Alvega
Pego 28 118 Gavião
Atalaia 18
Fratel
9 São
18 Miguel
IP2 Nisa 463
364 Nisa
São Bartolomeu
São Facundo 244
Monte da Pedra
Vale
das Mós 26 Sôr
Longomel
Torre das
Vargens
Chança
Ponte de Sor 14 2 369
119 Vale
de Açor 27
23 25 Valongo
IC13 Galveias Seda
Aldeia 244 370
Velha 30
Cabeção 15 243
Casa Branca
Pavia
251
14 Tera
20 São
Gregório 370
Sabugueiro
Gafanhoeira
Arraiolos 4
eira 23 22
Nossa Senhora da
Graça do Divor E90/802
Santa 21 17
Sofia
370 16
Nossa Senhora 114
da Boa Fé 380 Évora
32
São Brás do 254
Regedouro
Aguiar
257
Viana do Alentejo 384

Montalvão
Nossa Senhora da Graça
de Póvoa e Meadas
Barragem
da Póvoa
Beirã
Castelo
de Vide
246 246-1
118 Alpalhão Marvão
Gáfete 245 18 IC13
Tolosa 6
Vale Alagoa
do Peso 14 21 16 359
Fortios
Aldeia 119 Portalegre
da Mata Crato 1027
12
Seda
Alter
Pedroso
413
Alter
do Chão Cabeço
17 de Vide Assumar
369 29 27 371
Vaiamonte
Figueira Fronteira E802
Avis e Barros 243 19 Monforte
19 243
11
245 243
Cano 243 Veiros
13 Sousel 372
São Bento
do Cortiço
372-1 Santa Vitória São Lourenço
do Ameixial de Mamporção
15 Orada
21 Arcos
Vimieiro Estremoz 12 E90
25 27 18 33 Glória Borba
Évora-Monte Rio de Moinhos
19 Ossa
Igrejinha 653 Serra de Ossa
Azaruja
8 381
254-1
254
São Miguel Redondo
de Machede
Nossa Senhora 31
de Machede 381 Terena
Santa
18 Susana 255
Machede Casas Novas de Mares
Monte das IP2 Montoito
Flores 17 E802 Caridade
31 Barragem do
Monte Novo Vendinha
São
Espinheira Manços Monsaraz
Torre de 270 Reguengos
Coelheiros 12 de Monsaraz
Monte do Trigo 255
12 Campinho
Oriola E802 Mourão
Portel São Marcos do Campo
Vera Amieira

Embalse de Cedillo
La Atalaya de Santiago
Santiago de
Alcántara 621
Membrío
0 10 kms
de San Pedro Salorino
Valencia de Alcántara
Serra de São Mamede 12
San Vicente
de Alcántara
33 20
530
Alcorneo
La Codosera
Barulho Alburquerque
24
246 Esperança
Arronches
25 24
Senhora do Rosário Ouguela
15 Nossa Senhora da
Graça dos Degolados
Barragem do Caia
Santa Eulália Campo
14 Maior
Barbacena 246 373 371
13 18 19 19
Santo 243-1
Aleixo Vila Fernando
21 17 V
8
Orada 29 Elvas 20
15
Terrugem
373 São 27
Romão 36 436
Vila Viçosa Olivença
Bencatel
Pardais
Alandroal Embalse de
Piedra Aguda
San Benito de Olivenza
la Contienda San Jorge
de Alor
LLANOS DE
OLIVENZA 19
Aldeia de Táliga
38 Ferreira
Cheles Alconchel
436
17
256 20
15 436
Luz 385 Villanueva del
24 Fresno 27
Granja 4311
Estrela Godolín

Accommodation and food in Campo Maior

Hotel Santa Beatriz € *Av. Combatentes da Grande Guerra; tel: (068) 690 10 40, fax: (068) 68 81 09.* Up-to-date lodgings with all the basic amenities, they add charm with lovely handmade tapestries from Portalegre.

Restaurante O Faisão € *R. 1º de Maio, tel: (068) 68 94 95,* a friendly restaurant serving *petiscos* and full meals.

CASTELO DE VIDE❖❖

Turismo *R. Bartolomeu A. da Santa 81-3, tel: (045) 913 61, fax: (045) 918 27,* off Praça de Dom Pedro, very helpful and open even on holiday weekends.

Friday is market day in Praça Dom Pedro V, with food and pottery.

Easter Sunday is celebrated with a street procession; houses along the route are draped with richly coloured hangings.

The tourist office has a map with a good walking route from **Igreja de Santa Maria**, on **Praça Dom Pedro V**. The church's classical interior appears to be faced entirely in varying shades of marble, but it is imitation. The route leads up Rua de Santa Maria to the **Castelo**❖ *(open daily 0900–1900 summer, 0900–1700 winter),* within whose walled enclosure is the narrow Rua Direita de Castelo, lined with flower-draped whitewashed houses. Inside the castle yard is a round-topped cistern, a vaulted great hall and a keep you can climb for fine views over the old Judiaria (Jewish Quarter), directly below.

Bear left from the castle to explore the Judiaria, past vignettes of carved stonework and some very fine portals. These streets have kept much of their 15th-century appearance. The humble old **synagogue**❖ *(corner of R. da Judiaria and R. da Fonte, open daily 0900–1730)* is the oldest in Portugal, housing a small museum. Below is a fountain, Fonte da Vila, at the edge of the newer town, filled with elegant 17th-century houses with iron window grilles.

Right
The Fonte da Vila in Castelo de Vide

Northwest of town, near the intersection of the N246 and N246-1, is an area thick with megalithic sites. Several dolmen are within sight of each other, and the 8-metre Menir da Meada, the tallest in Iberia, is nearby. Follow signs from the N246 to *Antas* or *Megalíticos*. The area is not very big, and webbed with lanes and country roads through green farmland. Although you are almost certain to get lost at least once, you will find several of these ancient sites.

Accommodation and food in Castelo de Vide

Hotel Garcia d'Horta €€ *Estrada de São Vicente; tel: (045) 911 00, fax: (045) 912 00.* Big, full-service hotel manages to retain an old-world feel, from the stucco and yellow exterior to the handmade Portalegre tapestries inside. They have a very good restaurant (€€).

Marino €-€€ *R. Volta do Penedo 6.* Prize-winning Italian dishes, warm hospitality and a fine view.

ELVAS✧✧

Turismo *Praça da República; tel: (068) 62 23 36, open Mon–Fri 0900–1800, Sat–Sun 0900–1230, 1400–1730, or so the sign says. Reality is somewhat different.*

There is a large parking area at the Aqueducto, except on Monday, when the market fills it.

Nossa Senhora da Consolação *open Tue–Sun 0930–1230, 1430–1900, until 1730 winter.*

Castelo and **Museu Militar** *open daily 0900–1230, 1400–1730.*

Helena Lavores *R. de Alcamim 46, has a good selection of embroidery and needlework.*

Known for its sugary plums and good restaurants, Elvas is an exceedingly graceful town. Despite the magnificent defensive system that surrounds it (walk the 5km perimeter to fully appreciate its size and strength), it appears open and spacious within its armour. The main square, Praça da República, is paved in large stones that create the optical illusion of three-dimensional blocks. Above it looms the Sé, which, although no longer a cathedral, retains its title locally. Behind the somewhat grim façade hides a splendid 18th-century organ and a marble chancel. The south portal is Manueline.

Follow signs to *Castelo*, passing an ornate marble *pelourinho* with dragon-head hooks, in a sloping square surrounded by noble houses with crests and iron grilles. A portion of the original town walls is topped by a graceful loggia. **Nossa Senhora da Consolação✧**, behind the cathedral, is a rare example of a completely unrestored church, with painted swirls still visible on the pillars supporting its octagonal dome. The arched ceilings and walls are completely lined in blue and yellow *azulejos* in a Persian rug pattern.

The **castelo✧**, built by the Moors and improved upon by later monarchs, gives the best view over the impressive fortifications surrounding Elvas. Its **Museu Militar✧** has giant keys to all the city gates.

Dominating the western approach are the layered arches of the Aqueduto da Amoreira, built 1529–1622. To follow the great aqueduct to its beginnings at the springs of Amoreira, take the N372 west towards Vila Fernando, through Calçadinha, with the aqueduct crossing and recrossing the road.

Towards the end of September, the Festa do Senhor Jesus da Piedade brings markets, performances, processions and people, who fill every lodging in a 50km radius. Food-lovers should come in April, when restaurants vie with each other for their best spring lamb dishes; the tourist office posts menus from those participating.

Accommodation and food in Elvas

Estalagem Dom Sancho € *Praça da República; tel: (068) 62 26 86,* has the best location in town, pleasant rooms and a restaurant (€–€€) known for its cod fishcakes. .

Parque de Campismo € *Parque da Piedade; tel: (068) 62 37 72, open May–Sept.* Campsite, nothing fancy.

Bolota Castanha €€€ *Quintas das Janelas Verdes; tel: (068) 65 74 01.* Good restaurant with an interesting menu emphasising local products.

Girasol € *R. de Evora; tel: (068) 62 44 94,* modest, but with excellent lamb dishes and *feijoada* (meat and bean stew).

O Assador € *R. de Melo; tel: (068) 62 61 15,* is a friendly restaurant with a good selection in the lower price ranges.

ESTREMOZ**✧✧**

ⓘ Turismo de Estremoz *Rossio, open daily 1000–1230, 1500–1800,* is far more useful than the one in Elvas.

It is easy to picture King Dinis, who was known as the Farmer King, happily surveying farmlands of the surrounding valley from the tall square keep of his castle at Estremoz, now one of the loveliest *pousadas* in Portugal. Unlike the one in Evora, this *pousada* welcomes the public to see its grand ground floor. Next door, through a wrought-iron gate, is the **Capela da Rainha Santa Isabel✧**, commemorating the wife of King Dinis, the sainted Queen Isabel of Aragón, with *azulejo* scenes from her life. The Sala de Audiencia de Dom Dinis has Manueline vaulting and a beautiful Gothic colonnade. Opposite is the **Museu Municipal✧**, with examples of local pottery, including Nativity figurines.

The smaller **Museu Rural✧** faces the Rossio, with handcrafted miniatures depicting life in small Alentejo villages. The Rossio, a vast main square, is marred by ugly green semi-permanent market stalls of corrugated tin. Pottery, the main local craft, can be found in shops and at the huge Saturday market that fills the Rossio. The Câmara Municipal, an imposing building facing the square, is a former convent; from its courtyard rises a grand staircase bordered with *azulejos*.

Accommodation and food in Estremoz

Capela da Rainha Santa Isabel open Tue–Sun 1000–1300, 1500–1900 Apr–Sep.

Museu Municipal € open Tue–Sun 0900–1145, 1400–1745.

Museu Rural € open Tue–Sun 1000–1300, 1500–1800 Apr–Sep, until 1700 Oct–Mar.

Pousada Rainha Santa Isabel €€–€€€ *Largo Dom Dinis; tel: (068) 33 20 75, fax: (068) 33 20 79.* One of Portugal's loveliest *pousadas*, its large rooms furnished with elegant antiques – carved beds, early folk arts, Arraiolos rugs. The dining room (€€) is the best restaurant in town.

São Rosas €–€€ *Largo Dom Dinis; tel: (068) 33 33 45,* has a good selection of dishes and a pleasant dining room under low-arched ceilings, but the staff lack cordiality.

Café Alentejo € *Rossio; tel: (068) 228 34.* Upstairs, above the busy café is a somewhat quieter dining room serving local dishes.

MARVAO✧✧✧

Turismo de Marvão, R. Dr António Matos Magalhedes; tel: (045) 931 04, fax: (045) 935 26, open 0900–1230, 1400–1800, very helpful, with good booklets (€) on São Mamede park, nearby.

P Parking is at town gates; during quiet seasons you can drive to the *largo* by the castle.

Museu € in the Igreja de Santa Maria, www.cm-marvao.pt open daily 0900–1230, 1400–1730. Those interested in nearby prehistoric sites should look here for information.

Ruinas da Cidade Romana de Ammaia, open Mon–Fri 0900–1230, 1400–1730, often at weekends.

Even if Marvão did not have one of Portugal's best castles to explore, it would still be worth visiting to wander in the narrow stone lanes between whitewashed houses with carved windows and wrought-iron balconies. But the castle at the far end is irresistible, with its vast courtyard, high walls, towers and battlements. Just inside its entrance gate, steps lead to the huge vaulted cistern; beyond, through the second gate you can see the channel that fed rainwater into it. Go inside the *artesanato* to see the gigantic oven. In the keep, do as the clever Portuguese did when defending the castle from larger Spanish armies: talk loudly so your voice echoes, sounding as though many more people are inside.

The castle is open all night, and one of the many joys of staying in Marvão after the day-trippers leave is the chance to wander inside the castle after dark. It is lit, but a torch is handy on the stairs, and where darkness lurks in the corners.

Below the castle gate is a sunken garden with benches shaded by trees and bright flowerbeds surrounded by boxwood hedges.

The former church of Santa Maria houses the **Museu da Marvão✧**, whose bright, well-displayed collections include a complete *azulejo*-lined chapel with a polychrome wooden altar, artifacts found in excavations of local dolmen, medieval gravestones, local costumes and arts, and a bridal trousseau of handmade lace and needlework. There is an exhibit of medicinal herbs, and an entire room of Roman artifacts, most labelled in English. It is one of the best local museums in Portugal, especially strong on Bronze Age sites.

Outside the town gates, Nossa Senhora da Estrela has a good Manueline doorway. The ruins of the Roman town of **Ammaia✧**, in the valley below, are impressive. Remains of the town continue to emerge with the help of an archaeological team stationed there.

Unlike many picturesque walled towns, Marvão is not filled with

● **Artesanato Milflores** behind tourist office has a very good selection of pottery, as does **Artesanato O Forno** inside the castle.

Market day is Thur, in *Largo de Olivença*.

souvenir shops and cute cafés. In fact, apart from being spotlessly tidy, it seems relatively unaffected by the tourists who wander through it.

A 7.5km circuit of footpaths connects Portagem, in the valley below Marvão, with two other villages, through forests of cork and chestnut trees, over a medieval bridge and roadway, past a convent and chapels and two medieval tombs cut into the rock. Ask at the tourist office for a map and brochure (€) describing the nature and wildlife, as well as the historical sites.

The **Festa da Castanha**, on Nov 11, is Marvão's chestnut festival with folk dancing, music, wine and plenty of roasted chestnuts for sale.

Accommodation and food in Marvão

Albergaria El Rei Dom Manuel € *Largo do Terreiro; tel: (045) 90 91 50, fax: (045) 90 91 59.* A warm welcome and attractively furnished rooms with many amenities (some with balconies) await guests at this new inn. So does an exceptionally good meal, but note that the dining room (€) closes 2130, as do most in Marvão.

Pensão Dom Dinis € *R. Dr Matos Magalhães; tel: (045) 932 36, fax: (045) 937 67,* could hardly have a better location; it overlooks the square just below the castle. Rooms are pleasant and hospitable and the restaurant (€) serves sumptuous *acorda Alenteja*, a rich soup.

Pousada de Santa Maria €€ *R. 24 de Janeiro 7; tel: (045) 932 01, fax: (045) 934 40.* A low-key inn in a row of three old town houses inside the village walls, with tasteful decorative details, rustic antique furnishings, and a good dining room (€€) overlooking red rooftops below.

Below
Marvão's Castle

VILA VICOSA❖❖

ⓘ **Turismo** *Praça da República; tel: (068) 983 05.*

🏛 **Paço Ducal** €€ *open Tue–Sun 0930–1200, 1430–1700, by one-hour tour.*

Museu dos Coches € *open Tue–Sun 0930–1200, 1430–1700.*

This marble town was the enclave of Portuguese royalty until the Bragança dynasty went into exile in 1910. Guided tours of the Bragança's **Paço Ducal**❖ vie with those at Mafra for the dubious title of most boring in Portugal, but the palace itself is interesting, with painted ceilings and its personal view of a royal family, including the king's rather good artwork on the walls. At the impressive royal stables is the **Museu dos Coches**❖, an outstanding collection of royal and everyday carriages and coaches.

The old convent next to the palace is now a *pousada*, and between the two buildings are the palace gardens. Formal vegetable gardens have been restored and herb gardens planted in beds on low terraces, with pools and a pergola. The gardens are open to the public even when the palace is not, and entry is free. In the wall of the palace grounds, alongside the street from Borba, the Porta do Nó pushes Manueline to the ridiculous by 'tying' the arch together with rope-carved stone.

Before the Dukes of Bragança built their palace, King Dinis (who seems to have had a hand in building every castle in Portugal) constructed the walled Castelo, surrounded by a moat and some picturesque whitewashed houses.

Suggested tour

🌙 **Pousada Flor da Rosa** €€–€€€
Mosteiro Flor da Rosa, Crato; tel: (045) 99 72 10, fax: (045) 99 72 12. In a 16th-century fortified monastery, Flor da Rosa is decorated with Portalegre tapestries and modern colourful furniture. Its gardens are being restored.

Total distance: 245km; 372km with detours.

Time: 5 hours driving. Allow 2 days for the main route, 3 days with detours. Those with limited time should concentrate on Castelo Vide and Marvão.

Links: This route starts at Evora (*see page 220*). The N246 and the IP2 connect Castelo de Vide to Castelo Branco, and the Serra da Estrela route (*see page 216*) to the north. Heading south, the N18 goes to Beja and the Lower Alentejo route (*see page 244*).

Route: From **Evora** head north on the N18, stopping at the tiny hilltop village of **Evoramonte** to see its huge round-towered castle, then continue to **ESTREMOZ ❶**.

Detour: To visit the rug-making town of **Arraiolos**, leave Evora on the N114 west and turn north on the N370. Head north from Arraiolos on the E4/IC10 to Vimeiro following the N372-1 to rejoin the main route in Evoramonte.

From Estremoz, continue north on the N245 through **Fronteira** and **Crato**, turning right (east) onto the N246 in Alpalhão. When the N246 branches southwards, follow the N246-1 east through rolling pastureland with rocky outcrops to **CASTELO DE VIDE ❷**.

Café dos Caçadores, *Esperança,* overlooks the sleepy main square.

Casa do Forno €€ *Monsaraz; tel: (066) 551 90,* with a huge oven at the entrance, a shaded terrace or whitewashed stone dining room, popular on weekends.

Below Monsaraz

Continue on the N246-1, turning left in the little settlement of Portalagem and uphill to **MARVÃO** ❸. Head south on the well-surfaced but twisting N258 through terraced olive groves to Portalegre. Then follow the more gently rolling N371 to **Aronches**.

Detour: In Aronches, turn left to **Esperança**, a pretty whitewashed Alentejo village with colourful borders around doors and windows. Follow the brown signs to *Pinturas Rupestras* (cave paintings) straight ahead to **Hortas de Baixo**, then right, and 2.2km later right again at a faded blue sign. The road ends at the short trail to the cliffs and cave paintings of **Lapas dos Gaivões**. Painted on the stones, at eye level, are three figures in red; after some searching you will see others, thought to date from 3000–2500 BC. Retrace your route to Aronches.

From Aronches, follow the N371 through some of the peninsula's most beautiful agricultural landscapes of olive and cork, broken by tidy whitewashed villages. The Delta Coffee plant on the left signals your arrival at **CAMPO MAIOR** ❹. The N373 from Campo Maior is lined with plum trees, bright pink in early April, as you approach **ELVAS** ❺.

Head west from Elvas on the IP7, turning left to **Borba**, and left again at its elegant marble fountain, passing quarry slag piles of enough chipped marble to line every loo in London. Carry on to **VILA VICOSA** ❻, then follow the N254 through **Redondo** to Evora.

Detour: From Redondo, take the N255 south to **Reguengos de Monsaraz**, following signs east through the pottery town of **São Pedro do Corval** and past the prehistoric **Cromleque de Xares**, a circle of standing stones. Not far from the cromlech is **Anta de Xares**, a large dolmen. On a rocky hill beyond, close to the Spanish boarder, **Monsaraz** is a completely walled hill town guarded by its 13th-century **castle**.

Also worth exploring:

Collect a set of the excellent and inexpensive walking brochures at any regional tourist office, covering each area of the Parque Natural da Serra de São Mamede, south of Marvão. The maps in these brochures are so thoughtful that they even include cafés in the tiny villages *en route*. The footpaths are signposted.

Maxieira
Fratel
São Miguel 463
Montalvão
La Atalaya de Santiago
Santiago de Alcántara 621

244-3 244
Envendos
Maçao
IP2
18
Nisa
Nossa Senhora da Graça de Póvoa e Meadas
Membrío
Salorino

E806
Mouriscas
Alvega
Pego
Gavião
Atalaia
359
364
Barragem da Póvoa
Castelo de Vide
Beirã
0   10 kms
de San Pedro
Valencia de Alcántara

São Bartolomeu
São Facundo
Vale das Mós
Monte da Pedra
Tolosa
Gáfete
118
Alpalhão
246
Alagoa
246-1
Marvão
IC13
San Vicente de Alcántara

244
Longomel
Torre das Vargens
Chança
Aldeia da Mata
Crato
Fortios
359
Portalegre 1027
Serra de São Mamede
530

Ponte de Sor
119
Vale de Açor
369
Alter Pedroso 413
Cabeço de Vide
Assumar
371
La Codosera
Alburquerque

IC13
Valongo
Galveias
244
Alter do Chão
370
Vaiamonte
369
Senhora do Rosário
246
Barulho
Esperança
Arronches
Ouguela

Aldeia Velha
Benavila
Figueira e Barros
Avis
Fronteira
243
E802
Monforte
243
Nossa Senhora da Graça dos Degolados
Santa Eulália
Campo Maior

Barragem de Montargil
Barragem do Maranhão
Maranhão
370
Cabeção
243
Cano
Casa Branca
245
243
IP2
Veiros
372
Barbacena
243-1
246
373
371

Mora
Pavia
251
São Gregório
370
Sabugueiro
Gafanhoeira
Arraiolos
4
Sousel
Santa Vitória do Ameixial
372-1
São Bento do Cortiço
São Lourenço de Mamporcão
Orada
Arcos
Santo Aleixo
Vila Fernando
243-1
Elvas
436

Vimieiro
18
Estremoz
Glória
Rio de Moinhos
Borba
E90
Terrugem
São Romão
373
436

Évora-Monte
A6-IP7
Serra de Ossa
Ossa 653
Bencatel
Vila Viçosa
255
Pardais
Alandroal
Olivenza
Embalse de Piedra Aguda

Nossa Senhora da Graça do Divor
E90/802
Igrejinha
Azaruja
254-1
São Miguel de Machede
254
Redondo
Terena
255
San Benito de la Contienda
San Jorge de Alor

emor-tovo
Santa Sofia
370
114
Évora
Nossa Senhora de Machede
Santa Susana
Casas Novas de Mares
Montoito
Aldeia de Ferreira
LLANOS DE OLIVENZA
Cheles
Alconchel
Táliga

Santiago coural
Branca
Nossa Senhora da Boa Fé
380
IP2
Monte das Flores
E802
São Manços
Vendinha
Caridade
Monsaraz
436

São Brás do Regedouro Aguiar
254
Torre de Coelheiros
Espinheira 270
Monte do Trigo
Reguengos de Monsaraz
255
256
Mourão
436

257
Viana do Alentejo
384
Oriola
E802
Portel
São Marcos do Campo
Campinho
Luz
385
4311

Torrão
Vila Nova da Baronia
Alvito
Vera
Amieira
Estrela
Granja
Villanueva del Fresno

Lower Alentejo

Ratings

Historical sights	●●●●○
Architecture	●●●○○
Museums	●●●○○
Art and craft	●●○○○
Castles	●●○○○
Nature	●●○○○
Outdoor activities	●●○○○
Villages	●○○○○

Often passed off as no more than a waystop *en route* to the Algarve, the southern Alentejo is Molly-in-the-middle, without the mountains of the north or the beaches of the south to draw tourists. Its open landscapes dotted with olive orchards and groves of cork oak are at their best in the spring, when entire meadows are yellow or pink or blue with wild flowers. The open habitat is favoured by storks, whose untidy nests can be seen in trees and on electric poles along the roadsides. Whitewashed towns and small cities are far apart, looking more and more like the Algarve with their bright-coloured trim and increasingly ornate chimneys. The weather is pleasantly mild in the winter, perfect in the spring and autumn; in midsummer, travellers from northern latitudes might wish to be elsewhere.

BEJA❖❖

ⓘ **Turismo** *R. Capitão João Francisco de Sousa 25; tel: (084) 236 93, open Mon–Sat 1000–2000 (1800 in winter).*

ⓜ **Museu da Rainha Dona Leonor** € *Largo dos Duques de Beja, open 0930–1230, 1400–1715. Same ticket admits to Museu Visigótico. Printed guide in English (free Sun).*

Right
Rainha Dona Leonor
(Queen Leonor)

Too often ignored because of its remote location, Beja is an attractive city, centring on the Largo dos Duques de Beja. In the square, a loggia is filled with splendid Roman stone bulls and a giant carved capital, like an advertisement for the treasures behind it, inside the 15th-century Convento de Nossa Senhora da Conceição. The former convent's church, chapels and cloister, setting for the 17th-century *Letters of a Portuguese Nun*, form a perfect venue for the **Museu da Rainha Dona Leonor**❖. The building is a mix of Gothic and Manueline, with baroque and rococo chapels. *Azulejos* of the 16th

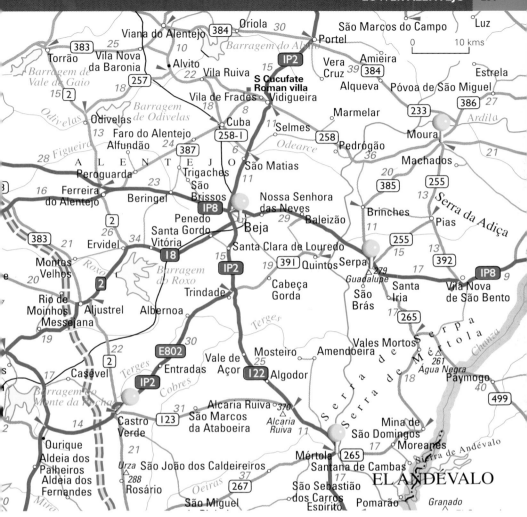

and 17th centuries line the cloister and chapter house, which has a lovely painted ceiling. The collections are worthy of the setting: Roman mosaics and Bronze Age artifacts from local excavations, medieval relics, and fine 16th-century paintings. A graceful bronze Rainha Dona Leonor stands in front of the museum.

Igreja Santa Maria, below the plaza, looks Moorish, and in the back you can see its 7th-century Visigothic foundations. Consider each of its chapels separately, since styles vary greatly; the highlight is a Jesse tree of free-standing polychromes, springing from a placidly sleeping Jesse.

Praça da República, at the other end of Rua dos Infantes, has fine

Castelo de Beja (€ Keep) *Open Tue–Sat 1000–1300, 1400–1800, in winter 1000–1200, 1300–1600.*

Museu Visigótico € *Antero de Quental, just outside the town walls from the Castle, open 0945–1230, 1400–1715.* Combined ticket with Museo Dona Leonor.

Ovibeja Feira do Borrego, *mid-March,* an exhibition of cattle, horses and sheep with regional crafts, music and food.

Festas de Cidade, *May,* brings various festivities.

Festa de São Lorenço e Santa Maria *second week of August,* with singing, dancing and general good times.

buildings, a *pelourinho* and, at the far end, the Misericórdia with a market portico.

Impressive **Castelo de Beja*** has the highest keep in Portugal, and there are good views from the crenellated walls. Inside the keep is a fine bronze of King Dinis. Close to the castle, just outside the walls, is the Igreja de Santa Amaro, parts of which may date from the 6th century, and the **Museu Visigótico***.

At **Pisões*** *(daily 0900–1230 and 1400–1600, 1800 summers),* west of the city, extensive mosaics have been unearthed, one room with several different patterns. Roman baths and a hypocaust have also been uncovered and excavation work continues. To reach Pisões, leave Beja on R. Almeida to the roundabout, the follow the IP2 for about 4km to the road to Penedo Gorda. At the edge of town turn right and almost immediately left, signposted *Pisões.*

Accommodation and food in Beja

Residencial Cristina € *R. de Mértola 71; tel: (084) 32 30 35, fax: 32 98 74.* A pleasant in-town hotel with friendly staff and comfortable rooms. Continental breakfast included.

Right
The Castelo de Beja

Alentejo € *below Largo dos Duques de Beja*, busy and cheerful; fish grilled in salt is a speciality. Large quantities, well prepared.

Monte da Diabroria € *Beringel, off the north side of N121 5km west of Beja; tel: (084) 9 81 77, fax: 9 61 35.* In the quiet countryside, a Turihab with nine attractive rooms in beautifully converted farm buildings.

Pousada de São Francisco €€-€€€ *Largo D. Nuno Alvares Pereira; tel: (084) 32 84 41, fax: 32 91 43.* In town, this former convent has a 12th-century chapel and it is close to all attractions. Fine appointments and all amenities. The restaurant (€€€) is probably the best in town.

Nova Mundo € *R. Mértola 41; tel: (084) 32 97 86,* downstairs, this bright blue and white dining room is run by a pleasant family.

O Infante €€ *R. O Infante.* Sample the braised quail.

CASTRO VERDE✥

Hotel Apartamento de Castro €-€€ *R. de Seara Nova; tel: (086) 32 72 13, fax: 2 28 14.* A large modern single-level hotel with a palm-shaded pool. It has its own restaurant (€-€€) and snack bar. Rooms have air conditioning and TV.

Overlooking the main street is the 18th-century Basílica Real, on a raised plaza. Behind its rather plain façade, walls are covered from floor to ceiling in *azulejos*, patterned tiles below and pictorial panels above, depicting the battle of Ourique. The tiles frame a fine gilt baroque main altar and discrete side altars. The nearby Igreja Matriz has 18th-century *azulejos* half way up the walls, also under a painting of the battle of Ourique. Next to the Igreja Matriz is a pleasant little park with an amphitheatre and a café where you can enjoy ice cream under the shade of an olive tree.

Ever since the 17th century the Feira de Castro Verde (*third Sunday Oct*) has celebrated the harvest with a market selling sheepskin clothing, shepherds' crooks, woollens, woodenware, dried fruit, cheese and much more.

MERTOLA✥✥

Turismo *Largo Vasco da Gama at R. Alves Redol; tel: (086) 6 25 73, 0900–1200, 1400–1700,* are the hours posted; hours open are not necessarily the same. Tours of the old town are at 1030 and 1500 Sat–Sun and holidays.

Public conveniences and showers are under the weaving workshop.

The old town sits inside partial walls, high above the confluence of Rio Guadiana and the smaller Ribeira de Oeiras. Everything in the old town is steeply up or down. Poppies bloom inside the walls of the castle, at the very top with views over the valleys and surrounding hillsides. A passage leads down to the cistern – be careful, there is no rail at the bottom.

Below the castle is the starkly white Igreja de Nossa Senhora da Assunção, a mosque converted to a church after 1238. Its square shape, columns and mihrab (prayer niche) reveal its origins. Under the castle walls, extensive ruins of the Roman Forum and Moorish Alcáçova are being uncovered in ongoing excavations. Along the river are remains of the massive Torre de Rio Roman fortifications, a good vantage point for admiring the strong medieval walls.

With an extensive period of settlement to draw from, the Museu

Islâmico and Museu Romano show pre-Roman, Roman, Islamic and medieval artifacts. On the street to the castle, a restored old house serves as a museum for temporary showings of art and artifacts. Next to the tourist office is the Oficina de Tecelagen (weaving workshop) with exhibits of weaving and a number of looms where local women work. Handwoven woollens are on sale at the workshop. A small municipal market on Largo Vasco da Gama sells good local cheese, bread and dried herbs.

Annual canoe races are held on the River Guadiana. Anyone interested in hiring a canoe or kayak should try contacting the canoe club, Associação de Canoagem (*tel: (086) 6 22 53*).

Accommodation and food in Mértola

Casa das Janelas Verdes € *R. Dr Manuel Francisco Gomes 40; tel: (086) 6 21 45.* Three nicely appointed rooms with private baths, in a historic home in the old city, close to the castle. It has a pleasant garden.

Residencial Beira Rio € *R. Dr Afonso Costa; tel (086) 6 23 40.* Inexpensive plain rooms with shared bath, on the hillside above the river.

Below
Mértola and the
River Guadiana

Alengarve €-€€ *Av. Aureliano Mira Fernandes*, in the new part of town, serving Alentejo specialities.

Café Guadiana € *R. Alvares Redol at Largo Vasco da Gama.* A busy small café at the foot of the castle street, with a few tables outside – usually occupied by regulars – more inside.

MOURA✦

ⓘ Turismo *Largo de Santa Clara; tel: (085) 2 49 02. Open 0900–1300, 1400–1600.*

ⓣ Termas € *Praça Sacadura Cabral, open 0800–1300, 1500–1800.*

ⓦ Mourense O Carlos € *R. da República 37; tel: (085) 225 98, serves good, simple regional fare.*

Named after a legendary Moorish woman tricked by the wily Christians, this small spa town is best known for its splendid Moorish quarter at the west end of the Praça Sacadura Cabral. Wander through these narrow streets lined with white houses where housewives chat from open doors. The Igreja de São João Baptista has an unusual Manueline door with two armillary spheres and other devices. The 16th-century Igreja de Carmen was the first of many churches built in Portugal by the Carmelites. Once a popular spa, Moura still maintains its **Termas✦** (thermal spa) near Jardim Dr Santiago. Unlike many, it is open to casual visitors who can soak in its fizzy soda waters or help themselves to a drink from the marble fountain near the entrance.

SERPA✦✦

ⓘ Turismo, *Largo Jorge de Melo 2 (off Praça da República); tel: (084) 5 37 27, open 0900–1230 and 1400–1730 (1900 in high season). Friendly and helpful, with maps of town.*

ⓟ *Park outside the walls at Largo do Corro near the Museu Ethnográfico and walk south, entering on the R. dos Fidalgos which leads straight to Praça da República.*

◉ *A large market, last Tue of the month, R. de Santo António, past the road to Moura, sells everything, including handicrafts. The municipal market on R. dos Arcos, a good place for picnic supplies.*

Growing from the gently rolling Alentejo countryside, Serpa is known for its cheese and strong flavoured wines. Its massive crenellated medieval walls stand out above the plain and provide a view of the farms around the city. Stark whitewashed houses filling a warren of streets verify its long existence. Enter through the fortified Porta de Beja on the west side with twin round towers. A part of the arched aqueduct rides over the walls.

In the centre is Praça da República, the busy heart of the city, leading into the smaller Largo Jorge de Melo. Stone stairs climb to the Igreja de Santa Maria. Behind the church, which has a fine Manueline door, a narrow lane leads to a gate in the crumbled walls, a romantic entrance to the **Castelo✦** (*open daily 0900–1730*). The keep houses a small **Museu de Arqueologia✦** (*open 0900–1200, 1400–1730*) with exhibits going back two millennia, and a surprising *Last Supper*, in plaster.

The **Museu Ethnográfico✦** (*open Tue–Sat 0900–1200, 1400–1800*), in a converted market on Largo do Corro, displays and interprets everyday items from the Alentejo, including tools, farming implements and local costume.

At the feast of Nossa Senhora de Guadaloupe (early April) the statue of the town's patron saint is brought down from the chapel at São Gens and is carried in processions daily from Friday until Tuesday. Bright banners hang from windows and people along the route pin money to ribbons hanging from her palanquin. It is a colourful event thronged with local people. During the festival museums stay open longer hours.

Above
Alentejo landscape

Accommodation and food in Serpa

Herdade do Topo €-€€ *Herdade do Topo, Apartado 29, (28km south on N265); tel: 5 91 36, fax: 5 92 60.* Rustic elegance for horse lovers. It is part of a farm that raises sheep and Lusitana horses, with riding ring and arena. It has a restaurant (€-€€) and sports facilities.

Casa da Muralha € *R. das Portas de Beja 43; tel: (084) 54 31 50, fax: 54 31 51,* offers rooms in a typical local house.

Pousada de São Gens €€ *Alto de São Gens; tel: (084) 5 37 24, fax: 5 33 37.* On a hillside of olive trees, this modern building has air-conditioning, pool and poolside bar. The *restaurante* (€€) serves well-prepared local specialities.

Pensão Beatriz € *Largo do Salvador 10; tel: (084) 5 34 23, fax: 5 34 23.* A 2-star pension with air-conditioning, TV and phones in-room.

Alentejano € *Praça da República; tel: (084) 5 31 89,* is centrally located and inexpensive, café downstairs, restaurant upstairs.

O Casarão € *Largo do Salvador 20; tel: (084) 9 06 82.* Both fish and meat dishes well prepared, served in a homely setting.

O Ze € *Praça da República 10; tel: (084) 9 02 46.* A lively place popular with young people.

Suggested tour

São Cucufate *Tue 1400–1730, Wed–Sat 0900–1230 and 1400–1730, Sun 0900–1200, 1400–1730.*

Total distance: 207km; 308km with detours.

Time: 4 hours driving. Allow 2 days with or without detours. Those with limited time should concentrate on Beja.

Links: The IP2 leads north from Beja to Evora (*see page 220*) and the Upper Alentejo (*see page 228*). The N122 heads south from Mértola to the Eastern Algarve (*see page 246*).

Route: Leave **BEJA ❶** on the IP2 north, exiting at **Vidigueira** and heading west on N258, turning north at signs 2km past **Vila de Frade** to the ruins of a **Roman villa** at **São Cucufate**❖❖. This 4th-century site has a unique two-storey construction and vaulted gallery, as well as a number of frescoes. The remains of a temple are nearby.

Return to **Vidigueira**, continuing east on the N258 to **MOURA ❷**. Head south on the N265 to **SERPA ❸**, continuing southward on the N265 to **MERTOLA ❹**. About 10km west of Mértola, turn left on the N123 to **CASTRO VERDE ❺**, returning via the IP2 to Beja.

Detour: Turn off the N122 about 3km north of Mértola. After about 18km turn right and continue 8km to the waterfall of **Pulo do Lobo**❖❖ (Wolf's Leap). The great Guadiana River, constricted here in a narrow gorge, falls through rocks sculpted by millennia of falling water, an impressive sight.

Also worth exploring

The area around **Ourique**, southeast of Castro Verde, is more hilly, and a dam west of the town provides recreation areas. Ourique's castle is gone, replaced by a splendid pergola-surrounded **belvedere park** covered with trellises of sweet-smelling wisteria. A statue of King Dinis keeps watch over beautiful views to the south.

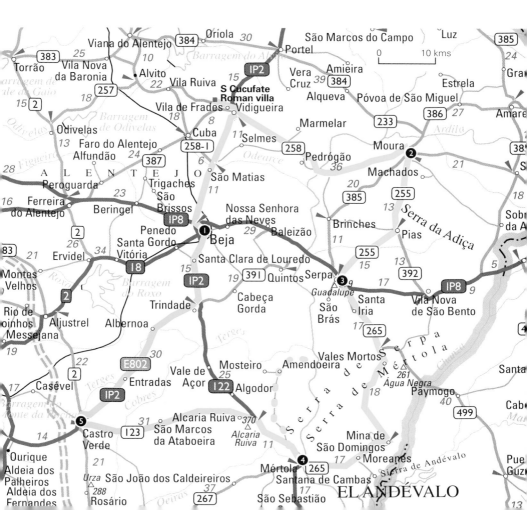

Eastern Algarve

Ratings

Beaches	●●●●●
Castles	●●●●○
Nature	●●●●○
Architecture	●●●○○
Children	●●●○○
Villages	●●●○○
Museums	●●○○○
Walking	●●○○○

Without the dramatic cliffs of its western counterparts, the coast toward the Spanish border can concentrate on what it does best: beaches. These surround the islands in the lagoons of the Ria Formosa, and stretch for an uninterrupted 20km from Cabanas to the mouth of the Guadiana River at Monte Gordo. Take your choice of lively beaches lined with cafés and filled with fellow holiday-makers or quiet almost deserted sands you may share only with the birds that nest there. Busy Faro, thrust by its airport into its role as the Algarve's arrival point, still retains its small-town air with spacious parks and wide pedestrian streets. Tavira, further east, is a gem of whitewashed churches and stately homes along a river, topped by a miniature castle. Many travellers find it the most appealing of all the Algarve's towns.

ALCOUTIM*

ℹ Tourist Office *Praça da República; tel: (081) 54 61 79.*

🍴 O Soeiro € *R. do Município; tel: (081) 46 241.* Enjoy the river view while your dinner sizzles on the grill. In the summer they rent modest rooms (€) to tourists.

O Rogerio € *R. do Município tel: (081) 46 185,* another choice for local dishes.

Opposite San Lucar, in Spain, Alcoutim is dominated by Castelo de Alcoutim, from the early 14th century. Recent excavations have found Roman and Moorish remains but habitation began even earlier. Now there are wild flowers growing from its ramparts.

Alcoutim was a centre for copper mining before 2500BC, and several ancient mine sites can be found in the mountains. Just south, in the hamlet of Montinho das Laranjeiras, are the ruins of a Roman villa and early Christian church. At Cortez Peiras, a few km north, are mines dating from the Bronze Age and Lavajo Menhir is the oldest known neolithic site in the region.

For a good view of the castle, go to Ermida de Nossa Senhora da Conceição,

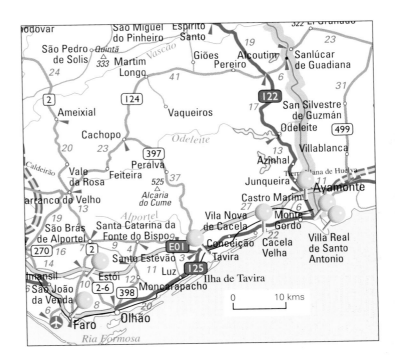

which has a Manueline doorway. The Igreja Matriz is best known for its carved capitals and 16th-century coloured bas reliefs of St John the Baptist. To visit San Lucar, engage a willing local boatman to cross the Guadiana.

CACELA VELHA ❖❖

ℹ Reserva Natural da Ria Formosa *Quinta do Marim, 1km east of Olhão. Open Mon–Fri 0900–1230, 1400–1700.*

☾ Camping Olhão € *Pinheiros de Marim, N125; tel: (089) 700 13 00, fax: (089) 700 13 90, reception open 24 hr. Tent pitches and caravan sites with pool, convenience store, cafeteria and playground.*

A handful of blue-trimmed houses surround a small square, blindingly white in the sun. Fishing boats will carry you across the creek to Fábrica, where white sand beaches stretch as far as the eye can see.

All that remains of the 13th-century structure of the Igreja Matriz is a small Gothic porch; the rest of the church dating from 16th- and 18th-century rebuilding. The tiny fort guarding the sands below was also rebuilt in the 1700s.

Surrounding the village is the Parque Natural da Ria Formosa, which includes the beaches, sandspits, islands, and lagoons of this watery ecosystem. Birds and plants attract nature-keen visitors to walk its beaches and trails. For the prettiest approach to tiny fortified Cacela Velha, drive to the neighbouring beach resort of Cabanas, off the N125, and walk eastward along the beach.

CASTRO MARIM❖❖

ⓘ Tourist Office *Praça 1° de Maio; tel: (081) 53 12 32.*

Castro Marim Sapal
National Parks and Reserves Service Office, Castelo, Castro Marim. Maps and lists of species. Park for the reserve west of the N122, south of Castro Marim.

ⓘ Castelo and **São Sebastião** *open daily 0900–1730, closed holidays.*

When the powerful military-religious Order of the Knights Templar was abolished in 1314, King Dinis of Portugal remembered their work in freeing his country from the Moors and invited them to Portugal, in the guise of a new Order of Christ. He gave them the fortress at Castro Marim as headquarters, where they could also keep an eye on Spain.

Today the knights' somewhat restored **Castelo**❖ is surrounded by much larger 17th-century ramparts, which you can walk for views over the town and river. Within the castle is the Igreja de Santiago, where Prince Henry the Navigator worshipped (he was Grand Master of the Order of Christ). **Castelo São Sebastião**❖ was built on a neighbouring hill, also with fine views over the river. Below the castles are the town's squat houses, with colourfully painted window and door frames.

Castro Marim Sapal is a large wetland reserve where nature enthusiasts walk along the dikes to see storks, flamingos, avocets, golden plover, oyster catchers, white-bellied boobies and more than 100 species of wild flowers in the salt-pans. These huge areas where salt is evaporated from sea water have been used since Roman times.

ESTOI❖❖❖

ⓘ Palácio do Visconde de Estói
R. de Barroca, gardens open Wed–Sat 0900-1200, 1400–1700. The main gate is closed; enter through a small gate next to the church.

Villa Romana de Milreu
€ signposted from the N125, open Tue–Sun 0930–1230, 1400–1800 May–Sep; closes at 1500 Oct–Apr.

This unprepossessing little town north of Faro has more than its share of the Algarve's blockbuster sites. Romantic in its neglect is the **Palácio do Visconde de Estói**❖, built in the 1700s by a noble family. Despite rumours of its restoration, it stands sadly closed, a derelict centrepiece for lavish and exuberant gardens. They, too, suffer from neglect, which only serves to make them more appealing. Nymphs only pretend to pour water from urns into shell-shaped lavabos, and crumbling stone steps lead from terraces to pools and walkways lined with *azulejo* scenes. Seek out the nativity group behind glass doors.

Not far west of town is the 1st-century Roman site of **Milreu**❖, thought to have been either an unusually grand private villa or a spa. The latter theory better explains the *nymphaerium*, whose imposing walls are still standing next to the entrance. This temple to the water cult was turned into a church by Visigoths. Most of the villa's outstanding statuary has been removed to the museum in Faro, but mosaic floors and extensive baths with elaborate heating and cooling systems remain.

Accommodation and food in Estói

Monte do Cacel **€€–€€€** *Estr de Moncarapacho; tel: (089) 99 01 40, fax: (089) 99 13 41, closed Dec–mid-Feb.* A fine old country home with rooms and suites; dining room (**€€€**).

Pousada de São Bras €€ *N2 North; tel: (089) 84 23 05, fax: (089) 84 17 26*, a newly renovated *pousada* with extensive views and a good dining room (€€€).

FARO✧✧

ⓘ Tourist Information *Arco da Vila, R. da Misericórdia 8–12; tel: (089) 80 36 04.*

ⓟ Park in Largo de São Francisco just east of the old city walls, unless it is filled with a fair (mid-Jul and mid-Oct).

⇨ Public conveniences are beside the café at the end of Jardim Manuel Bivar, opposite the neo-Moorish bank building.

Despite the sprawl to the north, central Faro is quite compact, its avenues converging at the graceful Jardim Manuel Bivar, shaded in tall palms, near the harbour. The old city, although no longer completely encased in walls, still feels as though it were, its narrow streets entered through the impressive Arco da Vila. Look up to its tower to see the storks' nest; you will see more on chimneys and towers inside the old city walls, and atop the adjacent Misericórdia.

At the centre of this old quarter is the **Sé✧** (Cathedral), rebuilt in the 1700s, and decorated with *azulejos* and a large baroque organ. You can climb its square 13th-century bell tower (€ *Mon–Sat 1000–1200, 1400–1900, Sun 0930–1300*). North of the old city the somewhat creepy **Capela dos Ossos✧** (€ *open Mon–Sat 1000–1300,1500–1700*), behind the Igreja do Carmo, is lined entirely with bones arranged in neat patterns. A smaller niche in the cloister is similarly decorated; stop to admire the church, for its brilliant carved gilt altars.

For more flamboyant carving, painting and gilding, go to the Igreja São Francisco, east of the old city, whose plain exterior gives no hint of the riot within.

The **Museu Municipal✧** (€ *Largo Alfonso III, open Mon–Fri 0900–1200, 1400–1700*) displays art, ceramics, a fine collection of *azulejos* and archaeological finds in a two-storey 16th-century cloister, one of the few to survive the 1755 earthquake. For local folklife, crafts and replica rooms and shops, see the **Museu Etnográfico Regional✧** (€ *open Mon–Fri 0930–1230, 1400–1700*) on Praça da Liberdade, which also shows Algarvian chimneys. The **Museu Marítimo✧** (€ *Capitania do Porto, open*

Right
Faro's Capela dos Ossos

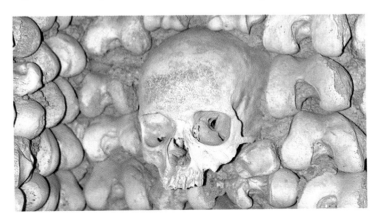

Mon–Fri 0930–1230, 1400–1700, Sat 0930–1300), next to Hotel Eva, has ship models spanning several centuries and exhibits on fishing.

The **Museu Antonino*** *(open Mon–Fri 0900–1300, 1400–1730),* at Santo António do Alto, just south of the N125, offers a quirky collection of artifacts relating (often tenuously, sometimes humorously) to the Portuguese saint. This is the highest point in the city and the view from the belvedere encompasses the city and lagoon.

Accommodation and food in Faro

Eva Hotel €€ *Av. da República 1; tel: (089) 80 33 54, fax: (089) 80 23 04.* Newly renovated, adjacent to the old city.

Residencial Madalena € *R. Conselheiro Bivar 109; tel: (089) 80 58 06, fax: (089) 80 58 07.* Rooms without breakfast, a block from the main square, very inexpensive.

Low-priced local restaurants cluster on Praça da Feira de Almeida.

Lady Susan Restaurant € *R. 1º Dezembro 28; no tel, closed Mon.* Excellent seafood at very low prices for central location.

Restaurant Adega Rocha € *R. da Misericórdia 48, no tel.* Look for the daily specials, hearty and cheap.

Below
Tavira's fishing port

TAVIRA✦✦✦

ⓘ Tourist Information *R. da Galeria 9; tel: (081) 32 25 11.*

⊗ Bike Rentals *R. do Forno 22; tel: (081) 32 19 73,* provide a good way to explore this level part of the coast.

⊞ Castelo do Tavira *open Mon–Fri 0800–1700, Sat–Sun 0900–1730.*

Churches in Tavira are often closed; ask at TIC or nearby cafés for times and location of keys.

◗ The produce market is open every morning, around it stalls sell honey and sundries. For crafts, see **Porta de Reixa Artesanato,** *Praça da República 9.*

Patrician homes, unique architecture, pleasant streets for strolling, a plethora of fine churches, nearby beaches, and a riverfront setting lined with cafés and restaurants add up to an irresistible base for exploring the eastern Algarve. So pleasant in fact, that you may get no further.

River banks are bordered by fine old homes in pastel colours, many with delicate iron balconies and some converted to gracious lodgings. Seven arches of a Roman bridge span the river, where colourful fishing boats chug in and out to the fish market.

To see Tavira's graceful towers and unusual gabled rooftops, walk the walls of the small **castelo✦** behind the tourist office. Inside is a well-kept garden, profuse with bright blossoms. From here you look directly at the twin towers of Santa Maria do Castelo, one with a giant clock face and the other with a cockerel weathervane. Of its days as a mosque, only the Arabic tower, refitted with a clock, remains. Inside, along with 18th-century tiles and gold, are tombs of crusaders who freed the city from the Moors.

But below the castle the Moors left their mark in the streets that wind between pale walls, feeling distinctly Arabic. The statue-crowned doorway of the **Misericórdia✦** is considered the finest Renaissance church portal in the Algarve. Of the city's many other churches, **São José do Hospital✦** has a carved baroque high altar, *trompe-l'oeil* painting and fine 18th-century carved statues. The **Igreja do Carmo✦**, across the river, has a carved and gilded baroque high altar that is just short of astonishing.

The Renaissance doorway of the Igreja Matriz in nearby Luz da Tavira to the west, overlooks the central square, while its equally splendid carved Manueline side door faces the N125. Village houses are decorated with painted floral or geometric borders and topped with ornate white chimneys.

Ilha de Tavira⁺, an offshore island 11km long and only 500 metres wide, is all sandy beach at its eastern end. To get there, follow R. José Pires Padinha past the market to catch the ferry (May–Oct) .

Above
Taviran rooftops

Accommodation and food in Tavira

Mare's Residencial € *R. José Pires Padinha 134-140; tel: (081) 31 58 15, fax: (081) 32 58 19.* Bright high-ceilinged rooms with balconies overlooking the river; friendly staff, central location opposite Ilha de Tavira boats. The restaurant (€–€€) serves *cataplana* and other seafood specialities.

O Pequeno Castelo € *Poço das Bruxas, Santo Estavão; tel: (081) 96 16 92, fax: (081) 96 16 92.* Friendly, quiet B&B in a charming home 6km outside Tavira.

Restaurant Imperial €–€€ *R. José Pires Padinha; tel: (081) 32 23 06.* Well-known among locals for good seafood and regional dishes, on the river near the market.

Vila Real de Santo Antonio⁺

Riosul €€ *Monte Gordo; tel: (081) 51 02 00, fax: (081) 51 02 09.* Cruise along the Guadiana River, with Spain on one side, Portugal on the other. Boats anchor at Foz de Odeleite for a swim and lunch at a local *quinta*.

No narrow streets winding up to a castle here; this town is table-flat and the picture of modern planning, built in five months with pre-cut stones shipped from Lisbon. The grid plan translated the ideals of the Age of Enlightenment into architecture. The focal point, Praça Marquês de Pombal, is paved in radiating stripes and surrounded by gracious well-matched buildings. Note especially those at the corners. Cafés fill the corner leading to Rua Dr Teofilo Braga, lined with the shops displaying household goods that attract Spanish shoppers.

Facing the square, the Igreja Matriz has baroque decoration and 18th-century statuary by the sculptor Machado de Castro. The Museu

Museu Paroquial €
open Mon–Wed, Fri
1100–1500.

**Restaurant
Pombalina** € R.
Zuzerbarão, no tel, just off
the main square, with a
cool dim interior and
sidewalk tables.

Hotel Guadiana
€€ Av. da República
94; tel: (081) 51 14 82, fax
(081) 51 14 78. Grand old
hotel with elegant marble
entrance and bright
traditionally decorated
rooms, some with large
windows overlooking the
river.

Fine lace is still made
in the region, although
most you'll see hanging in
the streets is imported.
Look for marionettes, a
newly popular craft. Most
shops remain open at
midday, some close
1300–1500.

Manuel Cabanas, also on the square, contains the woodcuts and paintings of the local artist after whom it is named.

Where river meets sea stands a lighthouse overlooking Monte Gordo Bay and the largest sand beach in southern Europe. It is sheltered here from heavy seas and the water is warmed by Mediterranean currents.

It's hard to resist riding the colourful old ferry (€) that crosses the River Guadiana to Ayamonte in Spain leaving Vila Real every 40 mins (0745–1900). Time in Spain is one hour ahead and all but restaurants and cafés close from 1300–1600.

Suggested tour

Total distance: 195km; 230km with detours.

Time: 4 hours driving. Allow 3 days; those with limited time should concentrate on Estoi and Tavira.

Links: The N125 connects Faro to the Central Algarve (*see page 256*); the N122 continues north to Upper Alentejo (*see page 228*).

Route: Leave **FARO ❶** on the N125 east past **Olhão**, turning left (north) on the N398 to **Moncarapacho** to visit the baroque Capela de Monte Cristo. Its unique **Museu Parroquial**◆ of archaeology and folklife, the collections of the parish priest, has everything from a Roman milestone to slave shackles.

Right
Vila Real de
Santo António

Guaditur €€ *Foz de Odeleite; tel: (081) 45 336,* operates riverboat tours.

Cova dos Mouros €€ *Vaqueiros; tel: (089) 99 92 29, open 1030–1800 Mar–Oct, 1030–1630 Nov–mid-Dec, mid-Jan–Feb.*

Miradouro de Caldeirão, at Barranco Velho, is a scenic picnic site.

Museu Etnográfico do Traje Algarvio € *R. Dr José Dias Sancho 59 Open Mon–Fri 1000–1300, 1400–1700, Sat–Sun 1400–1700.*

Above
The Guadiana river ferry linking Portugal's Vila Real with Spain's Ayamonte

Return to the N125, following signs to **Luz de Tavira** and on to **TAVIRA ②**. The N125 continues past **CACELA VELHA ③** (take turning opposite the Eurotel). Grapevines, small farms, and whitewashed villages line the road, and 1km south are the beaches of **Manta Rota** and **Lota**, the former with a small fishing village. The resort of **Monte Gordo** lies on the long beach before **VILA REAL DE SANTO ANTONIO ④**

Turn north on the N122 to **CASTRO MARIM ⑤**, then **Odeleite**, where basket makers may display their works along the street. The road climbs to a viewpoint of the mountains, and small roads branch eastwards, ending at the river villages of **Foz de Odeleite**, **Guerreiros do Rio** and **ALCOUTIM ⑥**. Follow the N124 west through **Pereiro** to **Martim Longo**.

Detour: At Martim Longo, turn south on the N506 to **Vaqueiros**, visiting the **Cova dos Mouros✶**, a mine that's been active since the Romans extracted copper here. You can see shafts, equipment, reconstructed buildings, and a donkey breeding station with rides. Backtrack to Martim Longo.

From Martim Longo, continue south on the winding N124. In spring this plateau is covered in blooming flowers. On reaching **Cachopo** you may see weavers working at **A Lacandeira**.

Detour: From Cachopo, turn west towards **Redonda**, to **Mealha** and the megalithic tomb of **Anta das Pedras Altas**. Its capstone has fallen, but supporting stones are still in place. Round stone structures with thatched roofs, used to store hay, are reminiscent of those used in Celtic hillforts. The road continues to **Almeixal**, where it meets the very scenic N2, rejoining the main route in **Barranco Velho**.

South of Cachopo, turn eastward 1km at the **Castelão** signpost to see a stone hamlet that seems to have dropped there from another age. The N124 continues south to **Barranco Velho**, where a left turn takes you to **São Brás de Aportel**. The **Museu Etnográfico do Traje Algarvio*** – folk life and traditional costumes housed in a prosperous 19th-century home – is worth a stop. The N2 continues through **ESTOI** ❼ to Faro.

Also worth exploring

The rugged country in the centre of this circular route, cut by the several tributaries of the River Guadiana, is webbed with roads which intrepid travellers with a good map will find fascinating. It's an altogether different Algarve, with villages unchanged by centuries and farms still worked by hand. Expect to meet the occasional mule-cart as well as ancient automobiles. Begin on the N397 from Tavira.

Central Algarve

Ratings

Beaches	●●●●●
Castles	●●●●○
Children	●●●●○
Nature	●●●●○
Walking	●●●●○
Outdoor activities	●●●○○
Scenery	●●●○○
Coastal villages	●●○○○

The central coast combines the honeycombed rock formations and cliffs of the western Algarve with the flat low tidelands of the east. It is the most crowded section, the result of both its abundance of good beaches and its proximity to the region's only airport, at Faro. At its centre, Albufeira is the undisputed king of the package holiday tours, a mecca of nightlife and fun-in-the-sun pleasures, but with an old town at its core and a beach lined with bright fishing boats. Smaller resort towns offer beaches with more elbow room, but less après-beach excitement. Inland towns like Alte are quieter, with ample opportunities for hiking and enjoying nature. Silves adds the dimension of history, with a past rich in Moors and crusaders (even Richard the Lion-Heart) and the Algarve's finest castle to explore.

ALBUFEIRA*

Tourist Information
R. 5 de Outubro; tel: (089) 58 52 79.

Zoomarine €€
N125, Guia; tel: (089) 56 03 00, e-mail: lgarve@zoomarine.com An interactive oceanographic park for all ages.

Market day is the first and third Tue of the month; the produce market is open Tue–Sun mornings.

Buildings in the centre of Albufeira give the impression of tumbling down the hillside like a spilled sack of white toy blocks. Stone-paved streets descend between them under Moorish archways to converge in a square of colourful café umbrellas. Like other resort towns, to get to this old core you have to drive the gauntlet of incongruous new hotels on its outskirts. But Albufeira fishermen still haul up their colourful boats filled with the day's catch under the cliffs at Praia dos Barcos, and mend their nets by the shore. And on Aug 15 they honor their patron saint with a procession to the chapel of Nossa Senhora da Ourada.

Both the Misericórdia and Igreja São Sebastião have Manueline doorways. The town is short on 'sights' but long on beach and related pastimes of shopping and café-sitting. Lunch on fresh-caught sardines grilled alongside the street.

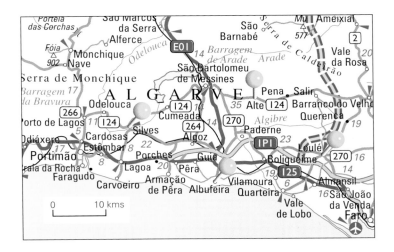

The bathing beach is accessed through a tunnel near the tourist office or you can join the fishermen on their beach. To claim a larger patch of private sand, drive west to Gale (popular with water-skiers) or walk to Xorino, with interesting rock formations and caves.

Nightlife in Albufeira stretches along the road towards Montechoro, a hurly-burly of clubs, bars, noisy discos and pubs where you'll hardly ever hear Portuguese spoken.

Accommodation and food in Albufeira

Residencial Vila Bela € *R. Coronel Aquas 15; tel: (089) 51 21 01*. Rooms are bright and airy, and there's a swimming pool.

The best dining bet in this ever-changing resort scene is to browse the posted menus along the fishermen's beach or in the streets nearby, not on the Montechoro road.

ALTE✣

From Alte it is an hour's uphill hike to the multichambered caves of **Buraco dos Mouros**, where Moors once hid. Mind the bats that take refuge there now.

Although tourists do find their way to this hilltop village, they haven't changed Alte's character. Its narrow flower-bordered streets are ideal for wandering and the Igreja Matriz is one of the most remarkable in all Portugal, with its lining of blue *azulejos*, the 18th-century pictorial tiles peculiar to Portugal. Blue angels play musical instruments in tiles that cover every surface, even inside the dome, where the panels are separated by ribs of stone. Polychrome statues and delicate gold scrolls flank the high altar.

Walk along the street past the series of natural springs, each set in a fountain of blue figural tiles. Fonte Grande, further on, has picnic tables, more springs and a path following a stream up into the mountains.

Accommodation and food in Alte

Alte Hotel €€ *Montino; tel: (089) 685 23*. Plain comfortable rooms and sports facilities overlook sweeping views. The restaurant (€€) serves good traditional dishes, including local game.

Casa d'Alvada € *Quinta do Freixo, Benafim; tel: (089) 47 21 53, fax: (089) 47 21 48*. Modern rooms on a farm, with pool and bright dining room with a view, 3km north of the N124.

Below
Typical Algarvian architecture

LOULÉ❖❖

Tourist Information R. de Paio Peres Correira 17; tel: (089) 46 39 00.

Park at Largo de São Francisco; parking is almost impossible on Saturday.

Museu Municipal R. de Paio Peres Correira 17; tel: (089) 41 50 00, open Mon–Fri 0900–1230, 1400–1730

Igreja São Clemente Largo Batalhão dos Sapadores do Caminho, open daily 1000–1300, 1400–1900.

The Algarve's only real Carnival is here, just before Lent, and its largest religious procession is also in Loulé, on Easter and the following Sunday.

The craft centre of the Algarve, Loulé is usually overlooked by tourists bent on beaches. It's a shame, because the town is charming and retains the tiny artisan shops that once filled most Portuguese cities. However, on Saturdays tourists do come in droves to the flea market (over-rated, unless you're short on T-shirts and plastic gimcracks).

Along with castle walls and towers, Loulé's skyline is crowned by white chimneys in the distinctive Algarve style, decorated by lace-like filigree work and relief designs. Built into the remnants of the Moorish castle walls, the **Museu Municipal**❖ includes a traditional kitchen along with tools and pottery from local prehistoric graves.

Igreja São Clemente❖ has fine gold altars and *azulejos* lining its interior walls. The 11th-century stone bell tower, originally a minaret, is one of the few to survive in Portugal.

Some of the interior elements of this church were brought from the **Convento da Graça**❖ (*Largo Tenente Cabeçadas*), destroyed by the 1755 earthquake, but worth seeing for its surviving Gothic doorway. More tiles line the interior of the **Ermida de Nossa Senhora da Conceição**❖ (*R. Paio Peres Correia 22*).

The market is a revival of the Moorish style that once filled the city. Its exterior is brightened by art nouveau tiles and the colourful stalls inside spill out on to the street. The streets between the market and the tourist office are filled with artisans selling leather, brass, iron, basketry and copper work.

Accommodation and food in Loulé

Loulé Jardim Hotel €–€€ *Praça Manuel de Arriaga; tel: (089) 41 30 94, fax: (089) 46 31 77.*

O Avenida € *Av. José da Costa Mealha 13; tel: (089) 46 21 06, closed Sun.* High quality menu for the price.

Bicavelha €€ *Rua Martim Moniz 17; tel: (089) 46 33 76, closed Sun.* Seafood stylishly presented in historic surroundings.

SILVES❖❖❖

Tourist Information R. 25 de Abril; tel: (082) 44 22 55, open Tue–Sat 0930–1230, 1400–1730, Sun 0900–1200, daily in summer.

Silves was the hub of Muslim Algarve, a vibrant, thriving cultural centre that in the 11th century surpassed Lisbon. It fell first to crusaders, then to earthquakes, but its castle is still the finest Moorish fortification in Portugal. Ten towers of the **Castelo de Silves**❖❖ are linked by an unbroken line of battlemented parapets, enclosing 12,000 square metres. Four towers have vaulted halls and Gothic doorways resulting from medieval renovations.

Park by the river near the arched medieval bridge to explore the old town on foot, since its streets are steep, narrow and connected by stairs.

Castelo de Silves € *open 0900–1700 (2000 summer). In off-season drive to the castle entrance, where there is limited parking.*

Museu de Arqueologia *€ R. Portas de Loulé, open 1000–1800 daily.*

For a different perspective on the Algarve, and a look at the historic route that made Silves important as a port, travel the Arade River between Portimão and Silves by boat. **Leãozinho Arade River Cruises** *(€€) Marina do Portimão; tel: (082) 41 51 56.*

Archaeological digs continue to uncover remains of the Moorish city, and its Roman and Phoenician predecessors inside the walls. One end of the enclosure is dominated by the vaulted roof of the gigantic cistern; narrow stairs lead deep down into the cavernous interior. Views from the ramparts extend over the tiled roofs of the town below, across orange and almond groves and out to the mountains beyond.

Just outside the walls at the entrance to the castle is the Sé Velha (Old Cathedral), begun in the 13th century. Walk around it to see the surviving original stonework. The interior is Gothic, with a fine Renaissance retable in one of the side altars. Just below the Sé is the Misericórdia, a smaller 16th-century church with a Manueline carved side doorway.

The castle is a tough act to follow, but the small Museu de Arqueologia* is worth seeing for its well-displayed artifacts from all periods of the city's long history. Although labelled in Portuguese, the exhibits are well illustrated and easy to understand. Islamic ceramics are excellent, but the highlight is the Moorish well, 18 metres deep and 2.5 metres across. The museum is built along a section of the old city walls, reached from the upper floor.

Beside the museum is the Torreão das Portas da Cidade, a massive gate tower in these walls that protected the medina of the old Moorish city. In its shadow is the Praça do Municipio, a pleasant square with cafés and benches. Step into the *pastelaria* under the arcade to see the fine old tile murals on the walls.

Under a sandstone portico by the N124 is the Cruz de Portugal (Portugal Cross), carved of stone in the 15th century.

Accommodation and food in Silves

Quinto do Rio € *Luisa Roberto Turismo Rural; tel and fax: (082) 44 55 28, 5km northeast of town.* Recently restored rooms in a peaceful setting among orange groves; dinner by reservation.

Recanto dos Mouros €€ *Monte Branco; tel: (082) 44 32 40, Thur–Tue,* serves traditional Algarve dishes in a rustic atmosphere, with sweeping views of the castle walls.

Casa Velha de Silves € *R. 25 de Abril; tel: (082) 44 54 91,* close to the TIC, serves *piri-piri* and fresh fish specials along with omelettes and sandwiches.

Suggested tour

Total distance: 105km; 137km with detours.

Time: 2.5 hours driving. Allow 2 days. Those with limited time should concentrate on Silves and its castle.

Left
Castelo de Silves

Capela de São Lourenço dos Matos *Almancil, open irregularly 0900–1300, 1430–1800; if closed, ask anyone nearby for the key.*

Museu do Cerro da Vila € *Vilamoura, open daily 1000–1200, 1400–2000 (1700 in winter).*

Links: The N124 leads west from Silves to meet the Monchique–Portimão road (*see page 268*). To the east, Loulé is only 16km from Faro (*see page 249*).

Route: From **SILVES** ❶ follow the N124 northeast to **São Bartolomeu de Messines**, a whitewashed valley town of 17th- and 18th-century houses and archways over the streets. Visit the **Igreja Matriz** with its twisted columns of variegated local marble, a rare example of this early Manueline style, and the baroque carved stone pulpit is especially fine.

After crossing the E1, the main road north, continue to **ALTE** ❷, past fields of red soil bordered with stone walls and planted with almond and orange groves. In **Pena**, follow signs north to **Rocha de Pena**, a 480-metre limestone escarpment. It is a short climb on a well-marked trail. Begin at Café das Grutas, where you can get a trail brochure. At the top are views of the mountains and ruined windmills. On the southern edge are walls thought to date from the Iron Age.

Continue on the N124 through **Benafim** to **Salir**, stopping to walk around the ruined ramparts of the once-grand 12th-century castle that crowns it. After passing through the hamlet of **Besteiros**, follow an unnumbered road south (right), signposted **Querenca**. Stop there to see the **Igreja de Nossa Senhora da Assunção**, founded by the Knights Templar. Just south of Querenca, turn south (right) onto the N396 to **LOULE** ❸.

Keep heading south on the N396 to the N125. Turn left (east) to **Almancil** to visit the extraordinary baroque **Capela de São Lourenço dos Matos**✶✶✶. The entire interior – even the ceiling and dome – is lined with tiles from the early 1700s, one of few churches in Portugal retaining these in their original state. An unnumbered road leads to **Quarteira**, where there is a busy daily market and a beach lined with cafés, then on to **Vilamoura**. Near the marina is the **Museu do Cerro da Vila**✶, displaying tiles and artifacts at the Roman ruins where they were found. Head north from Vilamoura, watching for a left turn just before reaching the N125, connecting to the coastal road that leads to **ALBUFEIRA** ❹.

Continue along the coast from Albufeira on the N526, following it to **Pera**, whose two churches are much more interesting inside than you would think from the outside. Head north from Pera on the N524 to **Algoz**, where the **Igreja Matriz** has fine gold altars and a baptistery completely lined in 17th-century 'Persian-rug' design tiles. The N269 returns to Silves through hills of orange and almond trees.

Detour: From Pera take the N125 1km west to **Alcantarilha**, where anyone with a taste for the bizarre can inspect the **Capela dos Ossos** at the parish church, its interior faced with 1 500 human skulls. Others can explore the ruined castle. The N269-1 leads south to **Armação de**

Pera, where blocks of sleek new holiday apartments overlook one of the Algarve's longest beaches and a series of coves and scenic rock promontories west of town. Perched on one of these is the tiny hexagonal **Nossa Senhora da Rocha**.

The N530-1 leads to **Porches**, known for its bright rustic pottery, which you will see for sale beside the road. Turn left (west) on the N125 for 3km, taking an unnumbered road south through **Caramujeira** to one of the most beautiful stretches of the entire coast.

There are no roads leading to the most spectacular cliffs, caves and rock formations that form the backdrop to the beaches of **Praia Marinha**, but a path leads along the headlands from the colourful fishing village of **Benagil**. Wild flowers abound in the spring.

Work your way westward along unnumbered coastal roads to **Algar Seco⁺⁺⁺**, where the fantastic rock shapes that characterise much of this coast reach their epitome. From the lively seaside resort of **Carvoeiro** head north on the N124-1 to **Lagoa**, and on to **Silves**.

Also worth exploring

Those interested in prehistoric stone monuments should explore the countryside around **São Bartolomeu de Messines**, where there are menhirs in **Monte de Alfarrobeira**, **Gregorios** and **Abutiais**, as well as a curious 100-metre-long series of carved depressions at **Vale Fuseiros**.

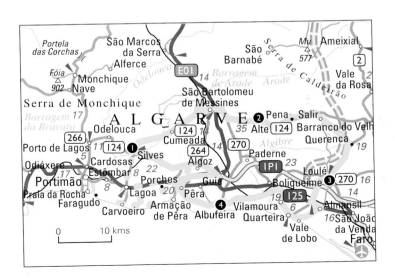

Western Algarve

Ratings

Beaches	●●●●●
Children	●●●●
Nature	●●●●
Scenery	●●●●
Walking	●●●●
Coastal villages	●●●
Geology	●●●
History	●●●

With the most dramatic coastline and the least crowded beaches, the coast from Portimão to Cabo São Vicente is the favourite of those who know the Algarve best. Coastal villages have retained their fishing port character and high-rise hotels are rarer. Cave-cut cliffs and deeply eroded sea stacks spring straight from the sea, or from the pale sands of secluded beaches. To the north, the entire coast of dunes and beaches are in a nature reserve. Inland, from the mountains of the Serra de Monchique, you can see the blue of the Atlantic and the white stripes of towns along the shore. The village of Monchique clings to the Serra's precipitous slopes, a centre for walkers and outdoor enthusiasts. The entire region is covered in walking paths, many along the clifftops bordering the sea.

ALJEZUR*

ⓘ Tourist Information
Largo do Mercado, (N 120); tel: (082) 998 229; open Mon–Fri. Park here to climb to the castle.

✊ Market Day is the third Monday of each month, in the plaza by the TIC.

Ⓟ Experienced riders can explore dune and mountain landscapes on Luso-Arab horses from **Sitio do Rio**, *Carrapateira; tel: (082) 971 19, fax: (082) 971 86; closed Nov.*

Whitewashed walls with brightly painted trim line old streets winding to the 10th-century Moorish castle, of which the walls, towers and vaulted cistern remain. Views reach to the sea and mountains, over an unspoilt landscape remote from the development of the southern coast.

From the castle you can also see Igreja Nova, a newer village, white amid surrounding fields. Inside the church are the skulls of the last two Moors killed when the castle was taken in 1249. Locals believe that touching them cures headaches.

The beach at neighbouring Arrifana, under high cliffs, is shared by fishermen and sun-worshippers. This area is a peaceful base for exploring the wild coastland of the newly designated natural park.

Accommodation and food in Aljezur

Vale da Telha € *Vale da Telha (near Arrifana), tel: (082) 998 180, fax: (082) 998 176*, closed Dec–Jan. A newly built hotel in an unfinished tourist complex near beaches.

Hospedaria O Palazim € *N120 north of Aljezur; tel: (082) 982 49*, is quiet and has a restaurant.

Tasca Borralho € *R. Dom Francisco Gomes 5, Igreja Nova; tel: (082) 991 158*, serves very inexpensive well-prepared dishes.

LAGOS***

Treading a fine line between the qualities that people love and do not love about the Algarve, Lagos combines mellow unhurried charm with up-to-date tourist facilities. If you don't seek solitude too rigorously, it's a good base for exploring the region; a pleasant town to come home to for dinner and a stroll.

Lagos stretches along a wide bay; a pleasant promenade separates the main streets from the marina, where fishing and pleasure craft

i **Tourist Office**, *Largo Marquês de Pombal; tel: (082) 763 031, open daily 0930–1230, 1400–1730, closed Sat pm and Sun in winter, in a pedestrian-only area; park at the waterfront, along the N125.*

Museu Regional € *R. Gen. Alberta da Silveira, open Tue–Sun 0930–1230, 1400–1700. Free on Sun.*

Forte Ponta da Bandeira € *open Tues–Sat 1000–1300, 1400–1800, Sun 1000–1300. Free on Sun.*

Igreja São Sebastião, *R. Conselheiro Joaquim Machado; tel: (082) 76 29 14, open by chance or ask hotel or tourist office to call.*

Market Day is first Saturday in the month, near the train station, but the food market opens Mon–Sat mornings opposite the fishing port. The best **shopping** streets are 25 de Abril and those radiating from Praça Gil Eanes.

Learn surfing and windsurfing at **The Watersports Centre**, *Meia Praia; tel: (0931) 83 05 91, fax: (082) 76 19 43.*

mingle. The caravels that equipped Prince Henry the Navigator's fleet in the Age of Discovery were built here.

Fall into the Algarvian pace at any of the cafés that fill the small squares, then visit the eye-boggling gold interior of the Igreja de Santo António, whose 18th-century gilded baroque woodcarvings merit closer inspection after the first overwhelming view. Adjoining the church, the **Museu Regional***‡* is worth visiting for its archaeological collections.

Follow R. de São Gonçalo into Praça da República, to see the Old Slave Market, the only one in Portugal. Further along the waterfront, cross over a moat to the 17th-century **Forte Ponta da Bandeira***‡*. The museum inside features shipbuilding, connecting Lagos with Prince Henry's navigation school at Sagres.

A peculiar and controversial statue on Praça Gil Eanes shows the boy King Sebastião as an oversized rosy-cheeked child in low-cut armour, helmet at his feet. Many think it captures this fanatical boy who ended Portugal's dreams of greatness. Others think it's just ugly. **Igreja São Sebastião***‡*, on the hill behind the market, has 18th-century tiles and a bone chapel.

For beaches and stunning coastal scenery, head south to Ponta de Piedade, a promontory reached from the EN125. Or walk the coastal path along the cliffs, with dizzying views and a succession of steep pathways down to secluded beaches. Red and ochre rocks are worn into convoluted shapes, caves, arches and seastacks, on which egrets nest. Coves separate the promontories, so from each dramatic headland there's a view of surrounding bays. Fishermen at Ponta de Piedade will take you into the sea caves in small boats.

A two masted schooner, *Bom Dia*, (€€ *tel: (082) 764 670*) also offers short trips to see the rock formations and caves, as well as full-day sails to Sagres. Other boats sell ticket near the marina.

Right
Lagos

Accommodation and food in Lagos

R. 25 de Abril is lined with eating places, cafés and tidy *pensões*, a good place to look if you arrive without reservations. Food prices are lower for the same quality just a block or two away.

Hotel de Lagos €€–€€€ *R. Nova de Aldeia; tel: (082) 769 967, fax: (082) 769 920.* Spacious, beautifully designed resort hotel a five-minute walk from the town centre; shuttle bus to beaches and golf. Landscaped pool, three restaurants (€€) café, shops and gardens.

Residencial Solar € *R. António Crisogono dos Santos 60; tel: (082) 76 24 77, fax: (082) 76 17 84,* opposite Hotel de Lagos, has pleasant, good-sized rooms, some with balconies.

Pensão Marazul €–€€ *R. 25 de Abril 11; tel: (082) 769 143,* offers bright rooms overlooking the central pedestrian-only street.

Parque de Campismo de Lagos € *Estrada do Porto de Mos; tel: (082) 760 031, fax: (082) 760 035.* Campsite.

A Floresta €–€€ *R. António Crisogono dos Santos 51; tel: (082) 76 37 19,* is our hands-down choice for dinner, serving generous portions of *cataplana,* swordfish, grilled meats and seafood prepared creatively.

O Cantina do Mar € *R. Soeiro da Costa 6; tel: (082) 76 77 22,* off R. 25 de Abril, serves typical dishes in a cosy atmosphere.

Restaurante Cangalho €€ *Quinta Figueiras, Barão São João; tel: (082) 672 18; lunch and dinner Tue–Sun.* Serves roast suckling pig, lamb and rabbit from their wood-fired oven on a farm northwest of Lagos.

Casa Doze € *R. das Portas de Portugal; no tel.* Tiny café-restaurant spills out on to the street, easily confused with neighbouring café. Serves three meals daily.

LUZ, BURGAU AND SALEMA❖❖

P In **Burgau**, turn right at the bus stop to park; don't drive down R. 25 de Abril to the waterfront. In **Luz**, park at the shore, on the east side of town.

While certainly not undiscovered, the shore between Lagos and Sagres retains its remote feeling, and the three fishing villages that punctuate it offer a pleasant blend of local colour and low-key tourist amenities. Just ignore the high-rise hotel dominating Salema's skyline. The best way to enjoy this coast is to walk along the coastal path that joins Salema, the westernmost village, to Lagos, 20km east.

The path from Burgau to Salema is filled with scenic headlands which you must climb and descend. Only one headland separates Burgau from Luz, an easier path. Miradouro da Atalaia, at Luz, has a sweeping panorama more than 100 metres above the sea. Also at Luz, the church (easily spotted by its tower) was one of the few whose gold-covered wood carving survived the 1755 earthquake. Luz and Salema are the most touristy of the three villages; at Burgau, the smallest, the seafront is crowded with bright painted boats.

Most tourists come for beaches, especially good at Luz (the most crowded) and Salema. Burgau's beach, while pebbly, is backed by cliffs. Birders should ask at the harbour for a fisherman to take them to the marshes just west of Salema.

Accommodation and food in Luz, Burgau and Salema

Casa Grande € *Burgau; tel: (082) 697 416*, quirky, atmospheric and full of antiques, a nice alternative to the new condo-style elsewhere. The restaurant (€€) – closed Sun and winter – is in a former winery.

Café Restaurant Atlántico € *Praia, Salema; tel: (082) 65 142*. On the beach, serving whopping portions of fresh seafood.

Opposite
Monchique

Ancora €€ *Largo dos Pescadores, Burgau; tel: (082) 697 102*, closed Mon. Expect more creative treatments of local seafood than in most Algarve restaurants.

MONCHIQUE AND CALDAS DE MONCHIQUE✥✥

The lower of these twin mountain villages, Caldas de Monchique, almost hidden in a deep ravine, found fame with its mineral waters. Its somewhat grim spa treatment buildings are lightened by the more frivolous candy-coloured houses and hotels. Free spring water is dispensed from a kiosk and trails lead to picnic spots beside the river. The upper town, Monchique, is more open, spilling down a steep slope along twisting streets. These converge in a pleasant square with a water wheel, garden, shops and cafés. The 16th-century Igreja Matriz has polychrome tiles and a Manueline doorway, its stone carved like twisted rope. Almost directly above town stand the decaying walls and towers of the 1632 monastery of Nossa Senhora do Desterro, a steep but interesting climb past flower-hung homes. You can peep into the ruined church, which until recently was used by a farmer as a livestock pen.

A road leads upward from Monchique through forests of cork oak, pine and eucalyptus to Pico da Fóia, the Algarve's highest elevation. It climbs past several restaurants serving spicy grilled chicken *piri-piri*; views from their terraces reach all the way to the ocean. While views from Fóia are panoramic, the summit is cluttered with antennae and facilities for coach tourists.

Walking paths connect Monchique with Caldas and Mt Fóia, leading along streams, past stone bridges, old mills, and farms, opening out to views of the mountains. Ask at your hotel or the tourist office for directions or follow the routes in the excellent book, *Landscapes of the Algarve*.

Accommodation and food in Monchique

Estalagem Abrigo da Montanha € *Estrada Foia; tel: (082) 91 21 31; fax: (082) 91 36 30, e-mail: abrigodamontanha@hotmail.com* Warm, inviting rooms decorated in rich colours perch in flower-draped layers with views to the sea. Hospitable English-speaking staff; begin dinner in the excellent dining room (€–€€) with salmon chowder.

Albergaria Bica-Boa € *Estrada de Lisboa 266; tel: (082) 91 22 71, fax: (082) 91 23 60, e-mail: inigma@mail.telepac.pt* Small pleasant inn with an outstanding restaurant (€€).

Café Central € *R. da Igreja 5.* A local landmark with walls covered in cards and notes from far-away admirers.

PRAIA DA ROCHA*

ⓘ **Tourist Information** Av. Tomas Cabreira; tel: (082) 41 91 32.

⊘ A shuttle connects to Portimão, preferable to fighting the traffic.

The Algarve's most photographed beach, this stretch of golden sand is surrounded by fantastic red and honey-coloured cliffs and rock formations. Even the ranks of new hotels and apartments encrustimg the clifftop cannot ruin the view. Don't look in this overbuilt enclave for peace and quiet, but for a lively restaurant and nightlife scene. The youngish set congregates at Bar e Bar, near the fortress and at Discoteca Katedral (*Av. Tomas Cabreira*), open until 0600.

The town is at the top, the crowded beach below, reached via long stairways. More private are beaches west of town, through the tunnel. The only sightseeing attraction is the 16th-century fortress of Santa Catarina de Ribamar, with a small chapel.

Accommodation and food in Praia da Rocha

Hotel Bela Vista €-€€ *Av. Tomas Cabreira; tel: (082) 42 40 55, fax: (082) 41 53 69.* Stay here at bargain winter rates; vintage tilework and beautiful ceilings are just as lovely then, as is the view from almost every room.

Taj Palace €-€€ *Av. Tomas Cabreira Miradouro; tel: (082) 41 84 58, dinner daily, lunch Tue–Sun.* Tandoori, curries and other Indian favourites.

Churrasqueira da Rocha € *Av. Tomas Cabreira; tel: (082) 41 74 52.* If you missed the *piri-piri* in Monchique, try it here.

SAGRES PENINSULA***

ⓘ **Tourist Information** R. Comandante Matoso, Vila do Bisbo; tel: (082) 62 48 73.

⊘ **Cabo São Vicente Cruzeiros €€**; tel: (082) 641 98 runs cruises and fishing trips along the coast, a good way to appreciate the grandeur of the cliffs.

Sheer cliffs plunging abruptly into the sea at the southwestern end of Europe would be enough reason for coming here. So would its place in history, as the seminal point in the Age of Discoveries. Add cliff-secluded beaches and sardines grilling over coals in the setting sun, and the peninsula is irresistible.

Except at the quietest off-season times, park outside the fortress at Ponta de Sagres and walk through the tunnel to the wide courtyard with its 43-metre wind-compass. The dreary little building nearby was not used by Prince Henry's coterie of navigators, cartographers, geographers and astronomers, but the land under your feet was. And the angry sea pounding at the cliffs beyond is the same one Henry set his caravels into when they discovered Madeira and explored the coast of Africa.

Be careful in a strong wind (there's always some wind), which could literally blow you off the edge. Paths weave through low sedums along the rim of cliffs, where the views west to Cabo São Vicente are incomparable.

Henry the Navigator

Geography and a half-English Prince (son of João I and Philippa of Lancaster) of extraordinary vision combined to make Sagres one of the most important places in 15th-century Europe. Three of the earth's plates converge just off these soaring cliffs, and to get past the violent tides, ships had to wait for the right wind. Sometimes it took weeks, and while they waited, Prince Henry offered sailors food, provisions for the voyage, and a chance to tell about the lands and seas they had explored. This added to the knowledge of the cartographers and scholars Prince Henry had assembled here, and together they fitted pieces into the puzzle of what lay beyond the horizon. They also designed the faster, safer caravel and better navigational instruments to help seamen push the limits of the known world. Without their work at Sagres, Vasco da Gama, Magellan and Columbus could not have succeeded.

Above right
Praia da Rocha

It's a short distance by road to this neighbouring cape, where you can stand at the end of Europe and ponder what it must have been like to sail into the unknown. Fishermen sit on the edge, feet dangling 75 metres above the sea.

Praia de Beliche, between Ponta Sagres and Cabo São Vicente, has calmer waters than most and some shelter from the unremitting wind. Be careful of strong currents anywhere here.

Accommodation and food in the Sagres Peninsula

Pousada do Infante €€ *Sagres, tel: (082) 62 42 22, fax: (082) 62 42 25.* A modern *pousada* in typical local architecture, overlooking the sea. Fresh seafood highlights the menu (€€).

Residencia Dom Henrique € *Sitio da Mareta; tel: (082) 641 33,* has bright, comfortable rooms with balconies facing the sea. The dining room (€) is also good.

O Pescador €–€€ *R. Comandante Matoso, Baleira; tel: (082) 62 41 92.* Best known for *cataplana*, but all the seafood is good.

Suggested tour

Alcalar Burial Chambers *open daily 0900–1700.*

Total distance: 172km; 182km with detours.

Time: 4 hours driving. Allow 2–3 days. Those with limited time should concentrate on Sagres and Lagos.

Links: The N125 continues east from Lagos into the Central Algarve (*see page 256*). The N120 (IC4) follows the Atlantic coast north toward Santiago da Cacém, south of Lisbon (*see page 276*).

Route: Follow the N125 from the **LAGOS** ❶ waterfront esplanade to **Espiche**. Turn left to **LUZ** ❷, then follow the coast road through **BURGAU** ❸ and **SALEMA** ❹, returning to the N125 just east of **Val do Bisbo**. Follow the N268 south to its end, going west 6km from the roundabout to **Cabo São Vicente**. Return to the roundabout and go south 1km to **SAGRES** ❺.

Backtrack north on the N268 through **Vila do Bispo**, continuing through the rolling, piney nature reserve past **Carrapateira**, where a short circular detour west through **Bordeira** brings fine views of steep headland cliffs. Shortly beyond, follow the N120 (IC4) north to **ALJEZUR** ❻.

The N267 leads west into the Serra de Monchique, through cork oak forests and the villages of **Marmalete** and **Casais**, ending at the N266. Turn left (north) to **MONCHIQUE** ❼, taking a sharp left uphill from its main square on Estrada da Fóia to **Pico da Fóia**. Backtrack,

Above
Lagos

following the N266 south to **CALDAS DE MONCHIQUE** ❽. Continue south on the N266, lined with mimosa trees, to the N125 in **Portimão**, turning right to return to Lagos

Detour: Instead of returning to Lagos via Portimão on the main road, turn right (west) off the N266 south of Caldas de Monchique, following signs to **Casas Velhas** and **Vidigal**. There follow brown 'Necropole' signs to visit the partially restored passage tombs at **Alcalar**❖, thought to date from 3 000BC. Continue south to join the N125, which leads west (right) to Lagos.

Alternatively, continue to Portimão, leave the N125 and follow signs to **PRAIA DA ROCHA** ❾, following the shore road to **Alvor**, at the mouth of four rivers. Here a raised footpath skirts the estuary and marshlands, a prime birding sight. The **Igreja Matriz**❖ in Alvor (*tel: (082) 45 91 51*) has one of the finest carved Manueline portals in the Algarve, as well as 18th-century polychrome tiles.

Return to N125 via the remains of the 4th-century Roman villa of **Abicada**❖ (*Quinta de Aguazul, open 0930–1230, 1400–1700 daily*) and then on to Lagos.

South of Lisbon

Ratings

Historical sights
●●●●○

Outdoor activities
●●●●○

Beaches ●●●○○

Castles ●●●○○

Nature ●●●○○

Walking ●●●○○

Coastal villages
●●○○○

Museums ●●○○○

Although within easy day-trip distance of Lisbon, this peninsula is largely overlooked by foreign travellers, leaving its sheltered sandy beaches, clear green harbours, breezy seaside cafés and soaring cliffs to the Portuguese. Hiking trails web their way through the Parque Natural de Arrábida, which is filled with wild flowers in the spring, many of them unique to these steep slopes. Travellers are more likely to visit the southernmost part of this route on their way to or from the Algarve. If southern Portugal is on your itinerary, Santiago do Cacém makes a good stopover, allowing time to see the outstanding Roman settlement under excavation at Miróbriga. To speed the inland route, take advantage of the A2 motorway; those with leisure will prefer to arrive in Setúbal via the ferry from the long sandspit of the Península de Tróia.

PALMELA✣

ⓘ **Turismo** *Castelo de Palmela; tel: (01) 235 21 22.*

High above the town, the **Castelo de Palmela**✣✣ is hard to miss. Fortifications predating the Moors were reconstructed by each new conqueror; museum rooms inside the walls expose excavations showing the process. Alongside, are boutiques selling *azulejos* and pricey local foods.

By the castle entrance is the ruined 12th-century Igreja Maria do Castelo with Renaissance touches and the Igreja de Santiago, built and rebuilt between the 5th and 18th centuries. The latter contains the Arrábida marble tomb of the last Master of the Order of Santiago as well as splendid 17th- and 18th-century *azulejos*. Its convent and cloister are now a *pousada*.

In the town below, by the 17th-century *pelourinho*, the Paço do Concelho has murals of the Portuguese kings. Opposite, on Largo

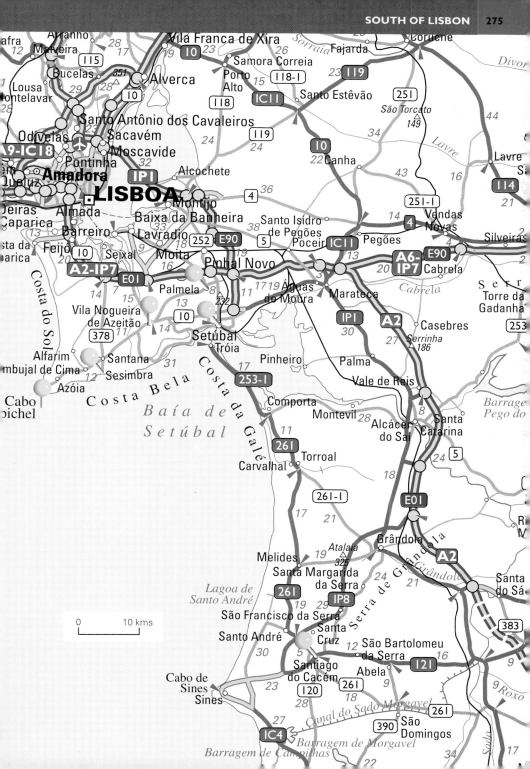

⊕ **Pinhal Novo**'s market fair is the second Sunday of each month.

⊕ For **horse riding** excursions, contact **Centro Equestre da Lagoinha**, R. General Ramalho Eanes, Quinta do Picadeiro; tel: (01) 235 13 87 or the **Centro Equestre de Lagameças**, Quinta de S Silvestre; tel: (065) 99 83 51.

⊕ **Festival Queijo, Pao e Vinho** Quinta do Anjo, Fri–Sun, third weekend of Apr. This bread, cheese and wine festival has tastings, sales, demonstrations and evening fado.

do Municipio, the interior walls of the Igreja de São Pedro are completely covered with tiles illustrating the life of Saint Peter, under a fine painted ceiling (if the church is closed, ask at the parish house).

Nearby, the fascinating necropolis, Caves do Quinta Anjo, has entry corridors and chambers carved into the stone. These were used for collective burials from neolithic times until the copper ages. To reach the burial ground, follow seplicoros and megaliticos signs in Quinta do Anjo, 5km from Palmela. Turn south at the traffic lights near the town square, go left at the fork, through the second intersection, then immediately left for 100m. Beyond Quinta do Anjo, the hills of the Serra do Louro rise to the south, in the Parque Natural da Arrábida, where there is a string of ancient windmills.

In September, the Festa das Vindimas, or wine festival, celebrates the harvest with a procession of grape-bearing vintners, blessing of the grapes, symbolic grape stomping and impressive fireworks over the castle.

Accommodation and food in Palmela

Pousada de Palmela €€-€€€ Castelo de Palmela; tel: (01) 235 12 26, fax: 233 04 40. A luxurious hotel surrounding the cloister of a 15th-century monastery of the Order of Santiago. The restaurant (€€-€€€) features tournedos with muscatel and salmon dishes.

Retiro Azul €-€€ R. Hermenegildo Capelo, near the Largo do Chafariz; tel: (01) 235 00 21, closed Wed, serves well-prepared local seafood and meats.

SANTIAGO DO CACEM❖

ⓘ **Turismo** Praça do Mercado; tel: (069) 82 66 96.

⊕ For horse riding, contact **Centro Equestre de Santo André** Monte Velho de Cima, Apartado 129; tel: (069) 7 12 35.

⊕ **Feira do Monte** first weekend of Sep.

The **Museu Municipal**❖ (open Tue–Fri 1000–1200, 1400–1700, Sat–Sun 1400–1700) on Praça do Municipio documents the area from pre-history and Roman times to the 20th century, with artifacts from Miróbriga, iron age coins and period rooms. On the Estrada das Comeadas, a **working windmill**❖ (open Tue–Sat 0900–1900, Sun–Mon 0900–1300, 1500–1900) invites visitors, and overlooking town is the ancient Castelo, rebuilt after 12th-century battles.

Santiago's treasure, however, is outside of town at , at the ruins of the Roman town of **Miróbriga**❖❖❖ (€ Chãos Salgados, just off N120, open Tue–Sat 0900–1230, 1400–1730, Sun 0900–1200, 1400–1730). Archaeologists continue to uncover a large settlement; already exposed are temple ruins, baths heated with a hypocaust, ruins of taverns and houses with mosaics, streets, stairways and a bridge. An unexcavated (but visible) hippodrome is 4km away; it is one of Portugal's three major Roman sites.

Right
Miróbriga's Roman road

Accommodation and food in Santiago do Cacém

Pousada de São Tiago €-€€ *Estrada de Lisboa; tel: (069) 2 24 59, fax: 2 24 59*. One of the older and more affordable *pousadas*, attractive, well appointed and in town. The restaurant (€–€€) serves especially good local lamb.

O Braseiro € *R. Professor Egas Moniz; tel: (069) 229 88*. Two dining rooms, one more upscale than the other but both good.

Martins € *R. de Lisboa 17; tel: (069) 794 81*, makes the definitive and savoury *bacalhau a bras*, also good lamb stew and curries.

SERRA DA ARRABIDA AND VILA NOGUEIRA DE AZEITAO✦✦

ⓘ Museu Oceanográfico e de Pesca € *Portinho de Arrábida. Open Tue–Fri 1000–1600, Sat–Sun and holidays 1500–1800.*

The Parque Natural da Arrábida rises abruptly from the sea, creating an environment for several plants unique to the area, and spectacular views over the Baía de Setúbal. Below the escarpment in tiny Portinho da Arrábida, the **Museu Oceanográfico e de Pesca**✦, in the 1670 fort of Santa María Arrábida, examines sea, river and ocean life and the fishing industry.

Quinta da Bacalhoa €
Vila Fresca de Azeitão, N10, 8km west of Palmela; tel: (01) 218 00 11, open Mon–Sat 1300–1700.

⬛ Market day in **Nogueira de Azeitão** *is the first Sun of the month.*

🌐 For **horse riding**, contact **Centro Equestre da Quinta do Ervideiro**, *R. do Poço, Venda de Azeitão; tel: (01) 218 16 75, fax: 218 16 75.*

The gracious **Quinta da Bacalhoa**✻, built in the late 15th century, combines Moorish and Renaissance styles with early *azulejos* portraying the great rivers. There is also a lovely loggia and garden containing the oldest figural tile panel in Portugal.

Nearby is **São Simão Arte**✻ (*R. Almirante Reis 86, Vila Fresca Azeitão; tel: (01) 218 31 35*), an *azulejos* studio and shop with hand-painted tiles, panels and medallions, both abstract and figural. They also offer a selection of hand-painted dishes.

The 18th-century Fonseca mansion and winery at **Vila Nogueira de Azeitão** is decorated with fine *azulejo* panels. Its **Museu de Vinho José Maria da Fonseca**✻ (*R. José Augusto Coelho 11; tel: (01) 218 00 02, open Mon–Fri 0900–1200, 1400–1630*) is included in winery tours. Tours – which include tasting – leave every half hour and last 40 minutes. It is advisable to make reservations.

The parish church of São Lourenço, across the street, has *azulejo* panels along the nave and a large painted altarpiece .

Accommodation and food in Serra da Arrábida and Azeitão

Quinta da Arrábida €€ *Casais da Serra, Azeitão; tel: (01) 218 34 33, fax: 840 22 69*, two small apartments furnished with antiques.

Quinta das Torres €€ *Azeitão, on N379 between Vila Fresca de Azeitão and Nogueira de Azeitão; tel: (01) 218 00 01, fax: 219 06 07*. A 16th-century *quinta* furnished in fine antiques. In the grounds and gardens is a large pool with a stone gazebo. The restaurant (€€) is beautifully appointed.

Pastelaria Fonte Nova € *Nogueira de Azeitão, on the main street opposite the Quinta Fonseca*, a good lunch stop.

Sesimbra and Cabo Espichel✻

🏛 **Museu Municipal da Arqueologia €** *Largo Luís de Camões, Sesimbra.*

Museu do Mar € *Largo Luís de Camões, Sesimbra. Open Mon–Fri 0930–1230, 1430–1730.*

🍴 **O Pirata €€** *R. Heliodoro Salgado 3; tel: (01) 223 04 01*, with more fresh seafood.

Locally excavated artifacts – from megalithic burial sites to medieval relics – are exhibited in temporary quarters at the **Museu Municipal de Arqueologia**✻. The **Museu do Mar**'s✻ collections relate to the area's fishing industry, showing nets, tools, boats and models of local vessels.

Sesimbra is most popular for its beaches, which stretch on both side of the 17th-century Forte de Santiago. Against the cliff at the harbour, fishermen repair nets by brightly coloured boats, a star or an eye painted on the bow. The empty Moorish Castelo overlooks the town and coast from its 260-metre perch.

At Cabo Espichel, the sheer cliffs drop over 100 metres into the sea. As well as the superb views, there is the 17th-century baroque Santuário de Nossa Senhora do Cabo, a lighthouse and the Capela da Memoria at the clifftops. The area is known for its fossilized dinosaur tracks.

Accommodation and food in Sesimbra and Cabo Espichel

Estalagem dos Zimbros €-€€ *Facho de Azoia; tel: (01) 268 49 54, fax: 268 49 56*. A modern full service hotel with balconies overlooking the large pool. Restaurant (€-€€) is reliable.

Ribamar €€ *Av. dos Naufragos 29; tel: (01) 223 48 53*. In and outdoor dining on fish and shellfish.

SETUBAL*

ⓘ **Setúbal Regioal Tourism** *Travessa Frei Gaspar 10; tel: (065) 52 42 84*, on a small alley between Av. Luisa Todi and Largo da Misericórdia. Look through the glass floor at Roman ruins.

Ⓟ There is parking along the busy Avenida Luisa Todi; buy a ticket for your windshield. There is also a carpark on the east end of the same avenue.

Ⓒ **Cruzeiros no Sado** *R. do Moinho, Lote 4-1D; tel: (065) 76 15 95*, cruises on the Sado River.

Natur Sociedade de Actividades Marítimo-Turísticas *R. António Feliciano Castilho 9; tel: (065) 52 49 63, fax: 52 49 63*, cruises along the Arrábida coast.

Planetaterra *Praça General Luís Domingues 9; tel: (065) 53 21 40, fax: 52 79 21*, for bicycle, canoe or jeep trips or rental.

SAL (Sistemas de Ar Livre) *Av. Manuel Maria Portela 40; tel: (065) 2 76 85*, guided hikes in Setúbal, Palmela, Sesimbra and the Trail of the Dinosaurs.

The royal family lavished gifts on the Igreja de Jesus, founded in 1490, and the finest example of emerging Manueline style with soaring twisted stone columns and 17th-century *azulejos*. The **Museu de Jesus*** (€ *R. do Balneario Paula Borba, open Tue–Sat 0900–1200 and 1400–1700*), in the former cloister, houses gold and silver treasure and art, most notably 14 remarkable panels from the 16th century salvaged from the altar during the 1940s government 'restoration'.

The **Museu Michel Giacometti*** (€ *Largo da República, open Tue–Fri and Sun 0900–0900–1200, 1400–1700*) features local industry, both commercial and cottage, with tools and machinery illustrating the processes of fishing, the tinning industry, lithography, metalwork, cheese making and basketry. The **Museu Regional de Arqueologia e Etnografia*** (€ *Av. Luisa Todi 162, open Tue–Sat 0900–1230, 1400–1730*) shows the area's archaeological history, relationships to the sea, fishing, salt evaporation processes, boat building, agriculture (including cork) and fabrics.

Contemporary art, especially that of José Bocage, are at **Casa Bocage*** (*R. E. Bartissol 12, open Mon–Fri 0900–1230, 1400–1800, Sat 1500–2000, closes 1730 June–Sept*). Outstanding 18th-century tiles and a splendid painted ceiling highlight the former church **Casa do Corpo Santo** (*R. do Corpo Santo 17, open Tue–Sat 0830–1200, 1400–1800*).

In the harbour look for traditional boats from the River Sado, particularly the *Ze Mario*, a former salt boat, and *Ritquitum*. Hiate de Setúbal is a replica built in 1994.

Ferry boats, taking about 25 minutes from loading to unloading, run regularly from Setúbal to the Península de Tróia (*hourly 0030–0800, half-hourly 0845–1915, less frequent until 2330*).

Feira Santiago, last week of July, first week of August, is an agricultural and business fair with amusements, crafts, folklore and bull fights. Later in the year, the Festas de Semana Sadina (mid-Sept), feature sports, cultural events and entertainment.

Vasco da Gama €-€€ *R. Vasco da Gama 34; tel: (065) 22 18 50.* Specialities include *caldeirada* (seafood stew) and *enguias* (eel).

O Cardador € *R. Vasco da Gama 5; tel: (065) 52 47 78*, small, serving good seafood and *petiscos*.

O Fernando €-€€ *Avenida Luisa Todi 510 (along the harbour); tel: (065) 52 71 02*, known for their *caldeirada de peixe* (fish soup), and other seafood dishes. A display of available fish awaits on ice.

Snack Bar Arcada dos Manos € *R. Vasco da Gama 66*, inexpensive meals; small portions available.

**Albergaria Solaris € ** *Praça Marquês de Pombal 12, Setúbal; tel: (065) 52 21 89, fax: 52 20 70.* Very pleasant, well-furnished rooms with views onto the praça and fountains. Air-conditioned and close to several restaurants.

Pousada de São Filipe €€-€€€ *Castelo São Filipe, Setúbal; tel: (065) 52 38 44, fax: 53 25 38.* Elegant quarters in a hilltop castle built by Philip of Spain in 1590. Their restaurant (€€) serves local seafood and fish, beautifully prepared.

Quinta do Hilario €€ *Estrada da Alcodeia, Setúbal, off of N252 west of the town; tel: (01) 236 00 77 and (065) 53 86 80, fax: (065) 55 16 82.* Five rooms and five apartments in a restored 18th-century farm estate with pool.

Suggested tour

Total distance: 263km; 290km with detours.

Time: 5–6 hours driving. Allow 2 days with or without detours. Those with limited time should concentrate on Palmela Castle and Miróbriga, in Santiago do Cacém.

Links: Continuing south from Santiago do Cacém, the coastal IC4 leads to the Western Algarve (*see page 264*). Two driving routes begin in Lisbon: Lisbon's Coast (*see page 67*) and North of Lisbon (*see page 80*).

Route: Leave **LISBON** ❶ on the IP1, over the stunning new Tagus bridge overlooking the Expo 98 grounds. Head south on the A2 to **Alcácer do Sal**, where the **Museu Municipal Pedro Nunes** (*Largo Pedro Nunes, open Mon–Fri 0900–1230, 1400–1730*) has a collection of archaeological finds, from megalithic to Visigothic and medieval.

Continue south on the IP8, past **Grândola** to SANTIAGO DO CACEM ❷, heading north along the coast on the N261 to the **Península de Troia**. Stop at the half-sunken Roman city of **Cetóbriga** just before taking the ferry to **SETUBAL** ❸.

Detour: Leave Setúbal on the N10-4 coastal road, which passes through the wild parts of the **Parque Natural da Arrábida** over the **Estrada de Escarpa**, a corniche road with spectacular views over the Baía de Setúbal. Turn left and descend into the village of **Portinho da Arrábida**, with restaurants overhanging the harbour. Return to the N379, rejoining the main route near Vila Nogueira de Azeitão.

From Setúbal, follow the N252 to **PALMELA** ❹, turning west on the N379 through **VILA NOGUEIRA DE AZEITÃO** ❺ to **SESIMBRA** ❻. Head north on the N377 to N378, connecting to the A2, past the statue of **Cristo Rei**, and over the Tagus bridge into **LISBON**.

Detour: From **SESIMBRA** take the N379 south past Zambujal to **CABO ESPICHEL** ❼, passing through farms at the foot of the Serra da Arrábida to the end of the peninsula and the lighthouse. Return as far as the intersection with the N377, heading north on the N378, where you rejoin the main route.

Also worth exploring:

Although bridges and ferries have made the southern shore of the Tagus part of suburban Lisbon, these little waterside towns still have their charms. **Seixal** is particularly attractive, with a fishing harbour, fine old buildings decorated in *azulejos*, tidemills harnessing the power of the water, and a boatyard museum.

Mafra 12
Arranhó
28
Malveira 17
Vila Franca de Xira
19 10 23
Samora Correia
26
29
Coruche
Fajarda
115
Bucelas 351
29
Alverca
Porto
Alto
15
118-1
23 119
251
São Torcato
149
44
Lousa 11
Montelavar 28
28
10
Santo Estêvão
118
IC11
Santo Antônio dos Cavaleiros
23
Sacavém
Moscavide
119
24
24
10
Canha
22
34
9
Odivelas
Pontinha
32
Alcochete
36
43
16
251-1
A9-IC18
25
Amadora
Cacém 26
Queluz
IP1
LISBOA
Montijo
4
Santo Isidro
de Pegões
14
Vendas
Novas
4
Oeiras
Almada
Baixa da Banheira
38
Pegões
IC11
4
Si
Caparica
Barreiro
33
Lavradio
252 E90
5
Poceir
13
A6-
IP7
E90
Costa da
Caparica
13
Feijó
10
Seixal
18
Moita
519
Pinhal Novo
16
Cabrela
20
S
To
Ga
A2-IP7
E01
Palmela 4
232
11
1719 Águas
de Moura
Marateca
Costa do Sol
14
7
15
13
10
3
IP1
A2
Casebres
Vila Nogueira
de Azeitão 5
14
Setúbal
30
27
Serrinha
186
378 11
Tróia
Pinheiro
Palma
Alfarim
Santana
31
17
Vale de Reis
Zambujal de Cima 12
6 Sesimbra
253-1
8
Santa
Catarina
7
Azóia
Costa Bela
Comporta
Montevil 28
Alcácer
do Sal
24 5
Cabo
Espichel
Baía de
Setúbal
Costa da Galé
11
Torroal
18
261
Carvalhal
261-1
17
21
E01
Grândola
A2
Serra de Grândola
Atalaia
Melides
19
325
Santa Margarida
da Serra
24
21
261
19 29
IP8
São Francisco da Serra
Lagoa de
Santo André
Santa
Cruz
12
São Bartolomeu
da Serra
16
Santo André
30
5
2
Abela
9
121
Cabo de
Sines
23
Santiago
do Cacém
120
261
Sines
28
18
0   10 kms
27
IC4
390
São
Domingos

Language

Portuguese has many words that are similar to French, Spanish or Italian, but the pronunciation can be difficult for English speakers. The letter s is pronounced like the s in sugar unless it is followed by a vowel; thus *carros* (car) is pronounced *carrosh*. When the tilde accent (˜) appears above the letters *ao* (as in *pão* – bread) it sounds like *ow* followed by a slight *oo* (powoo).

Hello	*olá*
Good morning	*bom dia*
Good afternoon	*boa tarde*
Good evening/night	*boa noite*
Goodbye	*adeus*
How are you?	*como está?*
See you later	*até logo*
Yes/no	*sim/não*
Please	*por favor*
Thank you	*obrigado* (male speaking)
	obrigada (female speaking)
It's OK, you're welcome	*de nada*
Excuse me (may I pass)	*com licença*
Excuse me (forgive me)	*desculpe*
I'd like	*queria*
How much?	*quanto custa?*
Do you have?	*Tem?*
Where is the...?	*onde e a?*
I don't speak Portuguese	*no fala Portuguese*
Toilets	*casas de banho*
Men's/women's	*homens/senhoras*

Getting around

What time does?	*a que horas?*
leaves/arrives	*parte/chega*
The train	*combóio*
The bus	*autocarro*
The boat	*barco*
for Lisbon	*a Lisboa*
A ticket (return)	*um bilhete (ida e volta)*

Eating

Breakfast	*pequeno almoco*
Lunch	*almoco*
Dinner	*jantar*
A table for	*uma mesa para*
two/four people	*dois/quatro pessoas*
No smoking/smoking	*não fumador/fumador*
May I have the bill please?	*Pode-me dar a conta, por favor?*

Hotel terms

Vacant/free rooms	*quartos vagos*
A room for one/two	*um quarto individual/duplo*
With/without a bath/shower	
	com/sem banho/chuveiro
A bed in a dormitory	*uma cama num dormitorio*
Hotel	*hotel*
Guest house, B&B	*pensao*
Youth hostel	*albergue de juventude*
I have a reservation in the name of	
	Tenho uma marcação em nome de

Tourist office terms

A map of the town/area	
	um mapa da cidade/zona
An accommodation list	*uma lista de alojamentos*

Communication terms

A stamp	*um selo*
A letter	*uma carta*
A postcard	*uma postal*
To make a telephone call	
	fazer uma chamada

Money terms

To change/	*trocar*
travellers'cheques	*cheques de viagem*
currency	*divisas*
How much commission is charged?	
	Que comissão cobra?

Driving terms

Unleaded/standard/premium	
	sem chumbo/normal/super
Fill the tank please	*Encha depósito por favor.*
Is there a car park near here?	
	Há um parque de estacionamento aqui perto?
I am looking for	*Estou à procura*
How do I reach the motorway/the main road?	
	Como vou para a autoestrada/ estrada principal?
Is this the right way to?	
	E este o caminho certo para?
the cathedral/the castle	
	a catedral/o castelo

Index

Acknowledgements

Project management: Dial House Publishing Services
Series design: Fox Design
Front cover design and artwork: Fox Design
Layout and map work: Concept 5D
Repro and image setting: Z2 Repro
Printed and bound in Italy by: Rotolito Lombarda Spa

We would like to thank Rogers Associates for the photographs used in this book, to whom the copyright in the photographs belongs.

Feedback form

If you enjoyed using this book, or even if you didn't, please help us improve future editions by taking part in our reader survey. Every returned form will be acknowledged, and to show our appreciation we will give you £1 off your next purchase of a Thomas Cook guidebook. Just take a few minutes to complete and return this form to us.

When did you buy this book? ....
....

Where did you buy it? (Please give town/city and, if possible, name of retailer)
....
....

When did you/do you intend to travel in Portugal? ....
....

For how long (approx)? ....

How many people in your party? ....

Which cities, national parks and other locations did you/do you intend mainly to visit?
....
....
....
....

Did you/will you:
❏ Make all your travel arrangements independently?
❏ Travel on a fly-drive package?
Please give brief details: ....
....

Did you/do you intend to use this book:
❏ For planning your trip?   ❏ Both?
❏ During the trip itself?

Did you/do you intend also to purchase any of the following travel publications for your trip?
Thomas Cook Travellers: Portugal ....
A road map/atlas (please specify) ....
Other guidebooks (please specify) ....

Have you used any other Thomas Cook guidebooks in the past? If so, which?
....
....

Please rate the following features of Signpost Portugal for their value to you (Circle VU for 'very useful', U for 'useful', NU for 'little or no use'):

The Travel Facts section on pages 14–23	VU	U	NU
The Driver's Guide section on pages 24–29	VU	U	NU
The Touring itineraries on pages 40–41	VU	U	NU
The recommended driving routes throughout the book	VU	U	NU
Information on towns and cities, National Parks, etc	VU	U	NU
The maps of towns and cities, parks, etc	VU	U	NU

Please use this space to tell us about any features that in your opinion could be changed, improved, or added in future editions of the book, or any other comments you would like to make concerning the book:

....
....
....
....
....
....
....
....
....
....
....
....

Your age category: ❏ 21–30 ❏ 31–40 ❏ 41–50 ❏ over 50

Your name: Mr/Mrs/Miss/Ms ....
(First name or initials) ....
(Last name) ....

Your full address: (Please include postal or zip code)
....
....
....
....
....

Your daytime telephone number: ....

Please detach this page and send it to: The Project Editor, Signpost Guides, Thomas Cook Publishing, PO Box 227, Peterborough PE3 6PU, United Kingdom.

We will be pleased to send you details of how to claim your discount upon receipt of this questionnaire.

Your guide to a great driving vacation

❖ A selection of the best regions for touring in Portugal. Includes Porto and the Douro Valley, Lisbon, Faro and the Algarve

❖ Ideas for exploring on your own

❖ Detailed guides to sightseeing and activities, together with accommodation, dining and shopping recommendations

❖ Attractions and areas all rated to guide your personal choice

❖ Road maps and town plans pinpoint driving routes and other tours

The
Globe
Pequot
Press

Thomas
Cook
Publishing